Everything
You Want to Know
About
Magick

Photo by Hillary Roney

About the Author

Shawn Martin Scanlon (Los Angeles) has studied, practiced, and taught magick for more than twenty-two years. He has worked with Enochian magickal groups, Thelemic and Golden Dawn orders, and taught private magick classes, sifting through many occult traditions to distill magick down to its most useful particulars. He teaches only what has brought him tangible results. Visit him online at www.whatismagick.com.

To Write to the Author

If you wish to contact the author or would like more information about this book, please write to the author in care of Llewellyn Worldwide, and we will forward your request. Both the author and publisher appreciate hearing from you and learning of your enjoyment of this book and how it has helped you. Llewellyn Worldwide cannot guarantee that every letter written to the author can be answered, but all will be forwarded. Please write to:

Shawn Martin Scanlon
℅ Llewellyn Worldwide
2143 Wooddale Drive
Woodbury, MN 55125-2989

Please enclose a self-addressed stamped envelope for reply,
or $1.00 to cover costs. If outside the USA, enclose
an international postal reply coupon.

Many of Llewellyn's authors have websites with additional information and resources. For more information, please visit our website at http://www .llewellyn.com.

Everything You Want to Know About Magick

But Were Afraid to Ask

SHAWN MARTIN SCANLON

Llewellyn Publications
Woodbury, Minnesota

FIRST EDITION
First Printing, 2012

Book design by Bob Gaul
Cover art: Background images ©iStockphoto.com/CTR design LLC
Cover design by Lisa Novak
Editing by Patti Frazee
All interior art © Llewellyn art department and Shawn Scanlon, with the following exceptions: Art on page 271 © *Devils, Demons, and Witchcraft*, Dover Publications, Inc., 1971. Art on page 139 © Eliphas Levi's *Dogme et Rituel de la Haute Magie*. Art on pages 107 and 127 © *Magic and Mystical Symbols*, Dover Publications, Inc., 2004. Rider Tarot card illustrations based on those contained in "The Pictorial Key to the Tarot" by Arthur Edward Waite, published by William Rider & Sons Ltd., London, 1911.

Courtesy of Liam Quin at www.fromoldbooks.org:
Seere sigils and seals on pages 230–232 © The Goetia: The Lesser Key of Solomon the King, translated by Samuel MacGregor Liddel Mathers, Ed. Aleister Crowley, 1904 (reprinted by Weiser, 1995). The Lamen of Frater Achad © *The Equinox*, Vol. III, No. I, Ed. Aleister Crowley, 1919. Sigillum Dei Aemeth © John Dee's original 16th century manuscript in the Sloane collection at the British Museum, reprinted in *The Complete Golden Dawn System of Magic*, Regardie, Israel, Falcan Press, 1984.

Llewellyn is a registered trademark of Llewellyn Worldwide Ltd.

Library of Congress Cataloging-in-Publication Data
Scanlon, Shawn Martin, 1972–
  Everything you wanted to know about magick but were afraid to ask/
Shawn Martin Scanlon.—1st ed.
    p. cm.
  ISBN 978-0-7387-3283-1
  1. Magic. I. Title.
  BF1611.S365 2012
  133.4'3—dc23
                    2012017114

Llewellyn Publications
A Division of Llewellyn Worldwide Ltd.
2143 Wooddale Drive
Woodbury, MN 55125-2989
www.llewellyn.com

Printed in the United States of America

For Nuit & Izabael

CONTENTS

IN+R⊕DUC+I⊕N

Real magick scares people as much as it fascinates them. Where does the power come from? Is it real? Is it safe? What are the limits? Can I learn to perform magick myself?

Everything You Want to Know About Magick (But Were Afraid to Ask) answers all these questions and every other question you may have about how to perform your very own magick.

Let's get started by answering some of the most common questions regarding magick, this book, and myself as your guide through the world of magick and the occult.

Questions About Magick

What is magick?
Magick is the science and art of using the subconscious mind to effect change in the material world. In more specific terms, magick is using conscious stimulation (i.e., rituals, symbols, gestures, chanting, lighting, incense, sex, etc.) to harness latent powers within the subconscious mind (i.e., gods, genii, intelligences, angels, daemons, etc.) to make changes in our bodies, our minds, and the world around us.

What is Hermeticism?

There are many schools of magick, under a variety of terms, but Western magick finds its roots most strongly situated in Hermeticism, the religion and philosophy of the Hellenistic culture. This term frequently comes up in this book because Hermeticism has strongly influenced modern magick both directly and through the many authors and magicians it has inspired, including John Dee and Aleister Crowley, both influential magicians we will soon be learning more of.

Does magick really work?

The magick in this book most certainly works. I present you with only the very best concepts and techniques gleaned from my twenty-two years of magickal practice and study.

The meditations and rituals in this book are drawn from the most respected sources in magick, including Hermeticism, the Golden Dawn, Aleister Crowley, Wicca, and various schools of shamanism. Combine these teachings with a modern view of psychology and the human mind, and you have the key to unlocking magickal results like never before.

Why use magick?

Everyone has problems and everyone wants answers, so why turn to magick to make lasting life changes? For starters, magick is rooted in humanity's ancient past. Magick includes concepts, teachings, and symbols that resonate to the deepest core of our subconscious minds. This is wisdom clearly articulated by Socrates, Plato, and Aristotle, which was then filtered and built upon by generations of mankind's greatest thinkers both in the East and West.

Magick works because it is the most up-to-date psychology that exists—and it does so by drawing on the traditions of our ancient past, not by denigrating them.

I am a great friend of science; however, it disappoints in its narrowness of scope and its inability to produce lasting harmony or growth in humanity.

Science is the blundering missionary bringing antibiotics to the local villages. While that is certainly useful, it is no replacement for the wise and beneficent tribe shaman who takes care of the emotional and spiritual needs of the villagers, curing psychological aliments as well as physical ones. Magick is the epitome of effectiveness when it comes to changing people's lives and making them happy.

Magick is about taking charge of your spirituality *now* and putting it to good use in your life where you can see, taste, and feel the changes it produces. Magick is more than a religion or philosophy as it takes from *all* philosophies and *all* religions—whatever works the best. That is the spirit of magick and the spirit of *Everything You Want to Know About Magick (But Were Afraid to Ask)*.

Who is magick for?

Magick is for everyone. It is for the butcher, the athlete, the painter, the musician, and the banker. It is for the lawyer, the doctor, and the mountain man. Magick is about taking your life, your art, your love, and your career to the next level, all the while increasing your joy and satisfaction with who you are and what you spend your time doing.

How can magick help me?

In concrete terms, the benefits of learning magick are too numerous to list, but here are a few advantages of using magick:

- Understand and maximize the full potential of your mind and body.

- Learn rituals and meditations to attract wealth (Chapter 4), health (Chapter 6), and any other earthly delight under the sun or moon. I personally stumbled into magick to help me with love (Chapter 7).

- Increase your communication skills, wit, and rapport with others.

- Vastly increase creativity and healthy spontaneity.

- Acquire exceptional self-esteem, confidence, and sex appeal.

- While traveling your own unique path in magick, you will acquire a deep-rooted sense of your own place in the world, increasing the *meaning* of your life, granting greater satisfaction in all you do.

- Perhaps most important of all, you will understand your heart's desires much better. You might even learn that it isn't sex (Chapter 9) you wanted at all, but just a clear connection to—dare I say it? Something a little bit spiritual.

How does magick work?

The subconscious mind has access to everything we are not aware of consciously and is therefore in a better position to manifest our goals than our conscious mind, which is generally ego-ridden, anxious, and short-sighted.

Magick works by giving more control to the subconscious mind. Bypassing the constant chitter-chatter of our conscious mind, magick plants seeds deep into our psyche where they can grow unhindered by bad attitudes and negative thinking.

In other words, by giving the subconscious mind a clear intent through a magick ritual, we are then able to let go of our desire and allow it to manifest. While we are keeping busy "in the moment," the subconscious mind will be leading us towards our desired goal without interference from the conscious mind.

Is learning magick difficult?

Not when you start at the beginning and learn the essentials step by step, just as I will teach you in the following pages. This book assumes no prior knowledge of magick. All that is required of you is to read the chapters and follow the exercises and rituals as best as you are able.

My hope is that by the end of the book you will not only be able to understand any other literature on magick but that you will be able to create your own effective magick rituals for any area of your life that you feel is lacking.

What is the difference between a spell and a ritual?

There really isn't a clear distinction. Certain occultists might favor one term over the other. In my mind, spells tend to be shorter and simpler than rituals, and are almost always for a practical purpose, but the difference between the terms is more in connotation than denotation. For example, you could call a ceremony to attract romance a "love spell," but you would most likely not call something like the Christian Mass a "spell" (though indeed it is).

What if I'm rational and just don't believe in magick?

I've been there myself. Jump to Chapter 8 where I discuss the seeming paradox of the god of magick, Thoth, also being the god of science and rational thought.

Is magick dangerous or evil?

No. If you follow the instructions in this book you can only have beneficial results for yourself and those around you.

How long does magick take to work?

It really depends on what you are trying to get and what sort of mental/emotional blocks you might have set up against getting it. Results could take days, weeks, or months. Magick is not necessarily a quick-fix solution—though oftentimes it is. What I am presenting here is a lifelong skill for getting what you want in all aspects of your life.

While this book is geared to help with the mundane problems of life, as you progress upon your path of magick, you will find that most problems take care of themselves—or didn't matter much anyway.

Questions About the Author

What is your background in magick?

I have been studying, practicing, and teaching magick for more than twenty-two years. You might even say I have done so ravenously. I have studied high magick, Wicca, Eastern religions, Hermeticism, and just about every other form of occultism or religion. I have worked with Enochian magickal groups, Thelemic and Golden Dawn orders, and private sex magick groups. To this day I am a student of all things magickal, and I am always hungry for new methods and ideas to further improve the efficacy of my magick and those I teach online and through private instruction and classes.

How did you get into magick?

The how starts with the why, and the why was quite simple: I really wanted a girlfriend.

Ever since middle school and up through my first two years of high school what I wanted more than anything was a nice girlfriend. It was just not happening—not at all.

In my junior year of high school, however, I had a conversation that changed my life. A friend mentioned that she had once practiced spells she learned from a book. *Real* spells. This was a revelation to me. Having been somewhat sheltered from such things by my strict Christian upbringing, I had never realized that there were legitimate books on magick, the occult, spells, witchcraft, and the like.

Within a week, I had shown up on the doorstep of my very first occult bookstore. I still remember the smell of incense, the tinkling of wind chimes, and rows upon rows of books in categories entirely exotic to me: Buddhism, astrology, witchcraft, shamanism, and the like. I was especially drawn to the high magick section, where I bought *Modern Magick* by Donald Michael Kraig (Llewellyn, 1988) and began practicing immediately.

Involving myself in magick was challenging as I had to hide my practices from the rest of my family for fear my mom would find out. However,

I persevered, studied ravenously, and, on the surface, continued my life as a regular kid.

My first two spells—love talismans made out of seashells—were both successful. One talisman brought the first and only girl to ever seduce me with flowers. The second talisman brought the first true love of my life.

I continued studying and practicing magick throughout college. In Albuquerque, I worked with a large Wiccan coven and a Thelemic/Enochian high magick group. Both magickal congregations were very different in focus and scope, but I've always felt a need to understand diverse magickal philosophies and harmonize them into something whole and practical.

Things were not always roses, however. Magick doesn't remove challenges from one's life, but rather makes us more able to rise to the occasion of dealing with them. After receiving my degree in English at the University of New Mexico, I was at a loss as to what to do next with my life. I was sick of writing and sick of Albuquerque. I wanted to live—to experience.

Once again I turned to magick. I began working in earnest with the *Goetia*, a book of 72 spirits, the most famous "grimoire" of them all. I worked with Bune for wealth, Uvall for love, and Seere, a spirit used to speed up any magickal process.

After the working, my life bottomed out. I was depressed so I traveled to Phoenix, Arizona to stay with a friend. This is where the magick kicked in and things worked themselves out. I learned to count cards at blackjack and would make regular trips to Las Vegas, which is how I supported myself for the next year. Once I became bored with that, I spent a year writing a novel, which detailed my magickal experiences of the previous few years couched in a dark-fantasy milieu, but I was still not ready to write a non-fiction instructional book of magick, though in the back of my mind I already wanted to do so.

At this point, I was out of love and money so I worked again with the *Goetia*, and within a month I had an answer to both problems in the form of a girl I met online. This was in 1999 at the beginning of the dot-com boom. With me as her web designer, we started up a website, which was such a big success I was able to move to Los Angeles and do nothing but work with this lovely girl who was my business partner and girlfriend. This cemented my absolute belief in the efficacy of magick.

Life was good. I continued to study magick, write, and enjoy SoCal, which is where I had always wanted to live since I was about fifteen years old. Eventually, however, I felt a need for something more—I wanted to take my magick to the next level. My relationship had ended and my work had grown less satisfying. I began experimenting with the legal entheogen *Salvia divinorum,* and my magick instantly took a shamanistic turn. It was also around this time in 2005 that I became active in online occult communities, including writing my short, but influential, e-book entitled, *So You Want to Be a Goetic Shaman?*

More detail of this time period is contained in Chapter 8, but the gist is that this was a major turning point for me. After a three-month magickal working I did in the summer of 2005, I met a woman who would not only become my wife, but my magickal soulmate. This ties directly into my extensive work with demonology, which is discussed in Chapter 8.

By this point I had been teaching online and privately for several years, and I was ready to write my own book on magick. So, continuing through the ups and downs of my first magickal marriage, I was able to write the book you now hold in your hands.

Why did you write this book?

There are many reasons to write any book, but the two most practical concerns were that, one, I always wanted a book with all the information I regularly use for rituals in one place. And two, I'm regularly asked for help with magick and book recommendations, and I've always had to suggest books that weren't quite what someone needed. Now finally, with *Everything You Want to Know About Magick (But Were Afraid to Ask)* the essentials are presented in such a way that a beginner can quickly get up to speed with magick.

More than all that, I hope to impress upon my readers that magick is not something you do; it's something you are. This world has so many problems, but all of them can be cured by understanding the connection between art, magick, creativity, and our deepest desires—not just those implanted by peers or mass media. I hope that my book helps rejuvenate the psyche of not just individuals but that of our troubled Earth as a whole.

Who are your sources?

Magick and Hermeticism have always been syncretic, and I follow in this tradition. The benefit of my twenty-two years as a magician is granted to my readers by cutting out the dross. I present only the gold of magick and Hermeticism. My teachings are based on the very best sources in magick and Hermetic literature including, but not limited to:

- Plato
- Rumi
- John Dee
- Paracelsus
- Eliphas Lévi
- Israel Regardie
- Aleister Crowley

The grand theme of magick and Hermeticism is to sift through the wisdom of the past and to consistently bring the most psychologically up-to-date methodology to bear on increasing the quality of life for all humanity. *Everything You Want to Know About Magick (But Were Afraid to Ask)* brings modern sensibility to an underlying Hermetic philosophy that has worked for hundreds, even thousands, of years.

Questions About This Book

Who is this book for?

Everything You Want to Know About Magick (But Were Afraid to Ask) is for anyone who has been interested in real magick but has been confused, scared, or overwhelmed by other books on the subject. Beyond that, this book includes subtexts and layers of advanced magickal thought that will appeal to intermediate and advanced students as well.

To illustrate the wildly varied experiences one can take from this book, I present two happy endings, but with completely different means to that end.

The first example is from a former student by the name of Emily. Emily was in the midst of severe money problems, legal problems related to her animal activism, and going through a mid-life crisis all at once. Emily did not grow up religious, did not pray, or have a religion or spirituality of any sort. She had a fear of most things "dark" or occult, but liked "good magick." Emily was only able to work with basic meditations and the simplest of rituals in the book; however, they were enough to turn her attitude and life around. Now she is working at a job in her new profession, and her first film is now in production in Hollywood.

Another student by the name of Natasha illustrates a more gung-ho plunge into magick. A bright, but uneducated girl, she grew up in a religious household, but had no real connection to her original religion. She was fascinated by all aspects of magick as presented in *Everything You Want to Know About Magick (But Were Afraid to Ask),* including charging talismans and plunging directly into work with *daemons* and astral entities. She found a "familiar" spirit who encouraged her to quit drugs and alcohol and inspired and guided her to turn her life around on all levels. This spirit is currently helping Natasha make her way through college.

While both students had completely different goals and levels of interest in magick, both were able to take what they needed from *Everything You Want to Know About Magick (But Were Afraid to Ask)* to rectify their spiritual and material problems and thereby resume enjoyment of their lives.

What subjects does this book cover?

This book teaches the underlying concepts of magick, i.e., the actual principles involved in creating a ritual for the purpose of having positive results in our life.

This book correlates and puts into perspective a diverse range of magickal and occult topics such as angels, spirit guides, Wicca, Paganism, witchcraft, Goetia, Thelema, Golden Dawn, Qabalah, alchemy, astrology, chaos magick, sex magick, and Hermeticism.

Here are some of the magickal topics you will learn by studying and practicing the rituals and exercises in this book:

- How to understand and utilize the Hermetic language

- How to heal oneself and others utilizing the chakras

- How to prepare your temple

- How to create rituals for any purpose

- How to increase your psychic and astral senses and abilities

- How to perform sex magick, both alone and with others

- How to work with angels and demons

- How to maturely and safely work with entheogens

The content and structure of *Everything You Want to Know About Magick (But Were Afraid to Ask)* serves up a solid magickal meal, presenting theory and practice sandwiched together in the most appetizing fashion.

Some of the other types of questions you will be able to answer by the end of the book include:

- Who is the granddaddy of modern magick?

- What should I wear when performing magick?

- Where is the best place to meditate?

- When is the best time to create a love talisman?

- How do I know if I did a ritual properly?

How will this book teach me magick?

Everything You Want to Know About Magick (But Were Afraid to Ask) provides straightforward answers to the most common questions related to practicing magick. It teaches with plainspoken language (no occult mumbo jumbo) and modern views of psychology and the subconscious mind.

Everything You Want to Know About Magick (But Were Afraid to Ask) also includes historical references for context and authenticity, and when needed, gives straightforward and modern explanations of how and why magick works. However, the focus of this book is tangible results and its salient features reflect this, including:

- Fun and easy meditations

- Step-by-step rituals with diagrams that make even complex magickal ceremonies easy to perform

- Answers to the embarrassing "newbie" questions

- Detailed footnotes containing helpful, interesting, and topical information without distracting from the natural flow of the lessons

- A powerful system of magick, simple enough for a beginner to get started, but robust enough for even advanced students of magick

I treat magick with utmost sincerity and seriousness, but always with a light-hearted touch. This is a fun book, not a dreary grimoire.

Do I have to believe in God or the occult for this book to work?

Everything You Want to Know About Magick (But Were Afraid to Ask) is technique driven, not belief driven. This book neither assumes nor demands that you have any specific spiritual or occult belief. Magick works regardless. This means you can hold whatever beliefs about the universe you like and incorporate the rituals and meditations as you wish. Atheist, Buddhist, Wiccan, or Christian alike can utilize the rituals and see what works best for them.

Is this magick "dumbed down"?

While there are simple and clear rituals and meditations to change every aspect of one's life, there is no dumbing down. Have I simplified and trimmed magick down to the essentials? Absolutely, but the core techniques and ideas are those passed down from Ancient Greece, filtered through a variety of occult geniuses, changed a little by me based on modern sensibilities, and then presented to you, the reader, in an easy-to-follow instruction book. Complex parts are broken down into small and manageable bite sizes, but nothing is lost. Clarity is paramount, but never at the expense of potency or nuance.

How is this book organized?

This book is organized in such a way to teach you the simple building blocks of magick in the first chapters, and how to arrange and create with those blocks by the final chapter. The book is also arranged in a more subtle and nuanced way based upon the Tree of Life, which you learn about in the following chapters.

How should I use this book?

Read it through and practice as many exercises and rituals as you can. Some parts of the book may seem confusing the first time through, and that is to be expected. By the end of the book, you will have completed your first circuit of a spiral leading ever upward into the highest, and deepest, vaults of occult knowledge and wisdom.

How do I start?

Take a moment to think about what you *really* want from life. Think about whatever it is that popped into your head as you read this. Yes, *that*. Magick can even help you get *that*. Continue on to Chapter 1 to start the path that will teach you how.

THE LANGUAGE
⊕F ᛖAGICK

*"My alphabet starts with this letter called yuzz. It's the
letter I use to spell yuzz-a-ma-tuzz. You'll be sort of
surprised what there is to be found once you go beyond 'Z'
and start poking around!"*—Dr. Seuss

A Brief History of Magick

Magick as it exists today is an eclectic collection of esoteric traditions from
all over the world, including everything from Buddhism to voodou. However, magick has its roots most firmly planted in a single source, the Hermetic Order of the Golden Dawn.

The Golden Dawn, as it is more succinctly referred to, is a magickal
order founded in 1888 by three Freemasons: William Wynn Westcott, Samuel Liddell MacGregor Mathers, and William Robert Woodman.

The instruction and rituals of the Golden Dawn are based on an elegant mishmash of Hebrew Qabalah, Sabian-Arabian astrological systems, Pythagorean philosophies, Gnostic traditions, Christian theology, and most notably, Hermeticism.

Hermeticism is a philosophy developed during the Hellenistic civilization, which draws upon the best of Greek philosophy, dating back to Plato (428–348 BCE), and what their sages understood of ancient Egyptian magick. Hermeticism also includes aspects of alchemy, astrology, and theurgy[1]. Hermetic symbolism is still the core language used by magicians today.

The Golden Dawn was instrumental in harmonizing all these various and divergent esoteric philosophies and presenting them in practical and usable form; however, it was a secret order so their rituals and meditations were not published until many years later, in 1934 by Israel Regardie. But by this point the cat was already out of the bag because the most notorious member of the Golden Dawn, Aleister Crowley (1875–1947), had already published many of the Golden Dawn secrets in his voluminous works on magick.

Aleister Crowley's influence on magick cannot be overstated. If it were not for his deliberate breaking of order vows, many of the rituals and documents of the Golden Dawn may never have been published. Crowley was a grand synthesizer of disparate beliefs, and his voluminous works, including *The Book of the Law*, *Magick*, and *The Equinox*, have influenced magick heavily to this day. In fact, it was Crowley himself who first coined the term "magick" spelled with a "k" to differentiate it from stage magic.

Crowley can even be credited as the primary source for Wicca, one of the most popular magickal religions today. Wicca was founded in the 1950s by Gerald Gardner, who was a student of Crowley. Many of the core rituals and ideology that Gardner presented as original have since been proven to have been lifted directly from Thelema and *The Book of the Law*. However,

---

1 The practice of using rituals to invoke divinity.

this is no slight on Wicca, as Wicca has evolved into a tradition both powerful and accessible, with many of its own developments further enhancing traditional Thelema.

So while some magicians and scholars like to differentiate magick into categories such as high magick, low magick, Hermeticism, Wicca, Paganism, shamanism, chaos magick, etc., I focus on similarities, not differences, and tend to pull from all sorts of esoteric teachings, including modern psychology. My goal is to teach you to do the same. Labels are ultimately irrelevant to successful practical magick and tend to foster discord, instead of a healthy syncreticism. The *underlying principles of magick* are what we are most interested in. This will allow you to understand any book on magick, no matter what flavor, and make it work in your day-to-day life.

So while this brief history may have thrown some unfamiliar names at you, all you really need to know is that *magick is magick*, and the only reliable gauge of efficacy is practical results. The goal of *Everything You Want to Know About Magick (But Were Afraid to Ask)* is to teach you the steps that are necessary to make magick work.

Why is this book so Thelemic?

Thelema is Crowley's philosophy and system of magick based on the teachings of *The Book of the Law*. While Crowley's system is unique, it is heavily rooted in Hermeticism as taught to him by the Golden Dawn. I have no intentions of making this a specifically "Thelemic" book; however, Thelema is *non-dogmatic*, meaning you can take or leave what you want from it. There is no strict formal code, other than to enjoy life the most you possibly can.

I quote from *The Book of the Law*, and reference Crowley in various other ways, because he not only offers concise and often poetic examples of the sometimes obtuse concepts in magick, but also because it will further introduce you to Aleister Crowley. Whether you like him or not is of no matter; he is such a lynchpin of modern occultism, one cannot escape the influence of his work, which is voluminous, complex, and erudite. I hope what you learn in this book goes a long way to understanding and using his magick if you are so inclined.

Crowley was a big proponent of doing your own thing and thinking for yourself. So in that way, I'm entirely in agreement with him. If you get anything out of my book, it is to be that way with your entire life. Learn, study, and analyze information from many sources and make your own decisions regarding magick, love, morals and ethics, government, etc. Make choices that enhance your life and those you love, anything else is the only "sin" you can commit.

The Hermetic Language

The "language" of Hermeticism is made up of symbols, formulas, and other magickal concepts, which we will soon be discussing in detail. The Hermetic language serves two primary functions. First, it is a method of communicating between magicians, and more importantly, it is the means by which we will communicate our desires to the subconscious mind.

Why doesn't our native tongue suffice for this? It's too tied to the mundane affairs of life, while the Hermetic language utilizes symbolism that hearkens back to our earliest scholars, most notably Plato.

So now I present the most commonly used symbols of magick, starting with simple and general principles and then moving into more detailed and complex ways to subdivide the universe. All of the following symbols are ways to classify and understand the universe and thereby transform it— while at the same time, the symbolism attunes and *harmonizes ourselves to the universe.*

Polarity

Polarity is the most simple energy to understand; it is the tension between two opposites such as male and female, Yin and Yang, positive and negative, etc.

Polarity is actively used in Wicca, for example, where the Goddess and the God are both venerated equally and often simultaneously.

Good and evil is another polarity, but it is a man-made moral concept. In nature there is no ultimate good or evil. What is good for one form of life, such as a parasite, may not be good for its host.

Polarity is not only utilized in magick and science but appears everywhere in our daily lives. Hot and cold, the nut and the bolt, the sun and the moon are all variations of polarity as it appears in the real world.

As Above, So Below

Another type of polarity is that which is within us versus that which is without us. This is another way of saying that which is above us (in the "heavenly" realm) is reflected in that which is below us (in the "material" world).

This concept is summed up in the famous Hermetic saying from the *Emerald Tablet*[2]:

> "That which is below is as that which is above,
> and that which is above is as that which is below,
> to perform the miracles of the one thing."

In occult circles this is usually simplified to "As above, so below." The ancients considered this maxim to contain a great secret of magick: If we make appropriate changes within ourselves, they must be reflected in our external, material world. This, indeed, is what a modern magician means when he says changes in his subconscious eventually have lasting and potent changes in the physical world. The essentials of magick and Hermeticism have not changed much over the centuries, simply the wording and conceptualization has evolved.

---

2 *The Emerald Tablet* is a popular alchemical and Hermetic text purported to have been written by Hermes Trismegistus ("Hermes the Thrice-Greatest"). Hermes Trismegistus was a combination of the Greek Hermes and the Egyptian god Thoth, both of whom were considered gods of writing and magick. Though no Greek original is existent, the *Emerald Tablet's* earliest Latin translation was in 1140, and Arabic versions exist that predate the Latin version by several hundred years.

The Alchemical Principles of Sulphur, Salt, and Mercury

Triple energies abound in magick and philosophy alike, including the three *gunas* from Hinduism, the Holy Trinity of Catholicism, and Hegel's thesis-antithesis-synthesis.

In this book we are most concerned with the alchemical principles of Sulpur, Salt, and Mercury.

What is Alchemy?

Alchemy is a philosophy and practice spanning thousands of years (5000 BCE for Egyptian alchemy) and dozens of cultures (Indian, Greek, Chinese, Islamic, and European). The ultimate goal of alchemy was the transmutation of "lead" into "gold." This was metaphorical as ancient alchemists were not looking for physical gold, but rather a way to transform the baseness of man into a perfected state of godhood. This solution was known as the "philosopher's stone."

The alchemical motto, VITRIOL, contains this belief: "*Visita Interiora Terrae Rectificando Invenies Occultum Lapidem.*" ("Visit the Interior Parts of the Earth; by Rectification Thou Shalt Find the Hidden Stone").

Don't let the word "alchemical" intimidate you. In modern parlance, many magicians might confess to performing "alchemy" of some sort, though very few are sitting near tables full of tubes, beakers, distillers, and alembics. Most modern alchemy is *psychological*.

In this book, all you need to know about alchemy is the following three principles[3] adapted for practical use in this book.

---

3 There are other variations of what Mercury, Salt, and Sulphur represent. For example, Paracelsus described Mercury as fusibility and volatility, Sulphur as flammability, and Salt as fixity and noncombustibility. I find these descriptions less useful in modern practice than the ones given here.

Symbol	Alchemical Principle	Meaning
☊	Sulfur	Symbolizes energy that is active. This type of energy is highly volatile and tends to be short lived and "burn up."
⊖	Salt	This symbolizes energy that tends towards stagnation, passivity, and heavy inertia.
☿ or ☿	Mercury	Mercury symbolizes lucidity, clarity, and poise. He is balance between the hyperactivity of Sulfur, and the slow-moving heaviness of Salt.

Magick is often about taking antagonistic energies and uniting them by a third concept harmonious to both. Imagine the opposites of Sulphur on one hand and Salt on the other. Who balances them? Mercury, the man, the magician:

A handy example of this is the atom, the once-thought-to-be indivisible building block of the universe. Now we know that the atom is made of three things: the proton (Salt), the neutron (Mercury), and the electron (Sulfur).

The Five Classical Elements

The five elements (Earth, Water, Air, Fire, and Aethyr) date from the pre-Socratic times of Ancient Greece (around 450 BCE). Other civilizations have similar categorizations, such as the Hindu and Japanese cultures, but we will be focusing on the traditional "Hermetic" elements.

These "elements" are not meant to be used and understood like the elements of the periodic table. These classical elements represent five categorizations of energies found in nature and, more importantly, within our own psyches and personalities.

Symbol	Element	Color	Meaning
△	Fire	Red	Symbolizes: the Will, energy, force, creation, destruction, libido.
▽	Water	Blue	Symbolizes: emotions, love, receptivity, understanding.
⟁	Air	Yellow	Symbolizes: intellect, strife, speed, travel, information.
⩒	Earth	Verdant Green (or Black)	Symbolizes: the physical body, the planet Earth, anything tangible, solidity, heaviness, the material plane, vegetative growth.
✹	Spirit/Aethyr	White/Brilliance	Spirit is "above and beyond" the other four elements; it's of another plane, another level completely. Spirit is also the true "essence" of something.

In practical magick we often discuss the "four elements" while leaving Spirit out. In this case, Spirit is still implied. Therefore, whether you see "five elements" or "four elements" in magickal literature, understand they both refer to the same concept.

A pyramid neatly symbolizes the five elements. The four base sides are the four elements. They are of the world. The fifth element, spirit, is the tip of the pyramid, above and distinct from the four elements below it, and yet attached to them from a place of superiority.

The Tetragrammaton

There is a magickal formula hidden in a four-letter Hebrew word. The Tetragrammaton is the "unpronounceable" name of God in the Old Testament and appears in dozens of other Hebrew God names:

The Tetragrammaton is the formula of the four elements.[4] In magick we often pronounce it by the names of the four letters that make up the name: *Yod-Heh-Vav-Heh*. Fire is Yod, the all-father. The first Heh is the mother, i.e., Water. Together they give birth to their son, Vav, who is Air, and their daughter, the "final" Heh, who is Earth. (Spirit is the tip of the Yod.)

This formula is considered to be circular, as once you get to the end, i.e., the daughter, she is to be set upon the throne of her mother to mate with the all-father and continue the cycle of energy.

The Four Quadrants/Quarters

The four elements also apply to the four directions of a compass. The usual magickal correspondences are that Air is in the East, Fire is in the South, Earth is in the North, and Water is in the West. Most magick rituals

---

4   This is true now; however, ancient Hebrews didn't consider Earth one of the original elements, but rather as a combination of Fire, Water, and Air. These three elements corresponded with the three Hebrew mother letters: Shin, Mem, and Aleph.

are performed facing East, since that is the direction of dawn. However, there are many occasions when a student may find it more appropriate to face one of the other cardinal directions. The fifth element of Spirit is often conceived of as being "above," hence, why the symbol of Spirit, a lamp, is hung over the center of the temple.

The cardinal directions are often referred to as quarters, or as quadrants, which mean the same thing. For example, you might hear "face the southern quadrant" for a ritual. That simply means face the southern part of your temple.

The Cherubim (Kerubim)

A cherub in this sense doesn't mean a cute baby with wings. These cherubim are pictorial metaphors for each of the four elements:

- Lion = Fire

- Ox/Bull/Calf = Earth

- Man/Angel/Water-Bearer = Air

- Eagle/Scorpion = Water

The four Cherubim pop up all over the place. They are mentioned in Ezekial (1:10) and Revelation (4:7). They appear in Golden Dawn rituals such as the Supreme Ritual of the Pentagram. They appear in tarot decks on the corners of Trump XXI: *The World* (and sometimes on other cards such as Crowley's Trump VII: *The Chariot* and the Rider-Waite Trump X: *Wheel of Fortune*).

The Cherubim are sometimes represented by just their heads and other times with winged bodies. It should also be noted that the Water sign shows a bird, and that the Air sign carries water. These two signs are inextricably linked in practical magick. In traditional Golden Dawn pentagram rituals, the invoking of Air banishes Water, and the invoking of Water banishes Air, as if they were inverse of each other.

Wherever the Cherubim turn up they represent the four elements as described above.

Why is Scorpio sometimes an eagle and not a scorpion?

Since ancient times the eagle has been associated with Scorpio as well as the scorpion, suggesting a dual nature to its symbolism. We will learn more about this when we discuss Path 24 of Tree of Life in the next chapter.

Elemental Pentagram

The five elements are traditionally applied to a pentagram as seen here. Depending on where one starts drawing the pentagram, and whether one moves clockwise or counterclockwise, a magician will invoke a specific elemental energy. You will use your first invoking pentagram in the next chapter, and the pentagram is covered in more detail in Chapter 5. For now you should understand that in magick, the pentagram is a symbol of all five elements coexisting in perfect harmony.

When you need a high-dose injection of a favorite element, you can perform a simple ritual given later in this book to invoke all the Fire, Water, Air, Spirit, or Earth that you need.

Why would I want to invoke elements?

While we will cover invocations later in the book, for now you might be interested to know that in magick, *like attracts like*. So when you "pull in" a specific energy, it will affect you psychologically and therefore your life. Each element corresponds to the following types of useful energy:

Spirit: Invoke for balance, perfect equilibrium, and dominance of the other four elements in a most sublime manner.

Fire: Invoke for energy, power, intensity, creativity, as well as for destructive and transformative energy.

Water: Invoke for openness, emotional harmony, intuition, love, and friendship.

Air: Invoke for intellectual pursuits, such as games, wars, simulations, debate, politics, verbal wit, help with school and college, and all pursuits that rely on "mental" energy.

Earth: Invoke for anything related to wealth, physics, geometry, architecture, as well as the carnal pleasures of the flesh.

If you are looking for creativity, they *all* provide an increase in creativity, it's just a matter of what type. You'll know instantly which element you most want to work with; however, if you are unsure of which element you need, but feel you are missing something—*that* is Spirit.

The Seven Traditional Planets of Magick

The seven traditional "planets" of magick are the five planets easily visible without a telescope plus the Sun and Moon. *The way the planets are used in this book has nothing to do with astrology or predicting fortunes.* It also has nothing to do with astronomy, so traditional astronomers will just have to forgive the convention of calling the Sun and the Moon planets.

Consider the planets to be specific archetypes living in our subconscious. In other words, each planet is symbolic of deeply rooted personality traits within the human psyche. Understanding these traits, which are essentially straightforward, will help a student understand other aspects of magick, such as the symbolism of the tarot and the Tree of Life.

These symbols are also psychologically powerful in themselves and their meanings are used throughout magick on a regular basis. These symbols are utilized in rituals and in the construction of talismans. They are also fundamental to the language used amongst magicians. The planets are shorthand for seven specific types of energy, a complete system by itself, even without the zodiac.

Symbol	Roman (Greek)	Symbolism
☽ or ☾	Diana (Artemis), usually known as Luna or the Moon	Mystery and intuition. Purity, grace, and inspiration.
♃	Jupiter (Zeus)	Royalty, expansion, benevolent rulership, stability.
♄	Saturn (Kronos)	Time, Karma, and death. Heaviness. Life lessons. Discipline.
♂	Mars (Aries)	Destruction, violent change, and power. Typical "male" energy.
♀	Venus (Aphrodite)	Love and romance, but also sometimes debauchery. Nurturing protection, Mother Nature, and vegetative growth. Typical "female" energy.
☉	Apollo (Apollo), usually known as Sol or the Sun	The center. Warmth, sight, light, and healing. Music and joy.
☿ or ☿	Mercury (Hermes)	Wit, intellect, speed, alacrity, and trickery. Mercury is also sexually ambiguous—it's never clear if he has no gender or both. As you'll learn as you make your progression through this book, Mercury is a wily one—seemingly everywhere at once, yet impossible to pin down.

These definitions are a bit succinct so if you wish to know more about a specific planet's energy, just research the corresponding Greek or Roman god in any mythological resource. Other gods from different pantheons are also appropriate. For example, Krishna from Hinduism fits under the Sun, while Loki from Norse mythology is a trickster, thus putting him under the dominion of Mercury.

Introduction to the Zodiac

The basis of the modern astrological signs goes back to the Babylonian period (around 1000 BC), but they were refined into their present state by Hellenistic Greece.[5] They are twelve in number and are represented by the symbols of the ram, the bull, the twins, the crab, the lion, the virgin, the scales, the scorpion, the centaur archer, the sea-goat, the water-bearer, and the fishes.

These symbols are immediate, suggestive, and fertile for resonate interpretations. Why have these signs remained so popular (now used on t-shirts, key chains, etc.) for nearly 3000 years? They resonate as archetypes in our collective subconscious. They make sense to our minds as metaphor and so we continue to use them.

Do you believe in astrology?

It's a fun way to get to know people, and it is a good way to familiarize yourself with the zodiac, but if taken too seriously, like other forms of divination, astrology can be a distraction from real magick. Magick is about taking action based on being present in the moment. Though I love the symbolism of the zodiac (and the planets) for defining certain human tendencies, I prefer to define my own fate rather than look for it in the stars. However, if you eventually choose to practice astrology, the symbolism you learn here will go a long way in your studies.

---

5   The Dendera Zodiac, a relief dating to ca. 50 BC, is the first known depiction of the classical zodiac of twelve signs.

Beyond astrology as a form of divination, I find that many people subconsciously take on the traits of their Sun sign, so astrology definitely has a psychological validity. I find this to be true even in cases of those who know nothing of astrology. Everyone usually knows their zodiac sign[6] even if they don't know exactly what it means. These symbols resonate somehow, hence their continued popularity with mankind.

Cardinal, Fixed, and Mutable

The signs of the zodiac are broken up into the four elements, and then further subdivided into cardinal, fixed, and mutable categorizations:

	Cardinal	Fixed	Mutable
Fire	Aries	Leo	Sagittarius
Water	Cancer	Scorpio	Pisces
Air	Libra	Aquarius	Gemini
Earth	Capricorn	Taurus	Virgo

Cardinal signs are the onrushing energy of that sign. Fixed signs are the most stable versions of their element. Mutable signs are the element as they tend to change into something else. Therefore, cardinal signs tend towards starting things. Fixed signs tend to stay the same. Mutable signs are adaptable.

The Rulers of the Zodiac

Each of the twelve zodiac signs is "ruled" by one of seven traditional planets given above. This means that the ruling planet of the sign adds another level of interpretation to the zodiacal sign. Perhaps more importantly, the ruling

---

6 The Chinese astrological signs are in popular use as well.

planets show how to "stir up" the specific energy of the zodiac we are looking for. More on this in later chapters.

The Twelve Signs of the Zodiac
♈ Aries

The Ram: Ruled by Mars

Aries is the initial burst of energy that starts any new action or project. Aries is the fresh, new energy of Spring. Aries energy is direct, straightforward, and sometimes rigidly determined. This energy may be short-lived and can be destructively impetuous.

♉ Taurus

The Bull: Ruled by Venus

Taurus is steady, persistent, and durable. It is difficult to sway Taurus energy from its current path since it is Earth energy in its most stable and reliable form. There also is grace and beauty in this sign granted to it by its ruler Venus.

♊ Gemini

The Twins: Ruled by Mercury

Gemini is dual-natured, quick-witted, and intuitive energy. Mercury rules this sign and so Gemini's energy is fascinated by the power of language and responds well to savvy intellectual stimuli.

♋ Cancer

The Crab: Ruled by the Moon

Cancer is protective, secretive, nurturing energy. Being ruled by the Moon, the passion of the crab is stirred by mystery. This also suggests the mood and energy level of Cancer tends to ebb and flow like that of tides.

♌ Leo

The Lion: Ruled by the Sun

The Lion is "King of the Jungle." The royal Leo is as much the center of attention as the Sun is the center of the solar system. Leo loves to be the source of good energy, thus dominating everyone and everything in his sphere of influence.

♍ Virgo

The Virgin: Ruled by Mercury

Virgo, ruled by Mercury, implies refinement and verbal eloquence. Virgo energy is also prudent, detail-oriented, practical, and even a bit "picky." Deeper than all this, the virgin is pure potential, i.e., the potential to give birth. So this entire sign is about the hidden mysteries of procreation.

♎ Libra

The Scales: Ruled by Venus

Libra is all about balance, which includes energy tipping from one side to the other in the name of equilibrium. This includes energy moving towards a final result such as marriage or court cases. Ruled by Venus, Libra energy also exudes elegance, beauty, and harmony.

♏ Scorpio

The Scorpion and *The Eagle:* Ruled by Mars

Scorpio is passion and brooding intensity. Scorpio has the ability to destroy itself (Scorpion) or the ability to transcend (Eagle). This energy is magnetic and darkly seductive. Obsessive, sometimes dangerous, sexual impulses can originate with Scorpio. This is Cancer's only rival for "most secretive" of the signs.

♐ Sagittarius

The Archer Centaur: Ruled by Jupiter

Sagittarius is focused intelligence and directed action. Sagittarius energy is optimistic and freedom loving. Imagine the image of the centaur (body of a horse with the head and chest of a man). The centaur roams carefree across the plains, but when it's time to hunt, the archer is deadly accurate with his aim.

♑ Capricorn

The Goat-Fish: Ruled by Saturn

Capricorn, a goat with a fish-tail, ascends from deepest emotions (the fish-tail) all the way to the highest mountains of action and accomplishment (symbolized by a mountain goat). Capricorn energy is practical, yet still contains a certain emotional sensitivity. Capricorn is persistent, determined energy that will not be easily shoved aside from its ambitions.

♒ Aquarius

The Water-Bearer: Ruled by Saturn

Aquarius is original, independent thought. An intellectual sign, Aquarius is ruled by Saturn, suggesting that the grandiose ideas of the Aquarian are best governed by practical and realistic concerns.

♓ Pisces

The Fishes: Ruled by Jupiter

Pisces is mysterious, reflective, intuitive, and imaginative energy. The weakness here is that Pisces energy can be led astray by external influences. Also it can stagnate and lead to malaise.

What is the point of learning all these symbols and their meanings?

All the symbols used in this book, whether the elements, zodiac signs, or even the Hebrew letters themselves, are all part of a common language used in magick. Over hundreds (sometimes thousands) of years of use, they have been proven to have psychological resonance.

Each symbol is a "pointer" to a type of energy in our psyche. The more one uses the symbols, the stronger the connection to the actual energy. With a little time and practice, all these magickal symbols become a new language with which to speak to your subconscious as well as with other magicians.

Also learning simple concepts such as Fire and Water helps to make sense of more complex magickal symbols, such as the seven planets and the zodiac. These concepts will come in handy in Chapter 3 when we discuss the paths of the Tree of Life, which in turn make even the seventy-eight cards of the tarot deck comprehensible and manageable.

The Hebrew Alphabet

The most common alphabet associated with Hermeticism is the Hebrew alphabet. The twenty-two letters of the Hebrew alphabet look like this (from right to left):

אבגדהוזחטיכלמנסעפצקרשת

What does Judaism have to do with magick?

Magicians use the Hebrew alphabet, the Tree of Life, and other components from traditional "Hebrew mysticism."[7] This might give the appearance that high magick is closely related to Judaism, when ideologically it is not.

Magick tends to take from any religion or spirituality—if it works. You will find not only influences from ancient Hebrew, but also influences from all world religions and spiritual schools of thought including Arabic, Hinduism, Buddhism, ancient Egyptian, and even modern psychology.

The tools of magick presented in this book can be used without any specific belief in God or religion. ***This book focuses on techniques rather than dogma.*** There is no reason the exercises taught here couldn't be plugged into anyone's spirituality (or lack therefore). The magick works regardless.

What is gematria?

All Hebrew letters also have a numerical value.[8] By adding the numerical value of words together and comparing them you get philosophical correspondences. For example, the Hebrew word for Love (אהבה) adds to 13; so does the word for unity (אחד). Gematria suggests then that love equals unity.

---

7 Known as "Kabbalah." A full explanation of *Kabbalah*, and the magickal variant *Qabalah*, is given in Chapter 3.

8 See Chapter 3.

Gematria is commonly used in high magick as a mean of communicating complex magickal ideas, i.e., formulas. Gematria is also helpful in the construction of magickal tools, and in such things as choosing your magickal motto. Gematria is also sometimes used in the invocations of spirits to test their validity. You will become more familiar with gematria and its uses over the course of this book.

Other Magickal Alphabets

While a familiarity with Hebrew is helpful in magick, there is no reason to confine yourself to the use of a single magickal alphabet. There are others that are just as efficacious. For example, the Hebrew alphabet, along with most other alphabets, such as Arabic, Greek, and Latin are derived from the Phoenician (which is also read right to left):

ℱOᏨᏒᏢ᠙WXᎩᏗᏁᎷ⊘H ⊥Ƴᘰ◁ᐳ꒦

This alphabet was developed around 1,050 BCE and uses most of the same letter names and descriptions as the Hebrew, e.g., Aleph means "ox" in both alphabets. While modern magick is heavily laced with Hebrew, there is no reason not to use Phoenician instead, which I consider to be a powerful, if under-used, magickal alphabet.

Magicians often use a number of other alphabets, many of which are quite elaborate, such as the Alphabet of the Genii:

Magickal alphabets are not meant to be used like our usual day-to-day alphabet, but instead kept separate and used only for ritual purposes. This builds up a psychological resonance with the magickal alphabet, creating a powerful link to our subconscious.

While Hebrew is the most commonly used magickal alphabet in Western esoterica, for your practical magick, you may use any alphabet you see fit. You may even end up creating your own. More information on the actual application of magickal alphabets will be developed in later chapters, including the Enochian, which is not just an alphabet but an entire angelic language.

Other uses of magickal alphabets are more mundane but just as useful, such as using them as ciphers for hiding secret rituals from prying eyes.

The 22 Major Arcana and the Tree of Life

Twenty-two is an important number in magick. It is the number of letters in the Hebrew alphabet, the number of paths of the Tree of Life, and the number of Major Arcana in a standard tarot deck. We will discuss what all this means in Chapter 3, but as a central component of Hermetic philosophy, I mention it briefly now.

Relax and Keep a Journal

To finish off this chapter, I end with two important, if seemingly simple, concepts. Both are crucial to long-term magickal growth, but could easily be glossed over by beginners as unimportant.

Relaxation

Magick works by using symbolic language to communicate our desires to the subconscious mind. One way to get a proper message to the subconscious is by utilizing an "altered" state of consciousness. In this case, a relaxed and calm state of mind is all that is required. (Later in the book we will discuss altered states of minds produced by long rituals, meditation, sex, drugs, and the like, but for now, relaxing is more than good enough.)

How does relaxing help magick work?

Alpha waves are brain waves that appear when we are in a relaxed and wakeful state. These waves can be measured with an EEG or an MEG and originate from the occipital lobe of our brain. What this means in science isn't nearly as important for our purposes as what it means in magick. It means this is a built-in "altered state." When we are in a relaxed and meditative state it is an opportune time for magick.

As a corollary, our usual waking, oft-stressed-out state of mind, is the worst place from which to make life changes.

The moral here is *do not skimp on relaxation.* Enjoy it. Take time to indulge in relaxation before every ritual and all your magick will be successful and fulfilling.

The Importance of Keeping a Magickal Record

Magicians should be vigilant in keeping track of all meditations, rituals, and other magickal practices. Here are four reasons why you will want to keep a magick journal of some sort:

- It will make your magickal experiences more real and therefore more powerful to effect change on the material plane.

- It's a record that one day you will be glad you have when you want to see how various magickal acts affected your life, i.e., what worked and what didn't.

- It builds confidence as you will see how much work you've been putting in and how much you've improved.

- It may very well evolve into the most magickal thing in your life, causing lasting changes in ways you never expected. Never underestimate the power of writing. The Egyptian Thoth was the god of magick *and* writing.

Relaxing *before* a ritual and writing all your experiences down *afterward* form perfect bookends to all your magick rituals and meditation practices.

EXERCISE 1.1: KEEP A MAGICKAL JOURNAL

Every chapter of this book ends with at least one practical exercise. Unless otherwise noted, all exercises are considered to be required practice.

Your magickal journal, also known as your Book of Shadows, can be as simple or as complex as you like, but you must record all magickal workings (including your daily Equilibrating Ritual of the Pentagram, given next chapter). Write down the time and date and any other useful information as you see fit, which can include such things as your mood, the weather, what's on your mind, and what you saw or felt during the ritual, etc.

You can write in anything from a simple notepad to a fancy diary. If you already keep a journal or diary, you can add your magickal records to it or start a separate journal.

EXERCISE 1.2: RELAXATION RITUAL

If you know some other form of relaxation technique you may substitute that here. It is not so relevant what sort of relaxation ritual you do, so long as you take time to be restful before performing other, more complex rituals.

First, give yourself permission to relax. Seriously. Some people will find this easy, but others get stuck on this. Know now that the best thing you can do to make lasting life changes is to stop, relax, and do nothing.

So take your time. Get comfortable sitting or lying down. Shake out any tension. Relax. Get cozy.

Mentally go over every part of your body to check for tension. Check your legs, your feet, your toes. Check your shoulders, your spine, your arms, your hands, and your fingers. Check your gut. Check your neck and double check your shoulders. Relax. You can't do this exercise wrong. There is no need to relax "perfectly." Just take it easy for a few minutes.

Say out loud: *"As I now relax, I feel the subconscious power of my Divine and Higher Self arise, easily and without conscious effort."*

Count slowly backwards from eleven. Take at least one full breath between each count. (If you go so slowly that you lose track of where you are in your counting, that is good—that is a sign you are relaxing deeply.)

When you reach zero, just wallow in the comfort of feeling more relaxed than you were when you started.

Learn this simple ritual well as it is the first step in all further magick rituals given throughout this book.

THE EQUILIBRATING
RITUAL OF THE
PENTAGRAM

*"Give me a place to stand and I will
move the earth!"*—Archimedes

What is the LBRP?

The LBRP stands for the Lesser Banishing Ritual of Pentagram. This ritual
was developed by the Golden Dawn[9] and is based on traditional Hebrew
prayers and the writings of Eliphas Lévi, a 19th Century French occultist.

---

9 Most likely worked out as some sort of joint contribution between Mathers and Wescott with
   Mathers in the dominant role.

Because of its simplicity and efficacy, it has become a centerpiece of practical magick, and most ceremonial magicians use some version of it when performing magick.

What does banishing mean?

Banishing is a common term in magick, which means clearing your mental, emotional, and physical space. However, I'm not happy with this term. The more you practice magick, the less accurate and misleading the term "banishing" is. As your magick and perception of the universe grows, you will experience a distinct unity with the universe and cosmos. Therefore when you "banish" something, where does it go? It implies there is some garbage heap out there where you push unwanted energies, but that is just wrong.

A better word to describe the calming, balancing wave of energy that a good banishing ritual confers is "equilibrating." A banishing ritual is actually about balancing energies and centering us within our own body.

What is the ERP?

ERP stands for the Equilibrating Ritual of the Pentagram. The ERP is the version of the LBRP I am going to give in this book.[10] It is streamlined, pared down to the essentials of what is necessary for fluidity, safety, and practical results.

Why perform the Equilibrating Ritual of the Pentagram?

This ritual is the minimum requirement for any magickal progress with this book. You will perform it before doing any practical magick whatsoever. If you continue the path of magick, you will use it regularly your whole life (even if you eventually modify it to your own taste and style).

---

10   This includes the "Analysis of Keywords" section from a long initiatory Golden Dawn ceremony called the "Adeptus Minor Ritual." This invokes the holiest and highest aspects of yourself into consciousness.

To understand the power and sublimity of the ERP, you would ideally practice it for a minimum of one year. It was a traditional requirement of the Golden Dawn that a student practice the LBRP for one year before they could move on to other magick. However, I believe one month of daily practice is sufficient to begin working with the rest of the magick in this book.

Here are ten benefits the Equilibrating Ritual of the Pentagram has to offer:

1. It is the solid basis for all magickal work, including love and wealth magick.

2. As you must clean and arrange your temple's physical space, so does the ERP clear you emotionally and mentally for magick.

3. The more you practice the ERP, the more you define a sacred and spiritual space within your temple. Your magick will then become more potent and easier to perform.

4. It will center you in the world, allowing you to look inward for balance and completeness. You will not rely on others to feel good, which breeds independence and self-confidence. Your self-esteem will shoot through the roof.

5. The ERP builds character and discipline. To boldly stand in your bedroom, now turned temple with a few candles and some incense, to chant "funny words" while drawing "astral shapes" in the air requires a fair bit of determination and the ability to step outside your comfort zone.

6. It removes the stress and negativity of a "bad" day. With all your negativity regularly stripped away by the ERP, you will more naturally attract what you want into your life.

7. It will help you create a "default state" of calmness and joy that will stay with you during your days and nights even when not performing the ritual. This will increase your sense of well-being in even the most chaotic and stressful of times.

8. It's one of the best preventive measures against media and social brainwashing that you can find. Learn to live life on your own terms and not be dictated to by the world around you.

9. It will increase your visualization abilities, which is useful in all types of magick.

10. You have to start the path of magick somewhere. This is it.

Can I really do this?

This single ritual will weed out the dabblers from the practitioners. Few will try to learn, and those who try often get frustrated and give up. In this book, I hope to inspire you to want to learn and make it easy to do so.

I'm here to tell you right now that doubts and frustrations are a natural part of learning magick. *I get it.* I was there myself. My first few years of magick I learned through books only, and many times I was filled with embarrassment, frustration, and sometimes even downright contempt for myself and the idea of doing something as "silly" as magick.

Some tips that will help you through learning the ERP and all other magickal rituals in this book:

1. Learn to acquire a trust in a "higher power," whether you call it "God," the "universal consciousness," or merely your "subconscious mind." Why? Otherwise you are going to put way too much weight on your own shoulders. Doing magick is about doing your very best, but at some point you have to let go and trust that your actions are working on a deeper level than the conscious mind. A trust in something higher makes it easier to let go of your worries and will allow you to act with more confidence and fluidity because you won't put so much pressure on yourself.

2. Let go of your mistakes. If you make a mistake, don't stop and analyze it. Either forget about the mistake and move on, or you can calmly correct it and then move on. If you "completely

bungle" a ritual, you can start from the beginning, but I
suggest you always finish off whatever ritual you start, even if
it has many mistakes. Forward momentum is healthier and keeps
you from obsessing over every detail of the ritual, wondering if
you did it perfectly. *Your magick does not have to be perfect to work.*
In fact, your magick will never be perfect. That is just the ideal
we strive for. The most important quality to have is *sincerity* that
you are doing your best. That's it!

3. Patience. It will take time to get comfortable with any new ritual.
   The first dozen times may feel awkward. Don't worry about that.
   Always pat yourself on the back after you are done—even if you
   felt it didn't go as well as it could have.

4. Practice regularly, but never to the point of burnout or
   exhaustion.

5. Trust your own sense of style. No person's rituals are exactly like
   any other's. Trust yourself to fill in any missing spaces in rituals,
   in this book, or in any other book on magick, as you see fit. Learn
   to trust your own intuition over what is printed in any book. If
   you feel you need to add little touches to the ritual, such as
   blowing a kiss to each cardinal direction, then by all means do
   so. Don't let your rituals stagnate. Let them evolve with your
   personality and experience.

6. Have fun! Magick should be treated with respect, but that
   does not mean excessive solemnity. You can laugh during rituals.
   You can smile. You can dance around the circle instead of walk.
   Be as lighthearted as you want and express joy in your rituals as
   you see fit.

What do I need to perform this ritual?

The only thing you need to perform this ritual is a small, clear space to work
in. However, here are some optional items to include:

Candles: To make the room more atmospheric.

*Incense: F*or now, any scent will do.

A dagger: Any dagger will do so long as it has *never been used to kill anything* and will not be used again for any other purpose than magick. Run it under cold water for 5–10 minutes to purify it before its first use. If you don't have a dagger, you may simply point with your index finger.

What should I wear?

Being nude or wearing a simple robe is traditional, but use your imagination if you like. If you do wear clothing, make sure it will not be used again for any purpose other than magick.

How do I decorate my temple?

As you see fit. There are books, like Crowley's *Magick* and Regardie's *Golden Dawn,* that have extremely elaborate ways to construct your temple, but this is not necessary. You may add to the walls or ceiling of your temple with whatever empowers you. You may bring any objects you hold in deep reverence into your temple. You may use something as an altar for the center of the room—or not. These things will develop naturally as you get more into magick and learn more about what does and does not turn you on, spiritually speaking.

Help! I have no place to practice!

Everyone has a place to practice. Even if you cannot devote an entire room to your temple, you can use your bedroom, or even a bathroom if that's the only place you can get some peace. Also there is no reason you can't practice outside at a park, a backyard, or elsewhere in nature. Just make sure you feel comfortable and won't be interrupted for the duration of the ritual.

The Equilibrating Ritual of the Pentagram

First, relax for five minutes as you learned at the end of Chapter 1 (or with your own method). When you are rested and peaceful, stand in the center of your temple and continue:

Qabalistic Cross[11]

1. Face East.

2. Touch your forehead (with finger or dagger) and chant: "**AH-TAH.**"

3. Point downward in front of your groin area and chant: "**MAL-KUTH.**"

4. Touch your right shoulder and chant: "**VE-GEBURAH.**"

5. Touch your left shoulder and chant: "**VE-GEDULAH.**"

6. Clasp your hands together over your breast (and if using a dagger it should be pointing upward) and chant: "**LAY-OLAM. Amen.**"

Drawing and Charging of the Pentagrams

1. Still facing East, move forward to the edge of your circle. (If you are in a cramped space, simply stay in the center, but rotate your body.) Draw a pentagram in the air. You may see it or feel it, but that is not important. Just *know* that it is there, perfectly drawn and glowing brightly with energy. Charge the Pentagram with: "**Yud-Heh-Vav-Heh.**"

---

11   The Hebrew in this sections translates: "Thou art the Kingdom and the Power and the Glory, forever and ever. Amen."

How do I "charge the pentagram"?

Here are detailed instructions for charging a pentagram. Each of the four pentagrams are done the same way—only the God name will change for each:

    a. After you draw the pentagram, stand calmly before it.

    b. Exhale completely.

    c. Put your hands into the pentagram.

    d. Slowly inhale, pulling your hands up to the area of your head as you do so.

    e. When you have completely inhaled, take a step forward (either foot), and thrust your hands into the pentagram while chanting the God name. (In this case, it's "Yod-Heh-Vav-Heh.") Use your *entire exhalation* to chant the God name.

    f. Breathe in completely while pulling your foot and hands back in.

    g. Stamp your foot, and make the Sign of Silence. This means to put your forefinger to your lips in the "shhh" sign, but don't actually say "shhh." Alternatively, you can do this with your thumb, which is called the Sign of Harpocrates.[12]

    h. Know that your pentagram is now duly charged.

Optional Visualizations:

The most important thing is to concentrate on the steps just given. Don't even bother with these extra visualizations until you are comfortable with the base ritual.

On the inhalation, visualize the energy (of any color or "all-colors") flowing down into your lungs. Imagine the energy continuing to travel down through your body and into your legs, spiraling down into the red hot core of the Earth

---

12 Greek god of silence.

itself. Once it hits the center of the Earth, you may pause for a moment. Under-stand the God name has now become completely infused with power.

Now as you exhale, feel the energy rebound fiercely, flying up through the Earth, back into your body, and shooting outward from your outstretched arms and hands. This energy bursts through the pentagram, charging it, and contin-ues out to the ends of the universe as far as you can imagine.

Make the Sign of Silence, understanding that this final action is essential as it perfectly seals the charging.

After charging the pentagram, continue with Step 2:

2. Point at the center of the pentagram, and draw a line in the air as you move to the south end of your circle. (If you are in a tight space, just rotate your body.)

3. Draw another pentagram and charge it as before, but this time with the God name: **"AH-DOH-NAI."**

4. Point to the center of your pentagram and continue a line around to the West. Draw another pentagram and charge it with the name: **"EH-HEH-YEH."**

5. Point to the center of your pentagram and continue the line to the North. Draw the pentagram and charge it with: **"AH-GLA."**

6. Point your dagger or finger to the center of your pentagram and draw a line around to the East, thus completing your circle.

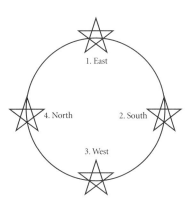

Invocation of Archangels

1. Move back to the center of your circle, facing East. Stand with your legs together and your arms straight out to the side (in the form of a cross).

2. Chant the following in your own style, but I highly suggest you save most of your exhalations for the Archangel names (written in all capitals with suggested pronunciation in parenthesis):

"Before me RAPHAEL!" (RAA-FAI-EL)
"Behind me GABRIEL!" (GAH-BRY-EL)
"On my right hand MICHAEL!" (MEE-KAI-EL)
"And on my left hand AURIEL!" (ORR-I-EL)

3. Chant, or roar with conviction:

"For about me flames the pentagram ... "

Imagine a pentagram flaming around your body.

"And within me shines the six- and seven-rayed stars."

Within your chest imagine *one* of these two six-pointed stars:[13]

Within your forehead, imagine this star:

Don't worry about keeping a perfectly clear image of these stars in your imagination. Just know that each one is in the right spot and leave it at that. If you are lucky enough to really see them in your mind's eye, then you can make them as bright as you like and you may choose your own colors.

Optional Visualizations:
Add these visualizations only when you feel you are ready. There is no hurry. They should add an enjoyable dimension to your ritual, not overwhelm it.

---

13   Both types of hexagrams are acceptable in magick. More detail on hexagrams in Chapter 6.

Raphael is Archangel of Air (and of Tiphareth). He carries a caduceus and the wind blows his yellow and purple robes.

Gabriel is the Archangel of Water (and Yesod). You may turn and look over your shoulder behind you to see him holding a large, overflowing cup of ambrosia. He wears blue robes, highlighted with orange, and may be seen standing upon a large body of water.

Michael wears fiery red garments edged with green. As your "right-hand man," his eyes are alight with God's glory, and he stands holding a large, flaming sword.

Aurial is silent and peaceful as he holds sheaths of wheat and other grains within his arms.

Qabalistic Cross
Repeat Qabalistic Cross as given above.

Drawing down the LVX[14]

| The Sign of "Osiris Slain" | "L" | "V" | "X" |

1. Stand in the center of your circle, arms outstretched in the Sign of Osiris Slain.

2. Chant: **"I. N. R. I."**[15]

---

14 In Latin, "U" is written as a "V." LVX means "Light."

15 INRI is an acronym of the Latin inscription IESVS·NAZARENVS·REX·IVDÆORVM. In magick, we consider all "dying/rebirth" gods to be of the same formula. This includes Jesus, Osiris, Krishna, etc.

3. Chant and draw at the same time, from *right to left:*

י ר נ י

YOD RESH NUN YOD

(So while it looks like this in the air, you would chant: YOD, NUN, RESH, and YOD, while drawing from right to left.)

4. Put your arms back out and say:

"The Sign of Osiris Slain."

5. Make the "L" sign (with your right arm straight up and your left arm straight out to the side) and say:

"L. The Sign of the Mourning of Isis."

Be sure to say "EL" for the letter "L". The same goes for letters "V" and "X" below (i.e., say "VEE" and "ECKS").

6. Make the "V" sign (both arms angled upward) and say:

"V. The Sign of Typhon and Apophis."

7. Make the X sign (arms crossed over chest) and say:

"X. The Sign of Osiris Risen."

Pause a moment, noting any mental or bodily sensations.

8. Say **"L"** and make the proper sign.

9. Say **"V"** and make the proper sign.

10. Say **"X"** and make the proper sign.

11. Still in the "X" pose, say:

"LVX![16] The Light of the Cross."

12. Stand in the Sign of Osiris Slain and say slowly, powerfully:

"Virgo. Isis. Mighty Mother."
"Scorpio. Apophis. Destroyer."
"Sol. Osiris. Slain and Risen."

13. Start slowly raising your hands up into the air. Say or chant:

"Isis. Apophis. Osiris."

14. By now your arms should be pointed directly overhead. Chant:

"IAO." ("Eee, Ahh, Ohh.")

Repeat this as many times as you like, building power and intensity as you do so.

15. When you feel the energy has peaked, thrust your hands downwards towards the ground and imagine the pure, white energy of Kether (i.e. God) coming down and infusing you and your entire temple with holy and divine presence. Say one final time:

"Eeeee!"

Feel the energy going through your head and shoulders.

"Ahhh!"

Feel the energy flowing down your torso.

"Ohhh!"

---

16   This is usually pronounced like the "u" sound in "lute," therefore "loox." If you prefer saying "lux" as rhymes with "bucks," that's fine too.

Feel the energy tunneling down your legs into the depths of the earth.

16. Stamp your foot against the ground and then breathe in, feeling the holy energy infuse you.

17. After a full inhalation, put your finger to your lips, making the Sign of Silence.

Qabalistic Cross
Repeat the Qabalistic Cross once more.

You are Done
Now you may meditate, start a practical working, or just get back to your regularly scheduled day. Don't worry whether or not you did it perfectly. If you finished it and did your best, that is enough. Congratulate yourself.

Frequently Asked Questions About the ERP:

I feel stupid! What should I do?
If you are unfamiliar with rituals, you may feel awkward or silly the first few times you perform the ritual. That's normal. Shrug or laugh it off and move on. Soon you will be performing the ERP with joyful equanimity.

Do I have to be loud when I do the ERP?
You should preferably do all your rituals in your most powerful chanting voice, but if you have to work in secret, you can chant more quietly or use what is called the "Great Voice." This is a fancy term for "chanting silently under your breath."

If you use the Great Voice regularly, make sure to occasionally go somewhere where you can really belt out the chants and feel their vibrations coursing through your body. Then you can more easily recall those sensations when using the Great Voice.

What does "vibrate" mean?

"Vibrating" is chanting a word or phrase with a full exhalation and at a pitch that seems to vibrate the air. I prefer the word "chant" as it is more suggestive to most people than the word "vibrate" and is more conducive to students defining their own chanting or "vibratory" style.

Chant your rituals at a pitch and tempo you feel is most powerful and comfortable to you, and use a full breath whenever I point it out as necessary. I only mention the word "vibrate" since it comes up in other magickal books and you should be familiar with what magicians mean by it.

What should I do if my visualization skills are poor?

This isn't a big deal. Like I said, just imagine the pentagrams around you as best you can. If you see them, then fine, but if you are just "pretending" they are there, that is fine too. Pretending is close to being "real" as far as astral work is concerned. The more important thing is to concentrate on what you are doing. Keep focused upon the ritual as much as possible, taking it step by step, without letting your mind wander too much.

What if I can't concentrate through the entire ritual?

No one has perfect concentration. Your mind will wander. When it does, just bring your attention back to what you are doing and keep going.

If you are neurotic or have obsessive thoughts about whether you are doing it right or "screwing it up," just let the thoughts arise and keep focusing on the ritual. You will never be completely rid of this "monkey mind," so focus as best you can and don't try to battle your mind; let it think whatever it wants while you focus on the ritual as best you can.

So what's going on in this ritual anyway?

In simplest terms, you are balancing yourself with the four elements, Fire, Water, Air, and Earth, and then drawing down the fifth element of Spirit into your presence.

Exercise 2: The Daily ERP

Learn the Equilibrating Ritual of the Pentagram as given in this chapter. Practice it once or twice a day. You should notice feeling more centered from it almost immediately, but the full effects of the ritual will continue to grow for months and years.

You will need to have this ritual down pat for all practical work in this book. So learn it now and learn it well. Perform it with joy and dignity. And don't beat yourself up over whether you've done it "good enough" or not. Just do your best each time, and you will evolve naturally into your own magickal groove.

THE TREE ⊕F LIFE

"The meaning of life is not to be discovered only after death in some hidden, mysterious realm; on the contrary, it can be found by eating the succulent fruit of the Tree of Life and by living in the here and now as fully and creatively as we can."—Paul Kurtz

The Tree of Life

The Tree of Life is a diagram of human existence—a roadmap of the mind, body, and spirit and their relationships to one another. It is also the cornerstone of most modern magick.

The first mention of the Tree of Life is in Genesis 3:22, which most scholars date to around the 6th century BCE, but the actual diagram came much later, developing and evolving throughout the Middle Ages. Diagrams similar to the ones we know today first appeared around the 13th century CE.[17]

The Tree of Life consists of 10 spheres, called **Sephiroth**, and 22 **paths** between them. Surrounding the Tree of Life is a "womb of nothingness" from which all life is born, collectively known as the "Three Veils of Negative Existence."

Don't worry if this chapter seems overwhelming and complicated. The Tree of Life is easy to work with, but it takes a little time for its simplicity and sublimity to sink in naturally. There is no deadline on comprehending the Tree of Life. It will evolve with you at your own level of understanding.

The version I use in this book is the arrangement used by the majority of ritual magicians. Be aware, however, that there exist other versions of the Tree of Life with somewhat different attributions.

What is the Qabalah?

The Tree of Life comes to us from the *Kabbalah*. In simplest terms, Kabbalah is Hebrew mysticism, i.e., the "magickal" side of Judaism. It is a collection of esoteric teachings intended to explain the relationship between the infinite, unknowable Creator, and the finite material world around us.

High magicians and Hermeticists, however, have done their own thing with traditional Kabbalah for a long time (since at least the 15th century[18]) and tend to use the spelling "Qabalah," when referring to their "Hermetic Qabalah" so as to distinguish it from Jewish Kabbalah.

---

17 Moses de Leon; *Sepher ha-Rimmon, 1287.*
18 Farmer, S. A, "Syncretism in the West: Pico's 900 Theses (1486)," *Medieval & Renaissance Texts & Studies,* 1999.

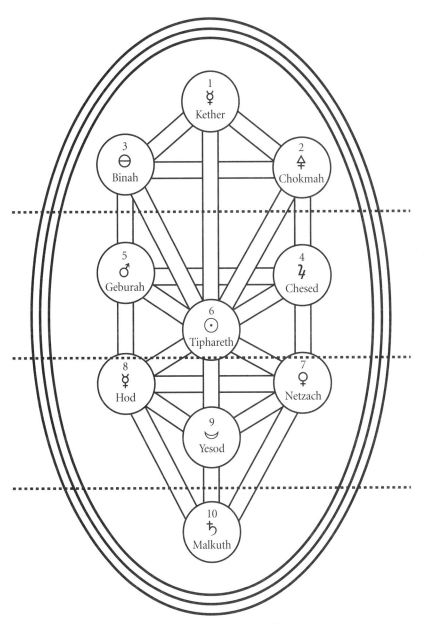

The Tree of Life with labeled Sephiroth

What can I get out of the Tree of Life?

1. A better understanding of the world. The Tree of Life is a classification system for *everything*. It's the structure upon which you may hang all your various knowledge resulting in improved comprehension of everything you will ever learn.

2. An improved memory and broader scope of mind. By having a classification system you will more easily be able to remember things. Ideas will naturally "pigeon hole" into their proper slots. Ideas, names, and concepts will not be lone entities scattered throughout your mind, but will instead be part of a web, or network, called the Tree of Life.

3. The Tree of Life will give you a common language to share with other magicians. Learning the attributions here will help you communicate quickly and easily with other students of esoteric thought. Moreover, it will place you in a position to understand other magickal books that may otherwise seem overwhelming (Golden Dawn and Aleister Crowley magick books for example).

4. The Tree of Life is an excellent basis for spells and meditation of all types. We will learn about this in upcoming chapters, but everything I've given in these first few chapters is the foundation for practical magick, i.e., magick for changing your day-to-day life and attracting things you want and need. The more you use these symbols, the more they sink into your subconscious, and therefore the more powerful your rituals and talismans become.

5. The Tree of Life will balance you and unclog any mental or emotional blocks you may have. Working regularly with the Tree of Life is akin to having a healthy circulatory system. When things are flowing, there are no problems in your life, because you will understand your place in the world and know where you are going. Everything will be exactly where you need it as

you need it. You will have *meaning*, and that will give you joy at all times, in all situations.

Introduction to the Sephiroth

In this next section, we are going to cover the "spheres," that is to say the Sephiroth (singular Sephirah), which is their technical name. When referring to the Tree of Life, "spheres" and "Sephiroth" are interchangeable.

Just what is a Sephirah? Traditionally, they are "emanations of God" or "things in and of themselves." If you like, you may consider the Sephiroth as actual "places" in the subconscious mind. The paths, which we cover in the next section, are the psychological means of conveyance between these places in our subconscious.

The Sephiroth evolve from simple unity (1) down to the complex material world (10).

One way to visualize this is to consider "1" as God and "10" as our material body. Together the ten Sephiroth make a complete map of the relationship between God and Man. To experience and sustain this sense of wholeness is one of the main goals of magick.

The good news is that while understanding all the theory behind the Tree of Life could take years, using it for real-life results is quite a bit easier. When it comes to practical magick, working with either the paths or the Sephiroth is simple. You decide which Sephirah (or path) relates to your problem and then use the appropriate correspondences to create a talisman or other magical ritual using the correspondences given. These correspondences are not necessary to memorize, but rather are to be referred to when creating a ritual.

If you are confused, don't worry. By the time you are ready to create your first talisman, you will have the confidence to succeed. I will be going over everything step by step, but if you struggle with any concept, just move forward. Eventually things will click.

How do I pronounce all these Hebrew words?

Pronunciation is flexible in high magick. No one really knows how original Hebrew sounded. I try to stay close to modern Jewish pronunciations of most words, but let me shock the purists right now: it's ok if you mangle the pronunciations. They will still work in rituals—perhaps even more so since you have made the words your own. I have given the usual Hermetic way of pronouncing the words in parenthesis in the following section.

The First Seven Sephiroth

Finally, we are ready to start "growing" your own Tree of Life. Just by reading and learning about the Sephiroth you will be planting seeds in your subconscious that will eventually allow a better understanding of your own place in the universe. Learning the Tree of Life will also bear fruit in later chapters when it comes time to perform practical magick. So here we go, the Tree of Life, from the bottom up:

10. Malkuth

(mal-KOOT)

מלכות

Colors: Black, Russet, Olive, Citrine

Scent: Dittany of Crete

Planetary influence: Saturn[19]

Metal: Lead

♄

Malkuth ("Kingdom") is the Earth, i.e., the material world around you, including your physical body. While seemingly the most solid of the spheres,

---

19 I have ascribed Saturn to Malkuth, which accords with traditional Golden Dawn attributions where Saturn often does double duty as the element Earth. Also the path of Saturn/Earth is Tau, which is the path straight up from Malkuth—indeed this path and Sephirah can hardly be differentiated in practice. The former is merely the entryway, while the latter is the mansion itself. Saturn is also sometimes attributed to Binah due to the supposed darkness and heaviness of the darker aspects of the Great Mother.

it actually contains the most transitory things. Malkuth is the end result of the Tree of Life.

"As above, so below" applies here. Your material world is a reflection and extension of the first nine Sephiroth.

The reason many humans are so unhappy is that they try to fix their problems from Malkuth, instead of from deeper within themselves (i.e., further up the Tree of Life).

Saturn is ruler of Malkuth. He was originally the Roman god of agriculture and harvest. Later on, however, he would acquire darker and "heavier" associations including his link to Karma, the passage of time, and even to death. (Saturn, like the grim reaper, was seen with a sickle.) All these associations are appropriate to Malkuth.

Ritual and talismanic uses: Good for grounding, especially bringing energy from the higher spheres down to earth.

What is Karma?

Karma means "action" or "deed" in Sanskrit. In its simplest terms, Karma is the law of *cause and effect.* For every action we perform, there will be corresponding results of some sort. These results lead to other actions, creating an infinite chain of action and reaction.

After the simple answer of what Karma is, things get more complicated. Karma means different things to various schools of Hindu and Buddhist thought, with some considering God to have a role in Karma, while others consider Karma to be a natural function of the universe, similar to the laws of physics.[20]

Westernized versions of Karma often compare it to a reward-and-punishment system, a sort of misunderstood 1:1 ratio in which "good" and "bad" acts are worked out in a single lifetime, but that idea is not very Hindu, as

---

20 Hinduism also subdivides Karma into different types of Karma, including "accumulated Karma" from all our lifetimes ("Sanchita") that we only deal with a fraction of in this lifetime, Karma we are accumulating from just this lifetime ("Kriyamana"), and Karma from previous lifetimes now coming into fruition ("Prarabdha").

the original concept of Karma is based on the notion of reincarnation and multiple lifetimes.

There is nothing inherently wrong with using Karma as a shorthand for "you reap what you sow," but do be aware that it has other uses and connotations in Hindu and Buddhist[21] schools of thought.

Note that Karma is *not* Fate; humans have free will to create their own destiny. However, the weight of our past actions weighing on our present and future may feel like our destiny at times! With magick we learn to efficiently take charge of our Karma and put it to good use in our lives. A magick ritual alters your future by taking into account the record of your past actions, i.e., your Karma, while implanting a new direction. More on this in Chapter 5 regarding the Earth Vessel, which is a symbolic representation of our Karma.

The Veil of Qesheth[22]

There are three traditional "veils" on the Tree of Life.[23] Veils are imaginary boundaries separating different levels of human consciousness.

The first veil, between Sephiroth 9 and 10, separates the physical world, including our body, from the rest of our being, which includes our mind, emotions, and spirit.

In a practical sense, this veil and the next two, can be highly important aspects of ceremony and ritual, especially initiatory ones. The veils are symbolized by actual partitions in the temple, screening off an area until the initiate is ready to see it.

---

21 In Buddhism, we can produce "good" and "bad" Karma all we want, but we will still be "trapped" in *samsara* (the endless cycle of birth and rebirth). Only certain types of actions lead to escaping the "wheel of samsara." So if you follow the tenets of Buddhism you don't want good or bad Karma, but rather Karma that leads to liberation ("nirvana").

22 The word *Qesheth* is formed by the Hebrew letters associated with the three paths branching out of Malkuth (Qoph, Shin, and Teth, which means "bow" or "rainbow" in Hebrew).

23 The dotted lines on the Tree of Life diagram.

9. Yesod

(yeh-SODE)

יְסוֹד

Color: Violet

Scents: Jasmine, Ginseng

Planetary influence: Luna

Metal: Silver

Positioned in between the physical world (Malkuth) and the realm of imagination (Tiphareth), Yesod is traditionally known as the "astral plane." Yesod is more tangible than Tiphareth, but also more impure. Yesod, like the Moon that influences it, receives its light indirectly from Tiphareth (whose planetary influence is the Sun).

What is the Astral Plane?

Aleister Crowley once wrote, "There is more nonsense talked and written about Yoga than anything else in the world."[24] The same can be said about the *astral plane*. The amount of rubbish written about it is staggering.

Forget everything you know about the astral plane, and start afresh by merely understanding that Yesod is the *indistinct* area between the mind and body. It contains the overlap of emotions, thoughts, visions, dreams, and any other sort of mental "picture making."

You will work with the astral plane during rituals when you imagine drawing pentagrams in the air, for example.

Some people will have a better sense of the astral than others. If you are a person with weak perceptions of the astral plane, it is of no major consequence. I also am of that type. Luckily, with magick, we are concerned about implanting seeds of desire much deeper than the astral plane. Later we will see how this is done, but in many ways Yesod is just a convolution of

---

24 *Eight Lectures on Yoga,* first lecture.

Tiphareth. Without the clarity of Tiphareth to enlighten it, Yesod is prone to delusion, deception, and false visions.

It's not completely unhelpful to think of the Tree of Life as "messier" the closer we are to the bottom. As we travel upwards we find more simplicity since we are moving from the actual to the ideal.

Ritual and talismanic uses: Improved astral senses and dreaming. Can be used for sex talismans—but a different flavor than those made by using Netzach.

8. Hod

(HODE)

חוד

Color: Orange, Yellow

Scents: Storax

Planetary influence: Mercury

Metals: Quicksilver, alloys

☿

Hod ("Splendour") symbolizes the rational mind, which might at first seem at odds with the idea that this is the sphere of Mercury, a.k.a. Hermes, the master of magick. But it is only contradictory when you think of it in modern terms. The great thinkers of ancient times[25] were spiritual—they were not "atheists" or "agnostics."

In ancient Egypt, the god of writing was also the God of Magick. His name is Thoth, and he has the body of a man and the head of an Ibis, and is usually shown holding a stylus and parchment. This implies writing *is* magick, but in modern times we tend to take writing for granted and so writing does not fascinate most humans like it used to.

However, even with the influence of Mercury's magick, the essence of this sphere is the logical and rational mind. Notice how far down the Tree of

---

25 Or more modern ones like Einstein, for that matter.

Life this sphere is, and note that it is off-center. Modern man often makes a crown of his rational mind, but this is a critical error.

Holding contrary ideas in our head at once is the hallmark of higher intelligence. Learn to accept magick *and* be skeptical of it at the same time. Then shall the lesson of this sphere go aright.

Ritual and talismanic uses: Good sphere to invoke when studying mysteries of any sort. This sphere grants exceptional skill at learning, writing, wit, and magick.

7. Netzach

(net-ZACK)

נצח

Color: Orange, Yellow
Scents: Benzoin, Rose, Red Sandal
Planetary influence: Venus
Metals: Copper, Brass

♀

Netzach ("Victory"), the sphere of Venus, is a tricky one. It is the Sephirah of love, but it is also the sphere of Copper, which was known as the metal of "external splendor, internal corruption."[26]

We do get Venusian qualities here, such as sexuality and seduction, but there is a tendency towards debauch, therefore the darker side of love and romance is here, including infidelity and disease.

Also the desire for fame and glamour can trap someone in Netzach.

Netzach is best balanced out by Hod. They are each other's complement—but the reaction between them is often violent and destructive as symbolized by the path of Peh ("The Blasted Tower"), which connects them on the Tree of Life (more on this in the next section). Therefore, there must be a third element, something higher than either, that can balance them out

---

26 Regardie, Israel, *The Golden Dawn, Fifth Knowledge Lecture:* "Copper is externally of the nature of Gold, but internally corrosive."

(in this case, Tiphareth, the next Sephirah). This is always true in magick. For every pair of opposites, there is a "higher" idea or concept that can reconcile the two.

If Hod is the sphere of the "nerd," then Netzach is the sphere of the "exotic dancer."

Ritual and talismanic uses: Love, romance, and sex spells easily fall under the dominion of Netzach. This sphere can teach deception—but of a different kind of trickery than Hod grants. Seduction, glamour, and sensual illusion all may be studied in Netzach.

The Veil of Paroketh[27]

Most people "live" in one of the four lower spheres (or just a muddled mix of them). The bottom four spheres are poor places to rule your life from. They are too far down the Tree of Life, and Netzach and Hod are off-center, which makes them even worse places to be stuck in.

Few people pierce the Veil of Paroketh, but behind it is the Sephirah where magicians, artists, and all enlightened beings prefer to reside as much as possible.

6. Tiphareth
(TIF-uh-ret)

תפארת

Color: Gold, Bright Yellow
Scents: Olibanum
Planetary influence: Sol
Metals: Gold

Tiphareth ("Beauty") is the pumping heart of the Tree of Life and encompasses every aspect of our imagination. All we can feel, hear, see, taste, smell, and experience come to harmonious fruition in this Sephirah.

---

27 This is actually redundant as Paroketh (PRKTh) means *hanging, covering, curtain,* or *veil* in Hebrew.

Understanding Tiphareth and its relationship to the other spheres is to experience the pure joy underlying every moment in the infinite universe.

Tiphareth is harmony and balance. Perfectly centered, it reconciles the highest with the lowest, and balances out the tensions of the left and right sides of the Tree of Life.

Tiphareth is the sphere of the magician, guru, or holy man. While Kether is the most pure representation of "God," and can occasionally be experienced in intense meditation, magick, or under the influence of entheogens, Tiphareth is the highest sphere in which we can experience the bliss of God and still maintain our day-to-day consciousness.

When I say "God" here, I don't mean any dogmatic representation of divinity. I simply mean a deep-rooted sense of connection to the universe. Feeling holy or spiritual is just a *general sense of well-being* you have with you at all times. Tiphareth is all about this good feeling.

You cannot find these good feelings through grasping or clinging to external things. You can find peace by focusing on "the now." As every second of your life unfolds, the moment of its unfolding is Tiphareth.

Tiphareth is always the present moment. To experience Tiphareth with all its harmony, balance, and joy, is merely to experience the present moment fully.

While Tiphareth expresses the beauty and clarity of a clear summer day, death is also here—in the form of resurrection. Tiphareth is symbolized by the sun, which "dies" every night and is "reborn" every morning. All Osiris-like gods (Jesus, Dionysus, Krishna, etc.) are attributed to Tiphareth. They exist. They die. They are reborn more powerful and enlightened than before.

I feel the message of Tiphareth is simple: Die to the moment and experience the beauty of "the now."

Even as you read this, the everlasting moment is now forever blooming before your eyes and senses. Be here. Be present. Stay with your senses. Don't hide. Don't think about your past; don't anticipate your future. Be bold enough to be right here, right now. Have fun. Find beauty in everything.

Do not think it complicated or difficult to feel the power of Tiphareth, i.e., the power of the moment. Instead, imagine a time when you were engaged in some enjoyable activity, whether a hobby, sport, a game, a work project, or whatever else. Imagine a time when you were completely in the "zone" and completely "on top of things." You felt that you could not be stopped or turned aside. You were excited and yet calm, lucid. You were completely "in the moment."

Recall that feeling now. This feeling is the essence of Tiphareth.

Ritual and talismanic uses: Invoke for inspiration and creativity and to connect with your higher self. All healing spells would do well to utilize Tiphareth as well.

5. Geburah

(Geh-BU-rah)

גבורה

Color: Red, Fiery Orange
Scents: Tobacco, Cinnamon
Planetary influence: Mars
Metals: Iron, Steel

♂

Geburah (also "Gevurah") means "severity." Geburah also implies strength, force, and fire. Though sometimes perceived of as "destructive," that is an illusion. The universe has perfect economy with the sum total of zero.[28] Nothing in the universe is created or destroyed—only transformed from one type of energy to another.

Mars, God of War, is attributed to Geburah. If Saturn is time and change, then Mars is the ability to roll with the punches life deals us, and how to re-

---

28 "The answer is that the total energy of the universe is exactly zero," from Stephen Hawking's *A Brief History of Time,* Bantam Books, 1988.

turn a few blows of our own. This is consistent with Geburah's other titles of "judgment"[29] and "power."

From a practical standpoint, it is no use denying that Geburah can feel violent and destructive at times. Like a warrior caught in the onslaught of Ghenghis Khan's legions, those on the receiving end of abrupt change may not like it—but they must adapt or die. That is the lesson of Geburah.[30]

Ritual and talismanic uses: Good for "war," whether in business, sports, love, or actual warfare. Geburah is also excellent for any ritual requiring intense transformational energy.

4. Chesed

(HEH-sed)

חסד

Color: Blue, Royal Purple
Scents: Cedar
Planetary influence: Jupiter
Metals: Tin, Aluminum

♃

Chesed ("kindness") is a source of stability and level-headed rulership. If Geburah is the king at war, out expanding his borders, then Chesed is the ruler at peace, working on the infrastructure and welfare of his kingdom. The number four here suggests stability and safety. Imagine four walls of a castle and you have the right idea of Chesed.

Jupiter is the supreme ruler of the gods in Roman mythology (known as Zeus in the Greek) and therefore we get all the royal associations of Chesed. Also this is the last sphere before we cross the Abyss. On the other side of the Abyss things cannot be "known," but they can be understood through direct experience or sensed intuitively, therefore Jupiter, as supreme ruler still makes sense—at least when viewed from Earth. Indeed, Jupiter rules from

---

29 One of Geburah's other titles is Din, which literally means "judgment."
30 Geburah is sometimes referred to by the title Pachad, which means "fear."

mount Olympus. Gods associated with this sphere are the highest conception of God we can have without crossing over the Abyss to abstract representations such as monotheism.

Chesed also implies luck and success upon the material plane. This is a better place to focus for financial gain than Malkuth. Not only will it manifest more easily, but you will have a better idea of what wealth actually is and how to use it in a wise and meaningful fashion since Chesed is directly ruled by the wisdom of Chokmah, the sphere above it.

Ritual and talismanic uses: Wealth, luck, and abilities regarding finance or money. Also spells to protect your home, spells calling for regality, and also any time you need the ability to govern large groups of people.

Veil of the Abyss

Of all the veils, the Veil of the Abyss is the most infamous. Magicians usually just refer to it as "the Abyss."

The Abyss separates the seven lower Sephiroth, which are considered to be of the "practical" world, from the top three Sephiroth. These top three Sephiroth are so different from the rest that they are considered "ideal." Because the top three Sephiroth are not part of the actual world in any sense that our minds can usually comprehend, the gap between them and the lower seven Sephiroth is traditionally considered an unfathomable chasm of space and time (as even the very concepts of space and time break down above the Abyss).

Why the dire associations with the Abyss?

We are talking about the complete destruction of the ego, and any personal concept of identity. Above the Abyss, the experience of existence is one of complete unity and harmony with the entire Universe. It's blissful there, but from the ego's point of view it is pure destruction. The more one is associated with one's fragile ego-mind, the more painful the experience of the Abyss will be.

When Crowley says give up your blood to Babalon[31] (his symbol for Binah, in this case), he's merely giving a poetic metaphor for the submission process of letting go of one's ego to one's True Self. Only our True Self can completely experience the top three Sephiroth. This is why Crowley said give up your blood *willingly* to Babalon. If you give up your ego on your own it's blissful to cross the Abyss—but if you are miserly and cling to your ego, it can indeed be uncomfortable as your earthly "crutches" are yanked from you.

The Abyss also has a bit of a reputation in the magickal world as a "frightening" place where one undergoes the "dark night of the soul." In his *Magick: Book 4*[32], Crowley goes so far as to say, "To him who has not given every drop of his blood for the Cup of Babalon all magic power is dangerous."

But don't be frightened by what you may read in other magick books on the Abyss. For one thing, you don't bodily experience the Abyss until you are an advanced student of magick, and second, you can work with the Tree of Life gradually so that there never is a "dark night of the soul." In fact, with proper preparation as you will receive in the book, the actual experience of the Abyss is exciting and liberating.

If the idea of letting go of your ego scares you, then you begin to see why the Abyss has a forbidding reputation—but don't worry. In this book, the Abyss is treated as an intellectual concept rather than as an initiation. All you need to understand is that the next three Sephiroth are in a class all by themselves.

---

31 Crowley's concept of Babalon and the Beast is a high magick twist on Babylon the Great riding her seven-headed beast in the Book of Revelation. Magickally, it's entirely congruent with Shakti and Shiva, and Binah and Chokmah.

32 Part 3, p. 267.

The Supernals: Binah, Chokmah, and Kether

The top three Sephiroth are collectively known as the Supernals. We are now approaching the simplicity of pure, idealized oneness. To completely comprehend any one of them is to automatically understand the other two, so closely are their concepts related.

There are no traditional metals listed for the last three Sephiroth—being not of this Earth, there is no metal that could properly represent the Supernals. Since these last three Sephiroth are so different than the other seven, I have also assigned them alchemical attributions instead of planetary[33] ones.

3. Binah

(BE-nuh)

בינה

Color: Black

Scents: Myrrh

Alchemical influence: Salt

Binah is the Great Mother, the ultimate female energy. Her color is black, symbolizing the darkness of her womb. Binah, impregnated by Chokmah, gives birth to the rest of the Tree of Life.

Binah is congruent with the Indian goddess Shakti, the personification of divine female energy in Hinduism. Shakti provides the universal womb for her consort Shiva (Chokmah energy) to impregnate her. Together they are the "divine couple" of Tantra.[34]

As we follow the process of creation down the Tree of Life, Binah symbolizes the womb, but there is another side to Binah. Climbing back up the

---

33   The five brightest planets are visible to the naked eye and have been known to mankind since antiquity. They have more powerful psychological resonance than the newer discoveries, which were never satisfactorily applied to the Tree of Life. Uranus, Neptune, and even Pluto have haphazardly been applied to the Supernals by various occultists over the years, but they don't really fit.

34   Usha, Brahmacharini (1990). *A Brief Dictionary of Hinduism*. p.77.

Tree of Life, which is an essential component of magickal initiation, she is also the destroyer. Initiations are meant to purify and cleanse our spirit. Binah has a critical function here as we must give up our ego-identity to return to the womb of our primal mother. Binah is the destroyer of the ego-mind, what most of us think of as our "self," and that gives rise to some of the more awesome and menacing aspects of the Great Mother.

Babalon is entirely congruent with everything just stated about Binah. Babalon is the Great Whore that takes all the energy of the Beast (Chokmah) and gives birth to manifested forms. As she initiates us, we are to give up our blood, which she receives into her Cup, the Holy Grail, which is said to hold the blood of Saints.[35] More on this subject will resurface throughout the book. For now just be aware that this is all symbolic for destruction of the ego and doing so willingly.

Ritual and talismanic uses: Good for any magick in which you are trying to cross the Abyss and experience the top three Sephiroth directly. Use it also when you need the supreme female energy.

2. Chokmah
(HOKE-muh)

הכמה

Color: Grey
Scents: Musk
Alchemical influence: Sulphur

🜍

Chokmah is Wisdom. He is the original male energy as Binah is the original female. I like to think of the grey color traditionally associated with Chokmah as the color of a wise man's beard.

Wisdom in this case is right action without reflection. Understanding is knowing why we made the choices we did. Chokmah is pure action. Binah is reflective upon its own nature; Chokmah does not have this ability. He is

---

35 This is revealed in *Vision and the Voice* and discussed in *The Book of Thoth*.

pure rushing, unadulterated force. Binah receives Chokmah's force and gives birth to the rest of the tree of life.

Chokmah is primal "fire." Binah is primal "water." Their son is air, Tiphareth, and their daughter is earth, Malkuth, so once again we see the formula of the Tetragrammaton.

Ritual and talismanic uses: Useful for works of wisdom, and anytime the supreme primal male energy is needed.

1. Kether

(KET-er)

כתר

Color: Pure bright white

Scents: Ambergris

Alchemical influence: Mercury

☿

This Sephirah is the source beyond all sources. This sphere has no polarity. It is complete in and of itself, and yet it is not—because only through incarnation into the physical world can it truly be appreciated. The story of the Tree of Life is Kether's development into the "imperfect reality" of Malkuth for the sheer joy of the experience.

Kether is pure oneness. It is the only perfection on the Tree of Life. Everything else is just emanations of the one perfection.

Kether is the singularity from which all life manifests. It is the simplest, most pure form of "God" that a human can contemplate. The experience of Kether is so profound, deep, and perfect, that any words about Kether itself must necessarily be false. Kether can only be completely understood through direct contemplation.

Mercury[36] is appropriate here not just as the unifying principle between Binah (Salt) and Chokmah (Sulfur), but because of his attribution as the

---

36 Mercury's ambiguous sexuality fits here as well. Kether has no polarity, but does contain the *potential* for both active and passive polarities.

Logos. Logos means "word" in Greek and it is symbolically considered to be *the* word that created the universe. Therefore, Mercury is both the Logos, and He who speaks it.

However, Mercury is nothing if not duplicitous. He partakes of the lowest and highest in every sense. Mercury, in the guise of *The Magus,*[37] is also the last illusion before God. He is a helpful initiator, but also a trickster. Mercury *is* God as well as the veil of illusion directly in front of God meant to mislead the profane and unprepared.

All these descriptions are highly symbolic and only useful in so far as they point to the real thing. While true of all descriptions in this book, it is even more true for Kether: Do not get hung up on descriptions of the Sephirah, but instead seek the underlying meaning that transcends words. Words are only pointers. It's too easy to forget that and start mistaking words for the "essence" of something.

Ritual and talismanic uses: Kether is too lofty for most talismans. Use Kether in your rituals when you need the highest and most pure form of divine energy available.

The Three Veils of Negative Existence

Besides the three veils I've just described, there is a further set of veils surrounding the entire Tree of Life. These veils are known collectively as the Three Veils of Negative Existence. They are the *ain, ain soph,* and the *ain soph aur.*

Ain, translated as "not," is the infinite void beyond comprehension of any sort, about which nothing can be known. *Ain soph* translates as "no end," i.e., the limitless, the infinite. *Ain soph aur* is "the limitless light." The easiest way to understand these veils is that together they are the unmanifested menstruum out of which the Universe is born. They are a sort of primal silence, a womb of nothing, which gives birth to everything.

---

37 Tarot Trump II (Path 12). More on this in the next section.

The Three Veils are "negative" ideas so if you have a hard time comprehending them, it's no wonder. Luckily, you won't use them much in practical magick. While crucial to theoretical discussions, we can leave the philosophical digressions on the Three Veils to another book.

The Three Pillars

The left side of the Tree of Life (which includes Binah, Geburah, and Hod) is known as the Pillar of Severity. This side tends towards discipline, control, and dominance.

The right side is known as the Pillar of Mercy (and contains Chokmah, Chesed, and Netzach.) This side tends towards mercy, compassion, and "letting things be."

The center pillar (which includes Kether, Tiphareth, Yesod, and Malkuth) is the "Pillar of Mildness." The center pillar, also known as the Pillar of Equilibrium, tends towards harmony, balance, and unity.

A popular axiom of the Golden Dawn is "Unbalanced Mercy is weakness and the fading out of the Will. Unbalanced Severity is cruelty and the barrenness of Mind."

The Tree of Life is about balancing this tension of opposites. Traditionally, the Pillar of Mercy corresponds to the left side of your body, while the Pillar of Severity corresponds to the right side of your body. I imagine my clenched right fist as Geburah, a good symbol for the entire Pillar of Severity. My open left hand is the mercy of Chesed. With myself in the center, I make wise and balanced decisions.

The Five Elements on the Tree of Life

As mentioned in passing, the formula of the Tetragrammaton can also be applied directly to the Tree of Life:

Kether is Spirit, the root of everything, pure potential. Chokmah (Fire) is the Father. Binah (Water) is the Mother.

Their son (Air) is specifically Tiphareth, but includes all six middle Sephiroth (Chesed, Geburah, Tiphareth, Hod, Netzach, and Yesod) known collectively as the Ruach[38] ("mind"). The Daughter is Malkuth. The daughter is to be set upon the throne of her mother, Binah, to mate with the father, Chokmah, continuing the cycle of energy.

Introduction to the Paths

Now that we've learned something about each Sephirah we can discuss the paths between them.

The twenty-two paths of the Tree of Life correspond to the twenty-two letters of the Hebrew Alphabet. The paths also correspond to the twenty-two tarot trumps (also known as "Atu" or the "Major Arcana") of a tarot deck.

The seven traditional planets (Mars, Venus, etc.), the twelve zodiacal signs (Aries, Taurus, etc.), and the three original Hebrew elements (Fire, Water, Air) also have their correspondences in the twenty-two paths.

It might seem confusing that the seven traditional planets are used to describe the paths as well as the Sephiroth, so let me clarify: The Sephiroth and the paths are much more than any single attribution assigned to them. All attributions just hint at the true nature of the path or Sephirah in question.

As an analogy, consider the paths a sort of "stew" of symbolism. For each path we consider its placement on the Tree. The Sephiroth on either end of the path contributes its own energy to the "stew" (for example Path 12 gets energy from Kether and Binah). That's the broth of the stew, but then we throw in the symbolism of the Hebrew letter (Path 12 is Beth, which means "house"). That changes the flavor a bit. Then we consider the path's planetary/elemental/zodiacal energy (in this case Mercury). This changes the flavor yet again. Finally, we consider the Tarot card (in this case *II. The Magus*),

---

38 Also known as the Ze'ir Anpin, "small countenance."

which adds its own packet of ingredients to the stew. Finally, we stir it up and taste the stew. That "taste" is the essential nature of the path.

There are some symbols, like Mercury, that are all over the Tree of Life. Aspects of Mecury affect Hod, Kether (as the alchemical Mercury), Path 12 (*The Magus*), Path 20 (because Mercury rules Virgo), and Path 17 (as he rules Gemini as well). Mercury, known to the Romans as "Messenger of the Gods," certainly gets around! The point is that none of these paths or Sephiroth are Mercury *exactly*—but they all partake of his essential energy in some way.

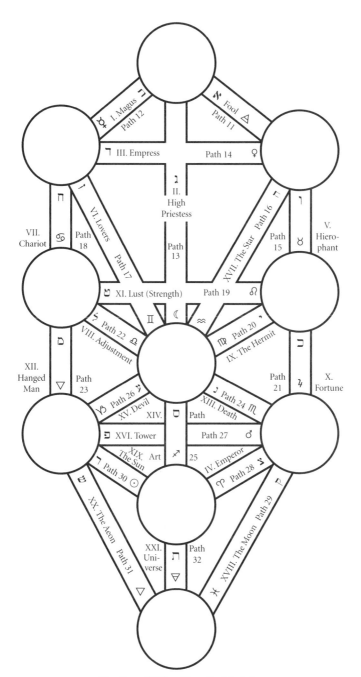

The Tree of Life with paths labeled

Tarot Trumps and The Twenty-two Paths of the Tree of Life

Once again you are about to be bombarded with a lot of information. I don't expect all this to make sense right away. I am providing the most useful attributions for each path. It will take some time for the symbols to be understood on their own, and even longer to appreciate the subtle interplay of energies upon the Tree of Life as a whole.

To make the visualizations easier, I recommend you buy a tarot deck like Crowley's *Thoth* deck that has the Hermetic attributions printed on the cards. If you don't want or can't buy a deck right now, just get online and take a peek at each picture of the tarot trump.[39] It will make the following paths much easier to understand.

I suggest not to completely rely on any one tarot deck to understand the energy of the paths. Study various tarot decks in conjunction with the underlying symbolism that is given here, and not only will you comprehend *any* tarot deck, you will even have the skills to design your own.[40]

So jump in and latch onto whatever symbols make the most sense to you. Any symbols learned now will help you understand further layers of symbolism down the line. For example, understanding the paths helps make more sense of the Sephiroth, and vice versa. Understanding the zodiac signs helps make sense of the Hebrew alphabet. All the symbols help clarify the tarot card titles, and the tarot helps make sense of the symbols as a whole.

For each path the following is given: the path number, the name of the Hebrew letter (and its pronunciation in parenthesis), the meaning of the Hebrew letter, the Hebrew letter itself (and its numerical value in parenthesis), the Roman numeral and the title of its respective tarot cart, and finally, the planetary or elemental symbol.

---

39 For example, a Google image search for "thoth tarot magus" brings up the tarot card just discussed.

40 Now painting them is another matter, and most famous magicians employed artists. However, even simply drawing the appropriate symbols on note cards can create a powerful tarot deck of your own. "Fancy" and artistic doesn't always make things more powerful in magick. Sometimes the more primitive and personal magickal items hold the most power.

Path 11: Aleph[41] (AH-lef), an "ox"

א *(1)—0. The Fool* △

The Fool from
The Pictorial Key
to the Tarot *by Arthur*
Edward Waite

Path 11 deals with "nothing" and therefore will have the longest description of all the paths. This card deals with such a simple concept that it takes many words to describe.

The most salient feature of this path is the concept of "zero." In magick, zero is a big deal! Zero[42] symbolizes the "nothingness" of pure being. This is the "zero" of a silent mind, where quiet divinity is revealed.

The shape of a zero symbolizes the egg, which is a symbol of spirit in magick. The egg is the *unmanifested* spirit, pure potential. This card therefore symbolizes the silence of the Yogi. This is the silence of pure being—the only place where the ultimate essence of life can be felt.

The Fool is the *divine* fool—drunk and mad on God's essence. He is also a "Fool" because he moves to the beat of his own drummer, and does not follow the "common sense" of the common man.

"Salvation, whatever salvation may mean, is not to be obtained on any reasonable terms. Reason is an impasse, reason is damnation; only madness, divine madness offers an issue … Mohammed … Napoleon … Karl Marx. There is only one thing in common among such persons; they are all mad, that is, inspired."[43]

The *contradiction* of folly being equated with wisdom is not uncommon in magickal symbolism. As obtuse as it sounds, most magickal truths are a

41 Aleph is often transliterated as "E" such as in the god names Elohim, El, Eheiheh, etc.
42 The album *Melon Collie and the Infinite Sadness* by the Smashing Pumpkins contains numerous references to both the Fool and zero, and of course Billy Corgan was famous for his "Zero" T-shirt.
43 Crowley, Aleister, and Frieda Harris. *The Book of Thoth: a Short Essay on the Tarot of the Egyptians, Being the Equinox, Volume III, No. 5.*, York Beach, Me.: S. Weiser, 1974.

seeming contradiction to the rational mind. It's just one of those things that takes getting used to.

The Fool is quite unlike other cards in not only the Major Arcana, but the entire deck of 78 cards. Why? It is the Fool that *travels* the paths. It is he who experiences the rest of the cards. He is the immaculate soul, and the rest of the cards are a parable regarding his decent into the World of Matter (and his ultimate return to divinity).

Like many of the Hebrew letters, it is not immediately clear what "ox" has to do with this path. Frankly, the Hebrew letter attributions can be a little confusing. These are best left to the student to study through meditation. I will sometimes give my suggestions as to how the Hebrew letter ties everything together, but my interpretations need not be considered to be writ in stone.

With regards to an ox pertaining to this path, remember that oxen can pull obstinate and almost unmovable loads. They are more sure-footed than horses and do not try to jerk the load, therefore, they can pull harder and longer than horses. This seems to me a hint that our soul is the ox. It is tireless in its slow march down the Tree of Life into manifestation. We each of us are the Fool bitten with wanderlust just as we each of us are the "dumb" ox on a long journey through the Tree of Life.

Interpreting a path's position between two Sephiroth also requires a fair amount of finesse, and once again interpretations vary depending on the student and the circumstances. I will give clues from my own experiences and interpretations. For example, on the Tree of Life, this path connects pure divinity (Kether) to wisdom (Chokmah.) To me this means wisdom comes from being able to find pure joy in every moment. *The Fool* is happy in any and all circumstances, because for him there is no final goal. Each moment of the journey is the meaning—the very reason for his existence.

As a final note, in most historical decks *The Fool* went unnumbered, considered to be distinct from the rest of the deck entirely. In 1870 America, the "Joker" appeared in a standard 52-card playing deck. Similar to *The Fool*, he is quite unlike the rest of the deck. He is the wildcard.

Ritual and meditational use: For "escaping" it all. For works of drunken ecstasy. Help with quieting the mind during meditation. Useful for combating fear, weakness, stagnation, and depression.

Path 12: Beth, (BET), "house"
‫ב‬ (2)—I. The Magus (The Magician) ☿

Mercury, also known as Hermes to the Greeks and Thoth to the Egyptians, is the God of Magick.

One of the great secrets of magick is indeed contained within this path: Beth=house=*The Magus*. *The Magus* is a master of acquiring things as well as traveling from place to place, so why is he attributed to a house, an immovable object valued for its stability? The secret is that when you move, you are always "home." In other words, "no matter where you go, there you are."[44]

You don't go to people or things. They come to you. This sounds so simple, but most people are constantly looking for things on the outside to make them feel complete on the inside. You will never actually go anywhere. You are and always will be the center of your perceptions. You cannot escape that. You can't quit having the experiences that constantly bombard you. All you can do is learn to change yourself internally, so that you may attract more and more pleasurable experiences.

"Every man and every woman is a star," a famous magickal quote from Aleister Crowley's *Book of the Law*,[45] is essentially the same idea. We are all of us the center of our own universe. We should not imagine we are in orbit around someone or something else, but rather, the world orbits around us.

In the magickal tradition, *The Magus* is the final veil before God, therefore Mercury is the ultimate illusion before God. He is the word or voice of God, but God's true essence is represented only in silence. Therefore, Mercury, for all his power and wit, falls short of the "Pure Fool" state of Path

---

44 This quote from the 1988 film *Buckaroo Banzai* is sometimes variously attributed to both Buddha and Confucius.

45 *The Book of the Law*, technically called *Liber AL*, Book I, Line 3.

11. *The Fool* is one step above *The Magus*, the master of magick. *The Fool* is beyond even the need of magick as in his eyes all things are blissfully equal.

In another sense, Mercury is an active form of *The Fool*. *The Fool* becomes *The Magus* through his experiences on the Tree of Life; *The Magus's* final goal is to become the Fool once more.

Ritual and meditational use: Improved wit, verbal and mental alacrity, help with winning at games, help with learning any science or language, multitasking, juggling competing interests, diplomacy, and anything regarding magick or writing. Also useful for business dealings of any sort, theft, trickery, deceit, etc.

Path 13: Gimel (GEE-mel), "camel"
ℷ (3)—II. The High Priestess ☽

This path is the longest path visually upon the Tree of Life. It is also the main path across the Abyss mentioned in the last chapter.

The Abyss is often referred to as a desert, and therefore the attribution of camel is appropriate here. This is a spiritual camel, capable of traveling safely from Tiphareth to Kether, no matter how long and dry the path.

That symbolism, however, is more appropriate when climbing back up the Tree of Life through pathworking (see Chapter 9). In a day-to-day sense, we understand this path not so much as Tiphareth up to Kether, but from Kether *down to* Tiphareth. In this sense, Path 13 is about the descent of "unknowable" divine energy descending into the "known" parts of our conscious mind. This is the connection from the nearly incomprehensible experience of Kether, brought down to Tiphareth, a more human-accessible conception of divinity.

There is something gracious and elegant about this path conferred to it by the Moon. There is no struggle here—no duplicity. Unlike the Magician on the last path, there is nothing "up her sleeve." This path is the moon in its purest and most lofty aspect (see Path 29 for a darker side of the moon).

The High Priestess is our intuition—a balanced and divine connection to our highest self (Kether). Imagine her as a pure white light descending upon you, blessing you with an enlightened comprehension just beyond your usual consciousness.

The High Priestess is virginal in the truest sense—she cannot be defiled.

Ritual and meditation use: For making a clear connection to our deepest intuition. This path is also used when absolute purity is required.

Path 14: Daleth (DAH-let), "door"
ך (4)—III. The Empress ♀

As Path 13 is the highest aspect of the Moon, Path 14 is the highest aspect of Venus. Therefore, this path is love, receptivity, harmony, and natural growth.

All this is symbolized quite succinctly by an empress resting languidly upon her throne, surrounded by fields of thriving grains, trees, and flowers.

This path does not benefit from over-analyzation, so I leave it to your own meditations to work out the attribution of Daleth, "the door." Do notice, however, that this path connects the primal male energy, Chokmah, with primal female energy, Binah.

Ritual and meditational use: Use this path when the very highest aspects of love are required, or when loving, nurturing mother energy is required.

THE STAR.

The Star from The Pictorial Key to the Tarot by Arthur Edward Waite

Path 15[46]: Heh (HAY), "window"
ה (5)—XVII: The Star ♒

Imagine looking out an open window, into a clear night sky and feeling refreshed and filled with a quiet hope for better things. That is the essence of

---

46 In some books on magick or Qabalah you may see this path attributed to Aries and *The Emperor* card instead of *The Star* and Aquarius. There are even some contradictions on this in Crowley's own writing because Crowley was not always in possession of the correct attributions, and earlier in his career he used the ones given to him by the Golden Dawn.

Path 15. Divine starlight and divine breath flow freely in through the window.[47]

The traditional symbol of Aquarius is that of the "man" or more specifically the "water-bearer." This card suggests that this water-bearer is not a man at all, but a woman, since in most versions of *The Star* tarot card there is a nude woman pouring out two cups, one onto the earth and one back into a lake.

In Crowley's version, the woman is Nuit, the Egyptian goddess who personifies the star-filled night sky. She pours one cup over her own face and the other cup back into the earth. One cup receives and one cup gives, thus completing the economy of the universe.

This path has a give-and-take quality to it. We must be active in our aspiration to the divine, but ultimately we must be passive, i.e., receptive, if we are to receive its guidance. This path travels from Tiphareth, our imagination, to Chokmah, our Wisdom, reinforcing this idea.

Ritual and meditational uses: Inspiration and guidance. Help with depression.

Path 16: Vav (VAW)
‎ו‎ (6)—V. The Hierophant (The High Priest) ♉

The Hierophant is the "high priest" and his goal is to bring his worshippers into the presence of the holy and divine. Thus, this is a path of teaching and guidance. It brings down the Wisdom of Chokmah into the Mercy of Chesed.

Through the attribution of Taurus, it symbolizes patience and toil. Ruled by Venus, the energy of this path is best managed with love and gentleness—not brute force.

---

47   A star appears to us as a point in the night sky. The Aquarius symbol is two wave forms on top of each other. Light is described this way in modern science, as both a particle and a wave.

This is congruent with being on the merciful side of the Tree of Life. If you wish to move the Earth, one should have patience and delicacy in the process.

While the Hierophant's job is to teach the mysteries of God to men, he is also concerned with the material plane, therefore the teachings of the Hierophant are both spiritual and practical.

This duality carries over to the influence of Venus, where *The Hierophant* is both spiritual and sexual. The Hierophant is not only a man of God, but also a man. In many religious cultures this sexual component has been repressed, causing perversion among the clergy, but in more sexually inclusive belief systems such as Tantra, Wicca, and Thelema, there is no contradiction. The Hierophantic task is to teach all secrets of God, including divine eroticism, to those who aspire.

Ritual and meditational uses: Helpful for increasing self-discipline and patience. This is a good path to use for help with extremely long or obstinate projects (or people).

Path 17: Zain (ZY-in)
ז (7)—VI. The Lovers ♊

This path is about the marriage of opposites. *The Lovers* symbolize two polarized energies, male and female, becoming joined through the act of love. The idea of twins (Gemini) reinforces this idea. Twins are separate individuals and yet are unified by virtue of their similarities. Famous twins such as Cain and Able, Castor and Pollux, etc., all find resonance within this path.

Gemini is ruled by Mercury; it is he who harmonizes the polarities. This is the same function Mercury displays as the intermediary between Sulphur and Salt as discussed in Chapter 1. Mercury symbolizes the thought process that can balance the tension between any pair of opposites, whether male vs. female, fire vs. water, or hot vs. cold.

Gemini is an air path, which is congruent with both the rulership of Mercury and the attribution of the sword. The sword is not only a traditional symbol of air, but also a weapon of division. It symbolizes the process of analyzation, of breaking down ideas for the chance to view them with fresh eyes, and a chance for new combinations.

This path therefore displays mental open-mindedness, because Mercury never gets overly attached to any one point of view. He is always able to see the opposite point of view, thereby opening up a range of new possibilities in the process. The theme of this card is to move beyond superficial polarities and into a full spectrum of possibilities.

Ritual and meditational uses: Helpful for solving difficult problems of any sort. It can shine clarity on the most confusing situations. This is the path to cut through a "Gordian Knot."

Path 18: Cheth (HET)
ח (8)—VII: The Chariot ♋

This is a path of conquest and victory. We have understanding (Binah) brought down to the sphere of power (Geburah).

The typical tarot attribution is a young man driving a chariot pulled by either horses or sphinx. The Thoth deck follows this symbolism, but adds one crucial element: The Cup of Babalon, which the driver, a knight, holds in his hands—while the chariot drives itself.

When you submit completely to the divine, i.e., give up all your ego-based wants, greeds, and obsessions, into Babalon's Cup, it becomes the Holy Grail. The history and mythology of the Holy Grail could fill volumes. The essential feature of the Grail, as far as we are concerned, is offering up the ego to the divine. The wine is our blood—given willingly. Therein lies true power.

This Charioteer has given up all his blood into the holy chalice, and therefore the Chariot guides itself perfectly, while he is free to relax in meditative repose. This is cognate with a quote by Indian spiritual leader Sri Sathya Sai Baba: "Give up all bad qualities in you, banish the ego and develop the spirit of surrender. You will then experience Bliss."

Like many of the paths, there is a paradox here. Even though this a path of conquering, and even domination, it is also a path of submission. The charioteer submits to the divine, and therefore is able to dominate and claim victory over that which is beneath him.

Cancer rules this path, so it is not surprising there are many secrets here. Crowley attributed the holy word "ABRAHADABRA" to this path. More on this in Chapter 6.

Ritual and meditational uses: A good path to help with meditation itself. Good for increasing self-discipline and control.

Path 19: Teth (TET), "serpent"

♉ *(9)—XI. Lust (Strength, Fortitude[48])* ♌

Strength from The Pictorial Key to the Tarot by Arthur Edward Waite

This path was originally called Strength, but Crowley changed it to Lust to imply not just strength, but the "joy of strength exercised."[49]

The image of this card is a woman taming a lion. She symbolizes our higher self gently dominating our lower passions.

This is an important card in Thelema, as in Crowley's Thoth deck the woman doesn't just tame the lion, but instead rides him with drunken ecstasy. This woman is Babalon, holding the Holy Grail we have discussed previously. The lion she rides is actually a creature with seven heads and the body of a lion (and the tail of a serpent because of attribution of Teth). This creature is "the Beast," and symbolizes all our human tendencies for power, passion, sex, adventure, romance, etc. The Beast is dangerous and wild unless tamed by Babalon who symbolizes our connection to our higher

---

48   Fortitude was one of the four Cardinal Virtues of Plato, three of which were titles of Tarot cards (Temperance and Justice are the others), and like the other two, Crowley changed the title. In this case, it's typical of Crowley's ironic sense of humor that he changed the title of this virtue to Lust, which was considered a Cardinal Sin.

49   *Book of Thoth*, p. 92.

self.[50] This path represents the joyous, blissfully ecstatic union between our lower self and our higher self.

Also, this path balances the opposing energies of Geburah and Chesed, giving it even more "oomph." With Geburah as power, and Chesed as Mercy, the woman's gentleness towards the lion seems to show that mercy dominates power if the energy is properly applied.

This path is the essence of carnal joy enlightened by our connection to the highest. In magick there is no contradiction between enjoying earthly pleasures and the pleasures of heaven. They are one and the same.

Ritual and meditational uses: This path is the very path of magick itself, and sex magick in particular is sacred to this path (among a few others). This is a different type of magick than that of *The Magus;* this is the pinnacle of success *below* the Abyss, and is good for spells of dominance, glory, grand beauty, and large indulgent displays of lust.

Also good for invoking fiery passion and a general "lust for life."

The Hermit from
The Pictorial Key to
the Tarot by Arthur
Edward Waite

Path 20: Yod (YOOD), the "hand" ʼ(10)—IX. The Hermit ♍

Once again, Mercury rears his ubiquitous head. Here we find him as the secret progenitor of the entire Tree of Life. How so?

Yod is the smallest Hebrew letter. Does its shape not suggest a spermatozoa? It is the root of the entire Hebrew alphabet. Through various elongations and contortions, the other twenty-one letters are formed.

Virgo is the spiritualized (a.k.a. mutable) aspect of Earth. What does that mean exactly? Earth is considered to be the "lowest" of the elements,

---

50 Babalon is attributed to Binah, therefore Babalon is our connection to the highest parts of the Tree of Life.

the basest, and the darkest. Here in Virgo we have the tendency for Earth to return to the highest. But how? By giving it a purpose, a direction, a part in the divine play of God. Earth cannot do it alone, however. It will need help.

Virgo means a female virgin, but a virgin is incomplete. What does she need? The same thing fallow earth needs: a seed.

The tarot card attributed to this path is the Hermit, an old man holding a light out to help guide the world.

Who is this Hermit? Why it is none other than Mercury, ruler of Virgo. Remember that Mercury in his highest aspect *is* God. Here he is in disguise, hiding his brilliance in rags to protect his ineffable holiness from the profane and also to protect the profane from being blinded by so intense a light. Instead, he holds aloft a lamp, shedding a tiny fraction of the infinite light of Kether out into the world so that we might find our own way in the darkness. In the deepest sense possible, Mercury is also the light *itself.*

So who is the virgin? Odd as it sounds, Mercury is simultaneously the old man and the young virgin. Mercury's gender is always ambiguous. As the light of Kether, he is the neutral state that contains both polarities. Here in Path 20, home of the mutable Earth sign Virgo, his polarity is expressed through the symbolic nature of *both* a female virgin *and* a wise old man.

Another way of looking at this path is that Mercury has come down to impregnate the fallow Earth with his seed, giving it intelligence, clarity, and purpose. The Yod is his seed and Yod means "hand." This path illustrates the idea that the hand of God is everywhere on Earth. There is nowhere the light of God does not reach. The Tree of Life grows everywhere, in everything, akin to a fractal.

Ritual and meditational uses: Confers practical wisdom. Help during the most difficult and dark of times. Help with meditation. Good for learning how to channel energy with solitary sex magick.

*Wheel of Fortune from
The Pictorial Key to
the Tarot by Arthur
Edward Waite*

*Path 21[51]: Kaph (KAHF), "palm of hand"
ב (20)—X. Wheel of Fortune ♃*

The Wheel of Fortune, also known as the *Rota Fortunae*, was a popular medieval concept symbolizing what they viewed as the capricious nature of Fate. The Wheel of Fortune originally goes back to ancient Rome, where it belonged to the Goddess Fortuna, who spins it at random, causing great windfalls for some and catastrophe for others.

The essence of this card is constant change. The Wheel of Fortune never stops turning, and therefore this card symbolizes the randomness of life, chance, and luck.

A vintage quote from the Roman philosopher Boethius perhaps sums it best: "I know how Fortune is ever most friendly and alluring to those whom she strives to deceive, until she overwhelms them with grief beyond bearing, by deserting them when least expected … Are you trying to stay the force of her turning wheel? Ah! dull-witted mortal, if Fortune begin to stay still, she is no longer Fortune."[52] Embrace change as the *status quo* and you will never be caught unprepared.

Ritual and meditational uses: To stay on top of life's constantly shifting situation you have to keep changing as well. Focus your meditations here if you wish to be able to more easily roll with life's punches. A magician cannot control the Wheel of Fortune, but he or she can become adept at maximizing its windfalls and learning how to turn Fortuna's many lemons into lemonade.

---

51 Let's do some simple gematria with the number 777. Some consider this a holy number, which it can be, and it is also known as jackpot to slot machine players. Now 7+7+7=21. Path 21 is the *Wheel of Fortune*, another game of chance. The number 21 is also the most important number in blackjack.

52 *Consolation of Philosophy*, c. 524. Translation by W.V. Cooper, 1902.

Path 22: Lamed (LAH-med), "ox-goad"[53]

ל *(30)—VIII. Justice (Adjustment)* ♎

This path is attributed to Libra, which means scales. Scales are not only an excellent symbol of balance, but are also a simplified example of the "laws of conservation."[54] This is most easily understood as a paraphrased version of Newton's Third Law of Physics: "To every action there is an equal and opposite reaction."

This is congruent with the idea of Karma, where our every deed has a consequence or reaction.

If you put an ounce of gold in one side of the scale, the other side will go up a proportionate amount. It's just the way the universe is. There is no conception of God doing the balancing. It is inherent in the nature of physics. This is why Crowley changed the title from *Justice* to *Adjustment*. He felt that *Justice* had too many negative connotations because of mankind's perpetual misuse of "justice." But were there such a thing as ideal justice on Earth, it would symbolize this path succinctly.

Ritual and meditational uses: For help with anything coming to a legal conclusion or requiring judgment, including marriages, divorces, and court hearings of any sort. It is also useful for balancing tricky situations. Because of the influence of Venus upon this path of balance, it can be invoked for creative and artistic endeavors, imparting elegance and harmony to the proceedings.

53　Lamed symbolizes the "ox-goad," that is to say the whip that keeps lazy ox (Aleph, Path 11) moving. In this sense, it makes sense that this is the card of Karma. Karma is what keeps the Fool moving forward. Every action produces consequences, which forces us to take more action, which causes more Karma. This is therefore the complementary path of Path 11. Together they spell AL, which is an important name of God both on its own and as part of other god names (Alhim, Eloah V'Dath, etc.). It is also an important name in Thelema. The *Book of the Law* is technically known as *Liber AL*.

54　In modern physics there are six laws of conservation: "conservation of charge, conservation of momentum, conservation of mass/energy, conservation of angular momentum, conservation of baryons, and the conservation of leptons."

The Hanged Man from
The Pictorial Key to
the Tarot by Arthur
Edward Waite

Path 23: Mem (MEM), "water"
ב *(40)—XII. The Hanged Man* ▽

The tarot image of this path is that of *The Hanged Man*. This path symbolizes "spiritual surrender." The energy of this path is giving up fixation on the material plane and letting go to the spiritual energies within us, i.e., our higher self.

Often people turn to God or spirituality when their lives are "falling apart." This path is about losing everything we thought important and finding something deeper and more meaningful just as things are at their worst.

This is usually a misunderstood path. It's not as uncomfortable as it is made out to be. In fact, it's quite a liberating experience. It can feel like diving into cold water—and losing your inhibitions that way, or it can feel like blissful submission to the unknown. Either way, it's finally being forced to let go of all our attachments. Although frightening at first, that experience *feels good*. It's free, "in the moment," and courageous. It is the feeling of nothing to lose and everything to gain. The quicker you submit to the energies in this card, the better they feel. The only thing that could make this path uncomfortable is overly resisting. Despite the title of this card, it is more of a baptism than a lynching.

Ritual and meditational uses: The very best card when desiring escape from the material, external world and entrance into a more spiritual, internal one.

Path 24: Nun (NOON), "fish"
ℷ *(50)—XIII. Death* ♏

This path is about sometimes drastic, yet natural and necessary transformations.

In Hermeticism, Scorpio has three different forms, representing various aspects of transformation:

The Scorpion—It was once believed that scorpions killed themselves when surrounded by a ring of fire.[55] This is not actually true, but humans do indeed kill themselves when surrounded by what they feel are insurmountable obstacles. This is the lowest form of transformation associated with Scorpio and in traditional Hermeticism it was considered a "bad" symbol.

The Snake—The snake, or serpent, was thought to contain both "good" and "bad" elements of transformation, and undulated between them. This was the intermediary level of Scorpio's transformation.

The Eagle—This is the "highest" level of transformation associated with Scorpio. It symbolizes leaving behind the earthly realm, and soaring high above in exaltation.

Scorpio is a Water sign, and it is not surprising to find that Nun means fish, symbolizing life beneath the sea. What is notable is that Mars, a fiery, aggressive planet, rules this path. This gives Scorpio its boiling intensity.

As far as the tarot, almost all versions of the *Death* card feature some sort of Grim Reaper, a skeletal figure with a scythe, cutting down human bodies, trampling them into the ground before him.

In one of the earliest surviving tarot decks, the Tarot de Marseille (1713), Trump XIII was numbered, but not labeled, probably out of superstition,

---

55 To the casual observer this still appears to be so, as the scorpion lashes about at unseen enemies giving the impression of stinging itself, but it actually dies from its sensitivity to the heat. The scorpion is immune to its own poison.

the same way some modern buildings "don't have" a 13th floor.[56] However, the *Death* card's bad reputation is due mainly to misunderstanding its true meaning. To this day, it is maligned in movies as an ill-omen, but this is simply not the case. Like other seemingly "destructive" parts of the Tree of Life,

*Temperance from
The Pictorial Key to
the Tarot by Arthur
Edward Waite*

any pain found here is purely imagined and caused from holding onto things too tightly with the ego.

Ritual and meditational use: Transformation. Help with shedding the past. Help moving forward and using current woes to transcend to a higher level of consciousness.

Path 25: Samech (SAH-mekh), a "prop" ◌ (60)—Art (Temperance) ♐

This card is about balancing opposites, somewhat similar to that in Path 17 *(The Lovers)*, except in this path, the opposites are not just paired, but *conjoined* back into one.[57]

The placement of this path on the Tree of Life is especially important:

---

56   The number 13 as an unlucky number goes so far back into antiquity that no one is positive how long it's been in use or what may have caused the original association.

57   Sagittarius and Gemini are opposite signs of the zodiac, so they themselves are "twins" of a sort.

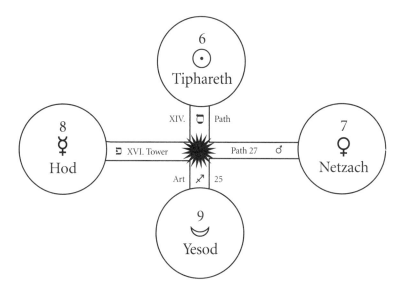

Not only does this path harmonize the polarities of the lunar vs. solar, but through the conjunction of this path and Path 27, it harmonizes the tension between the rational (Hod) vs. the sensual (Netzach).

Being so low on the Tree of Life the energy here is *practical*, and the harmonizing here is done *consciously*, that is to say through "art." Unlike the higher spheres, which are symbolic and distinct, now we are closer to the goings on of day-to-day life, therefore the separation between these lower spheres is a bit of a muddle. *Art* makes sense and harmony out of this jumble of tension and energy.

Ritual and meditational use: On this path, the ephemeral ideas of the imagination come to terms with the realities of the physical world. It is helpful for harmonizing internal, emotional messes, or external, physical ones. It is helpful for creating symmetry, beauty, and harmony out of the chaos that life so often presents to us.

Path 26: Ayin (AH-yeen), "eye"
ע (70)—XV. The Devil ♑

This path symbolizes blind, creative energy, and is fiercely related to the libido, hence many of its negative connotations.

The libido, if not hampered by guilt or outdated notions of morality, is the very wellspring of creative, energetic, and passionate juices. If these juices are flowing properly, they tend towards original, inventive, and powerful works of art and other forms of human expression. Voltaire sums this up succinctly, "You must have the devil in you to succeed in any of the arts."[58]

Capricorn is a sea-goat. His fish tail symbolizes his connection to the waters of the subconscious, while his mountain-goat upper body symbolizes his ability to climb the highest peaks of the Earth.

Everything about this card symbolizes going from the lowest to the highest[59] in the most direct fashion, therefore is it symbolic of the Kundalini, the energy that lays dormant sleeping in our spine, until it awakens, rising up through the spine and out the top of our head, where one is said to experience divine bliss.

Ayin means "eye" and this can refer both to the third eye, which becomes mystically awakened with the arising of the Kundalini, and the "blind eye" of the phallus. Crowley[60] correlated this path with the erect penis, which he boldly had painted on his version of the card. This is congruent with the Hindu *lingam*.[61] The lingam, as with the other symbols of this path, symbolizes the lowest rising to the highest and, at its pinnacle, releasing divine pleasure, whether it be in the form of art or orgasm.

---

58 Tallentyre, S. G., *Life of Voltaire,* third edition (Knickerbocker Press, 1903), p. 145.

59 And in another sense, from the highest to the lowest, both for reasons related to the complex relationship between *The Devil* and *The High Priestess*, and also simply because the greatest of sexual pleasures is sometimes found in the lowest, most primal incarnations.

60 "Veil not your vices in virtuous words—these vices are my service," is an apropos quote from *The Book of the Law.*

61 The lingam is a physical symbol of Shiva used for worship in temples in the shape of an erect penis.

This tarot card would be more appropriately entitled "The Goat-God," referring to Pan, the pastoral god of nature. Only in the middle ages did the superstitious and puritanical qualities of Christianity associate him with the Devil. The idea of obscenity as applied to erotic art or representations of sexual organs did not exist to the Greeks or Romans.

Ritual and meditational use: For help with creativity and anything to do with the arts. It helps with raising the Kundalini and increased sexual potency.

A certain type of fearlessness is granted through this path.

In many ways this path is a reverse polarity switch. There is a reprieve here from the purely rational mind. This path can help break through "writer's block" or other artistic blockages in any field.

Path 27: Peh (PEH), "mouth"
ל (80)—The Blasted Tower ♂

This path is known as *The Tower*, or more specifically *The Blasted Tower*, in the tarot. It is the explosive energy released when Netzach and Hod collide.

As previously mentioned, the conjunction of this path and Path 25 (*Art*) deserves special consideration. If you imagine the Tree of Life placed over your body (see Chapter 10) this area is below the heart and above the groin. It is not so much the stomach as it is the "gut," as in "gut instincts." It also includes our raging emotions, tension, and even anxiety. But ultimately this energy is our *power to change the physical world*.

Whether the tension here is felt as instinct, neuroticism, or power depends on how well we synthesize the various tensions of the lower spheres. This is why this path is so seemingly destructive on its own (ruled by Mars, you'll notice). It needs the harmonizing, and vertical, energy of *Art* to make sense and beauty of the endless conflicts of the material world.

Ritual and meditational use: Useful for breaking out of mental or emotional "prisons." There is powerful energy here for just about anything if channeled through the Tree of Life to exactly where you want it most.

Path 28: Tzaddi (TSAH-dee), "fish-hook"
צ (90)—IV. The Emperor ♈

This is active, male energy, but instead of being destructive, it finds outlet as calm rulership.

Aries energy is forceful and fiery. In this case, Aries's ruthless male energy is balanced by the number four, which, like Chesed, implies stability. Therefore, we get the fair and authoritarian rule of *The Emperor*.

Etymologically, Tzaddi is related to Tsar, Czar, Kaiser, Caesar, Senior, Seigneur, Signor, and Sir, all of which are cognate with *The Emperor*.

Like his counterpart, *The Empress*, the symbolism of this path need not be overstated. If Path 13 could be symbolized by the ultimate mother, then this path would be accurately depicted by the world's best dad.

Ritual and meditational use: Whenever calm leadership is needed, this path can be meditated upon or invoked. Helps confer authority and confidence in both voice and demeanor.

The *Moon from*
The Pictorial Key to
the Tarot *by Arthur*
Edward Waite

Path 29: Qoph (KOHF), "back of head"
ק (100)—XVIII. The Moon ♓

The Moon appears again, this time in her dark and mysterious aspect. This is the type of moon under which dark sorceries and menacing witchcraft are performed.

Nothing is what it seems here. This is the world of deceit, delusion, and madness. Not that some might not like it here for awhile—it can be darkly seductive. It's the grimy underworld of sex, drugs, and excessive indulgence. However, sooner or later, the lack of sunlight will kill any but the genuinely nocturnal.

It partakes of many of the more sinister aspects of Netzach (shallowness, superficial success, hollow fame) and brings it down to the material plane (Malkuth). The attribution of Pisces just enhances all this, with its worst aspects becoming prominent: weak-willed, easily led astray, and secretive to the point of deception.

This path polarizes with *The Sun* tarot card. This path is the "darkest" part of the Moon. *The Sun* card however, symbolizes the simplest, and brightest parts of the Sun. *The Sun's* Hebrew letter is Resh, which means the head—the center of our sensations, where all our experiences are processed. *The Moon's* Hebrew letter is Qoph, however, which means *back* of the head, implying that which cannot be seen, that which is behind us, and unavailable for conscious understanding.

Ritual and meditational use: Works of wickedness. Be careful they don't backfire.

Path 30: Resh (RESH), "head"
ר (200)—XIX. The Sun ☉

The Sephirah of the Sun is Tiphareth, which we discussed in the last chapter. This is the *path* of the Sun, so there are definitely similarities between this path and Tiphareth, including a natural sense of "wholeness." This path is simpler, though. It is merely the warmth and joy of being alive in the noonday sun.

This path symbolizes the general sense of well-being that is our natural birthright—before the ego-mind gets too greedy and neurotic, throwing a wrench into our internal harmony.

This is not a complicated path. You could draw a "happy face" on a note card and it would adequately symbolize the guileless joy of this path.

Ritual and meditational use: A good mood lifter, joy enhancer, and confidence builder.

Path 31: Shin (SHEEN)
𝕎 (300)—XX. The Phoenix (Judgment) Fire/Spirit △

This is yet another path concerning destruction and renewal, but in this path it feels entirely like a relief, entirely like a revelation. It is destruction that leads to a new order of things in short order.

Shin means tooth. Teeth "destroy" food in order to release the nutrients contained in food. This is congruent with the energy of this path, which destroys only to release some sort of new and more useful energy.

The title and design of both the traditional decks and Crowley's leave me unsatisfied. In the traditional deck the idea of a fiery rebirth gets bogged down in Christian dogma (and guilt) replete with Gabriel blowing his horn and people popping out of their graves.

While I'm content with all of Crowley's renames thus far, I'm not as enthusiastic about this one. I agree it needed a change, but Crowley's version, called *the Aeon*, is bogged down with complex Thelemic symbolism when this path is not that complicated.

This path is the energy of a lightning strike. It is purely a natural function of the universe— not God's judgment. There is no need to straddle this path with any dogma or overly complex symbolism.

If I were to rename the card, I would dub it *The Phoenix* with that selfsame bird as the image, burning himself up, being reborn from his own ashes.

Ritual and meditational use: Fiery rebirth when a completely new self is desired.

Path 32: Tau (TAHV), a "cross"
𝕿 (400)—XXI. The Universe (The World) ▽ *or* ♄

This path can be either attributed to Earth, or Saturn, or both. In this path, we are talking about the solidity, the heaviness, and the tangibility present in both their natures.

Satiety, completion, and wholeness are all represented by this path as its tarot trump is *The Universe.* As the first path, *The Fool*, symbolizes "nothing," so does this path symbolize "everything."

Magick, and the tarot in particular, is about transformations and changes. There is no ultimate end. The end of one series merely begins something new. In this path is the implicit desire to go from everything back to nothing.

In modern cosmology,[62] there are theories called "cyclic models" of the universe. In a cyclic (or "cyclical") model of the universe, the Universe undergoes an endless sequence of cycles, expand-

The World from
The Pictorial Key to
the Tarot by Arthur
Edward Waite

ing from nothing into everything (called the "Big Bang"), and then from everything into nothing (the "Big Crunch"). Each cycle could be trillions of years long.

Hinduism has held a similar belief for thousands of years. The universe never has a true beginning or end, but merely cycles. Brahma creates the universe. Vishnu preserves the universe while it is manifested in the present state we are familiar with. Shiva will ultimately destroy the universe, bringing everything back to nothing. Then the whole cycle starts over again.

This path symbolizes the four elements, symbolized by the four Kerubs in the corners.

A modern version of this card could proudly display the periodic table.[63]

Ritual and meditational use: Good for seeing the big picture. Useful for grounding energy and feeling "whole." Help with planning and finishing big or important projects. Can also be used in wealth talismans.

---

62 A branch of astronomy that studies the totality of the universe, including space, time, and all known phenomena.

63 Crowley's version does contain an obscure version of the periodic table, but it's hardly recognizable as such.

Regarding the Cornucopia of Symbolism Just Given

The previous descriptions are not meant to be completely inclusive. Though I list all attributions, I do not necessarily describe how each and every symbol fits in with the whole, but instead I focus on the most salient and understandable of the symbols, hoping the rest will make more sense to you with time and meditation.

For example on Path 16, the Hebrew letter means "nail," but I don't mention it in the text. So does the nail symbolize suffering? Or is it the will of Chokmah hammering down into Chesed? Or is it a symbol of the practical world—a way to hold things together in building and construction? It's all of these and more as you come up with your own ruminations upon the path.

I am also aware that all these symbols and attributions may seem overwhelming at first. Most likely some of the symbols resonate with you, but other comparisons I drew, perhaps, don't make a lot of sense just yet. This is the nature of the Qabalah. It grows not only at your own level of understanding, but the symbolism will be slightly different for every human. Therefore I encourage you to work with the traditional symbolism and let your own reasons for their connections evolve.

This is more of an art than a science. With time and persistence, the symbols will jiggle into place within your mind.

The point is to create a common language between your (literal) conscious mind and your (symbolic) unconscious mind. Whatever meaning works for you personally is a good meaning. Just don't cling too tightly to your interpretations. Let them evolve as your understanding grows.

What are the "final" letters?

Five letters of the Hebrew alphabet have "final" forms, those being Kaph, Mem, Nun, Peh, and Tzaddi:

Each one is an alternate way of writing the letter *only* when it comes at the end of a word. However, final letters aren't used consistently. The only one that comes up with regularity in magick is the final letter for Mem. אלהים (Elohim, a name of God) is a good example of when the final letter is *always* used. Also, the "Choir of Angels" names in the Appendix nearly all use the final letter Mem.

The "final letters" need to be recognized as they come up in magickal and Qabalistic literature, but how much you emphasize or minimize their effects on your own personal Qabalah is up to you.

Also note that Samech, ס, and final Mem, ם, look very similar. The main difference is the Samech should be more rounded off at the bottom edges, while the Mem has sharp corners. With many modern Hebrew typefaces, such as the one used in this book, only the bottom right hand corner shows any differentiation.

EXERCISE 3.1

Memorize the Tree of Life. This should include being able to draw the general shape of the Tree of Life and be able to label each of the Sephiroth.

EXERCISE 3.2

Memorize the 22 letters of the original Hebrew alphabet.

Learn to draw their shapes correctly with finesse and style. They will be a powerful tool in your magickal arsenal until the end of days.

Be open to discovering your own resonance with the letters. Draw them. Doodle them. Make art with them. Distort them. Make them into stick people—doesn't matter. The more you work with not only the Hebrew in this book, but all the other symbols, the more you will increase their power.

EXERCISE 3.3

Memorize the paths and all the attributions supplied. Memorize their place upon the Tree of Life in relation to the Sephiroth.

You will be perfect in this practice when you can draw a blank Tree of Life and label all the paths and Sephiroth. (See Chapter 10 for a completely labeled Tree of Life.)

Wait! You REALLY want me to memorize all that?

Yes. In this book I've kept what you need to memorize to the absolute minimum, but this much is necessary if the incredible symbolic power of the Tree of Life is going to sink into your subconscious.

However, I don't expect you to completely understand the barrage of symbols presented in this chapter. Memorizing the attributions is the chore of a week, but understanding their interrelations is the joy of a lifetime.

I presented them early not only so they can start sinking in while you finish reading the book, but also as a reference for you to flip back to when constructing your own talismans and rituals in the upcoming chapters.

Using some of the symbols in an actual ceremony will make a lot more sense of them. So just memorize the attributions and trust that with time this jumble of symbols will be useful, practical, and actually make a lot of sense.

WEAL✝H MAGICK

"Wealth unused might as well not exist."—Aesop

Welcome to the beginning of practical magick. I will teach you how to affect the material plane with ceremony and symbolism.

This chapter specifically deals with accumulating wealth, but many of the principles given here will be utilized in later chapters for acquiring health, love, and whatever else you are looking to attract into your life.

The Shri Yantra, a popular mandala found in Hinduism. It is a symbolic representation of Sri Lakshmi, the Hindu goddess of wealth, prosperity, and abundance on all levels.

The Abundance Mindset

The abundance mindset is the belief that there is plenty of wealth in the world to go around. It is the opposite of the more usual "scarcity mindset," which believes that not only is there not enough wealth but that acquiring it must be done through either Machiavellian or tedious means. This mentality leads to depression, futility, and greed.

The abundance mindset is liberation as it frees you to focus on your passions in life and let the wealth take care of itself.

What if I have trouble accepting the abundance mindset?

Admittedly, it's easier said than done to really feel it in your bones that there is more than enough wealth to go around. There is a certain amount of resistance from our mind to this idea. Here are a few tips to open yourself up to this liberating concept:

1. Be open to the idea of infinite abundance—at least accept that it *might* be true on some deeper level even if your rational mind balks at the idea.

2. Look around and focus upon abundance, both in nature and in the financial world. Niagara Falls, for example, can pump as much as 200,000 cubic feet of water *per second*, and has been around for more than 10,000 years. There are billionaires that in *minutes* make enough for an average family to live on comfortably for years. There really is *that* much abundance in the world.

3. There is no shortage of energy. In modern science, we know that energy is conserved, meaning nothing is ever created or destroyed, but only changes form. Learn to think of the abundance mindset as transforming one type of energy into another. There is always enough of *some kind* of energy going around—the trick is to convert it into the type of energy you require.

4. There is a certain amount of "surrender" when giving into the abundance mindset. Once again, a belief in some sort of "higher power" will greatly assist you.

5. Learn to give away what you have. Give away your love. Give away your creative ideas. Give away your time. Give away your last $10. By giving away the very things we usually cling so tightly to we clear our life of scarcity mindset blocks, and then real wealth and abundance will flow into your life.

If you are still having problems, then forget about it. The wealth magick given in this chapter will still work even if you do not accept the abundance mindset.

Ritual to Charge a Wealth Talisman

If you've made it this far and have been doing the exercises, you are ready to create your first talisman. A talisman is an object charged with magickal energy for a specific purpose, in this case, wealth.

There is endless variety and room for experimentation in most types of magick and talismanic magick is no exception. Nothing is set in stone about my instructions, but unless you have a good reason to change something, stick to what I give below. I've made the instructions as flexible as possible so you will get many chances to inject your own style and imagination into the proceedings.

Step 1: Define your intent

While it is not uncommon for a magician to make a talisman for a specific money amount, I don't consider this a particularly enlightened way to make talismans. It is usually more conducive to focus on the underlying issue, such as needing a new career.

Here are several ways to formulate an intent:

"I have _____."
"My true will leads me to _____."

"I will manifest _____ with naturalness and ease."
"My life is manifesting _____."
"I am being magickally led to _____."
"God allows me to manifest _____ right now, all the time."

In the following examples, I will use these two intents:

"My life is manifesting a meaningful
new job or career opportunity."
-and-
"I have a great job."

Normally, you only need a single intent per talisman. I am using two intents in this example for clarity's sake, and since the two intents are congruent, it is perfectly acceptable. What you do *not* want is competing intents. If you have two completely different goals, then you need two completely different talismans.

Step 2: Divine the appropriate Sephirah (or Path)

Decide which Sephirah (or path) best fits the type of magick you wish to perform. There are occasional overlaps, in which case you can use a mixture of Sephiroth/paths or use one or the other at your discretion.

In this instance, we are going to use Chesed to make a wealth talisman. As in Chapter 3, you'll see it has the following attributions, which we will take into account when making the talisman:

Chesed (חסד)
God name: AL
Color: Blue, Royal Purple
Scents: Cedar
Planetary influence: ♃ (Jupiter)
Metals: Tin, Aluminum

Step 3: Choose a material basis for your talisman

Creation of the actual talisman is a fun little art project.

For a wealth talisman, consider a pyramid-shaped object because of its stable, yet still spiritual structure. (The four sides are the four elements and the apex of the pyramid is Spirit.) You could make this out of wood as it is versatile and works with most talismans once you paint it an appropriate color. If you wanted to go all out, you could use tin to make the pyramid, or more simply use a square sheet of aluminum.

Several other options would be parchment, pasteboard, or cardboard cut into a square. If there are simply no other options, use plain white paper and cut that into a square.

Decide on an option that works for you and then move on.

Step 4: Turn your intent into symbols

Do Steps 4, 5, and 6 on scratch paper first because you will be experimenting and making mistakes. We will move our designs to the actual talisman in Step 7.

Synthesized Script

This method is similar to the one the famous occultist A. O. Spare[64] used. The underlying point of this method is to write out our intent and garble it into some interesting-looking symbols.

There is no right or wrong way to "synthesize" your handwriting, so let me just give you a couple examples in my own style, in my own hand, exactly as I have prepared successful talismans many times before:

---

64 An English artist and sorcerer contemporary with Crowley, but with a completely different style and methodology of magick (surreal, indulgent, and much more "low magick"). His influence upon chaos magick, mainly through the writings of Peter Carroll (the "inventor" of chaos magick), has been so great that he is considered the grandfather of chaos magick.

1. My life is manifesting a meaningful new job or career opportunity.

At each step, I become more abstract until I feel I'm done. I could simplify further, combining all the symbols into one, but in this example I like the design of the symbols already so I will stop here.

Simplify. Don't be afraid to drop lines or details. Take as many steps as you like. Abstract from your regular handwriting into unfamiliar symbols.

You may also remove duplicate letters first as in the following example:

1. I have a great job.

2. I have a great job.

Have fun with it and don't worry exactly how you got from one step to the other. Just simplify and abstract in any way you see fit.

Step 5: Prepare the appropriate God name

As noted in Step 2, the God name for Chesed is: "AL." You could use the Hebrew (אֵל) directly on your talisman. In which case you would be done with this step.

However, I'd like to get you comfortable with using magickal alphabets, so for our wealth talisman we will instead convert "AL" into two different magickal alphabets.

Using Magickal Alphabets

There are many "magickal" alphabets in common use, all of which are easy to use. We are going to use two in the following example, but see the Appendix for a large list of alphabets.

It does not matter which alphabets you use. Simply use the ones that appeal to you the most. The key to using magickal alphabets is changing something known and easily recognizable into something more symbolic and strange to the conscious mind. This helps our magick slip by the "censors" of the conscious mind and penetrate directly to the subconscious level.

The God name "AL" is easy to translate as it only has two letters to draw. Using the chart in the Appendix, convert "AL" into the magickal language known as "Theban."[65] You will find "AL" now looks like this (here written right to left, like the original Hebrew): ꙮꙮ

Now convert "AL" into "Passing of the River" and you will find it now looks like this:

---

65 First published in Johannes Trithemius's *Polygraphia* (1518) and attributed to Pietro d'Abano. Heinrich Cornelius Agrippa's *De Occulta Philosophia* (1531) is another early source of these alphabets and he also attributes them to Pietro d'Abano. Other magickal alphabets from the same source include "Passing of the River," Malachim, and the Celestial Alphabet.

You can write them out in either direction. In our examples, we went from right to left.[66]

Not only can you use the magickal alphabets with God names, you can use them for just about anything. For example, instead of using synthesized script in Step 4, you could instead translate your intent into one of the magickal alphabets.

What you *don't* want is anything written in your boring old native language. If you want to write "JUPITER" on your talisman, convert it to one of the magickal alphabets first.

Step 6 (Optional): Add any other appropriate symbolism you desire

Here are a few options of where to find even more symbolism for your talismans:

Olympic Spirits

Olympic Spirits come from the *Arbatel de magia veterum* (English: *Arbatel of the magic of the ancients*), a Latin treatise on ceremonial magick.[67]

The Olympic Spirits have a long history in magick. They were mentioned in John Dee's *Mysteriorum Libri Quinque*,[68] and were later used in the Golden Dawn.

Here is the Olympic Spirit of Jupiter, named Bethor:

---

66 Because Hebrew names often dominate my talismans, I tend to stick with writing from right to left for consistency; however, you might use the rationale that since an alphabet like Theban is based on the Latin alphabet, it should be written from left to right. That is also fine. Intent is more important than the direction we choose to write our letters.

67 Unknown author, first published in 1575 in Basel, Switzerland.

68 Transcribed between 1582–1583, discovered long after his death in the hidden compartment of a chest.

Archangels, Angels, and Angelic Choirs

Besides the God name, you can also add appropriate Archangel, Angel, or Angelic Choir names. These are all given in the Appendix and can be used either in Hebrew or converted into one of the magickal alphabets. These are associated with the ten Sephiroth.

For this wealth talisman, you would only use those listed for Chesed.

Heavens, Spirits, and Intelligences of the Planets

These can be used just like the God names, either in Hebrew or converted to a magickal alphabet. These are associated with the Planets rather than the Sephiroth so there are only seven rather than ten of each (see Appendix). The names are traditional, taught by the Golden Dawn, and also published in Crowley's *777*.[69]

In this case, you would use the Heaven, Spirit, and Intelligence of Jupiter.

Can I use symbols from other cultures, religions, and belief systems?

Absolutely.

For example, you could use the Sri Yantra on your wealth talisman. It might not be in the spirit of traditional Hinduism to use it in this fashion, but it is entirely in the spirit of Hermeticism to do so.

Taking symbolism, gods, chants, and anything else from various sources and using them in new and interesting ways is the hallmark of high magick and Hermeticism. The Golden Dawn itself is an "enlightened hodgepodge" of various sources, including Egyptian, freemasonry, John Dee's Enochian, and traditional Hermeticism. Crowley took magick to the next level for all serious practitioners with the publication of *777*, which classified various gods, beliefs, and magickal symbolism from nearly all known religions and spiritualities available at the time.

When you are satisfied you have enough symbolism for your wealth talisman, move on to the next step.

---

69 Crowley, Aleister. *777 And Other Qabalistic Writings of Aleister Crowley*. New York: Weiser, 1986. This book will come up repeatedly as it is a handy resource for practicing magicians.

Step 7: Decorate your talisman

Now that you have worked out your symbolism on paper, decorate the material basis you chose in Step 3.

Paint, markers, and pens are all fine depending on your medium. Consider using appropriate Qabalistic colors, in this case blue and royal purple. Using black or white for writing letters and symbols is always appropriate too. You may also use your intuition and sense of artistry to make color changes, but if you aren't sure, stick to what is given.

Here is a completed talisman using the example symbolism just given. Imagine this to be a blue pyramid:

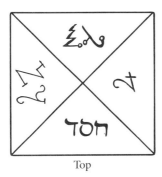 

Top   Bottom

You'll notice I used four astrological symbols around the corners of the bottom of the pyramid. When these four signs are used together they symbolize the four elements, which is appropriate to Chesed. Chesed is the fourth Sephirah and does indeed imply the stability of the four elements balanced with one another in harmony.

You will also note I added the Jupiter symbol and the word "Chesed" in Hebrew on the top of the pyramid.

You may make your wealth talisman exactly like this if you want, but I recommend that you at least rewrite the intent in your own words and abstract it yourself.

If you are feeling adventurous, then let your imagination run wild. Make this as fun as kindergarten and as professional as college and you can't go wrong.

Please note you do *not* have to be a great artist or painter to make a successful talisman. Draw or paint your talisman as best you can, but do not obsess over it. The sincerity with which you make the talisman is more important than how perfect it looks when you are done. In other words, even an incredibly sloppy-looking talisman, so long as you poured your heart into it, will still be powerful.

When you are satisfied with your talisman move on to Step 8.

Step 8: Ritual preparation

Temple preparation: Straighten up and clean the area you will be working in. You may choose to work outside somewhere, in which case I recommend "drawing" a ring around yourself in the dirt (such as by scratching into the ground with a stick, or by using a ring of salt, or rocks, or whatever else is handy and appropriate).

Temple preparation is flexible. Just understand that you are doing something important and very different from your normal state of affairs. Make your "temple" into something spiritual and holy to you, whatever that means to you. Even if you are in a tiny, cramped room with a bed in it, do your best to make it into a ritual setting.

You may decorate the temple with the same colors and symbols as you used for the talisman if you like, but that is not necessary.

As with all magick, the more effort you put into preparation, the more effective it will be—however, you need to balance that out with the imperfections and limitations of the material plane. Therefore, just do your best and move on.

What to wear: Whatever you have been wearing when you practice the Equilibrating Ritual of the Pentagram is fine. If you have the means and inclination to do something fancier, just use the general principles as laid down for Jupiter. For example, you might use a purple robe or draw the symbol of Jupiter on your forehead with paint. Use whatever works for you.

Day and time for the ritual: Despite what you might read in other books on high magick about having to do your rituals only on appropriate "planetary" days and hours, the time and day of your rituals is quite flexible. Some people like to choose the day of ritual based upon the traditional day of the week,[70] but this is a matter of personal choice.

Your priority is to choose the time of day that you will perform magick at your best. For some people this might be sunset, for others it might be midnight, and it may very well change depending on the type of ritual.

Except for purely solar rituals, I personally prefer all my rituals to be at night because I feel I'm more relaxed and open to the subtle influences and energies of the astral and magickal world. Ultimately, the time and date are up to you. Whatever you choose, make it meaningful to you.

One thing you can do is use an astronomy program to divine when your planet of choice is visible. In this case, you would do your ritual when Jupiter is in the night sky, preferably at its zenith.

If you are worried about doing everything "perfectly" for your first ritual, wait until the next full moon. There is something psychologically powerful about a full moon and this translates into effective rituals.

The altar: You don't need anything specific for the altar. You just need a place in the center of your temple where you will put the talisman during the ritual. If you are outside, you can make an altar using a large rock. It only has to be big enough for your talisman.

Candles: I love candles. Use them as you see fit. Just don't start any unintentional fires.

Incense: Try and find the incense as given in Chapter 3; in this case it is Cedar. Or you may use the incense of the "Goddess of the Starry Night Sky," Nuit.

---

70 Monday=Moon, Tuesday=Mars, Wednesday=Mercury, Thursday=Jupiter, Friday=Venus, Saturday=Saturn, and Sunday=Sun.

Nuit's incense is made of "resinous woods and gums."[71] This incense smells like a campfire. To acquire it, find a tree and gently remove dried bark that is already flaking or fallen to the ground. Any type of tree will do (but in the case of a wealth ritual, Cedar would be doubly appropriate). You will also occasionally find some sap dripping from trees; dried sap will burn beautifully and this is ideal. A charcoal censer is best for this, but in a pinch I'm sure you can find another safe way to light the incense.

Nuit's incense is good for any ritual or meditation where you want increase or abundance. Nuit is about abundance on all levels,[72] which includes all joys of the material plane.

Bell: If you have a bell you may use it at the beginning and end of the ritual as you see fit. This is optional. (I personally use two belly dance zills previously owned by a virgin.)

Music: For now, I recommend you don't use music unless you need it to mask out distracting background noise. In that case, use something relaxing and soothing. As you develop as a magician you can come to your own conclusions about how and when to use music. For now, we are concerned with staying centered and focused upon the ritual with as little outside disturbance as possible.

Other magickal items: As usual, bring anything you consider holy or magickal into your temple space for workings.

When you are content with the state of your temple, you are ready to begin. Make sure you will have no interruptions!

---

71 *From the Book of the Law, I.* 59: "My incense is of resinous woods & gums; and there is no blood therein: because of my hair the trees of Eternity."

72 "Ye shall gather goods and store of women and spices; ye shall wear rich jewels; ye shall exceed the nations of the earth in splendour & pride; but always in the love of me, and so shall ye come to my joy." *The Book of the Law, I.* 61b.

Step 9: Ritual for charging a talisman

This is a bare bones but effective method for charging a talisman. Learning this will teach you the core skills of ritual design, upon which you can drape any other layers of ceremony as you desire. There is an elaborate template for charging *any* type of talisman given in Chapter 10, which is an evolution of the ritual you are to learn now.

1. An extended relaxation ritual. Take a little more time than usual. You may also want to take a bath or do something else especially soothing or purifying.

2. Perform the Equilibrating Ritual of the Pentagram as given in Chapter 2, but at the final step you will make a change. Instead of saying: "May the divine light descend," you will instead finish as follows:

3. After saying "IAO," continue staring upward (your eyes may be closed for better visualization) with hands raised high.

4. Imagine a huge, glowing ball of blue or purple above your head. Chant "AL" repeatedly until you feel the ball of energy is at its peak. Trust your visualizations. If you are sincere, they will be more than good enough.

5. Take a full inhalation of air.

6. Lower your hands, and then touch or hold your talisman. Exhale while you imagine the blue or purple energy traveling down your arms and hands and into the talisman, filling it with energy. You may do this slowly, or quickly as in a burst of energy, but make sure you use an entire exhalation of breath.

7. Make the Sign of Silence.

8. The talisman is now charged. Repeat the entire ERP as you normally perform it, or simply end with the "Qabalistic Cross" if you prefer brevity.

Step 10: Forget about your talisman

Put the talisman away somewhere safe or keep it with you. You may forget all about the talisman, or you can obsess over it. It doesn't matter so much in the long run.

When your desire comes true, destroy the talisman by fire, or by crushing it and burying in the earth.

If your desire does not manifest after a certain amount of time, you should destroy the talisman anyway. While mileage will vary on such things, my talismans never worked until after I had destroyed them. This is because my mental blocks kept the magick from working until I had "given up" on them.

How long should you wait? I usually wait a month before destroying the talisman. You might want to wait longer depending on your goals. Pick reasonable timelines for your goals, and the talisman will reward you accordingly.

How do talismans work?

The process of construction and charging of a talisman creates a clear and concise message to the subconscious. The message allows the subconscious to lead us to our desire—in spite of mental and emotional blocks the *conscious* mind may have. The time-honored God names, symbols, and rituals used in magick are conducive to creating this clear message.

Ideally, you want to plant your new seeds into the subconscious, and then return to a Pure-Fool State, i.e., that state of completely and utterly enjoying what is around you, assured that you will be led to more and more happiness the more you submit to what is already manifested.

Is it spiritual to do magick for material things?

You may find as you progress in magick that you may not care as much for worldly things as you do now. However, baubles are shiny to infants and there is no use in denying aspiring magicians the skills to acquire the things they want—especially since it's the easiest way for them to master their new abilities and learn the underlying principles of magick at the same time.

Exercise 4

Construct and charge a wealth talisman using the instructions in this chapter.

If you don't want a wealth talisman, then start thinking ahead to how you would alter this ritual for something you do desire. By the end of this book, you will have the skills and resources to create a ritual for *any* goal.

MAGICK T⊕⊕LS
& WEAP⊕NS;
REVENGE MAGICK

"When patterns are broken, new worlds emerge."
—Tuli Kupferberg

This chapter covers a lot of ground related to the number five and Geburah, the fifth Sephirah.

First, we will discuss the pentagram and related topics, including the construction of the five magickal weapons. In the second half of the chapter we will discuss topics related to the seemingly destructive and sinister side of Geburah.

*Pentagram including
the Golden Dawn's elemental
attributions.*

Man and His Pentagram

The first known use of the pentagram is from Mesopotamian writings from around 3000 BC where it was used as a pictogram for the word "UB" which means "corner, angle, nook, or small room."[73]

The Pythagoreans were using it in 5th Century BCE as an important religious symbol, and by the time of Heinrich Cornelius Agrippa[74] the pentagram was well-entrenched as a magickal symbol.

The popularity of the pentagram as a mystic symbol continues into modern day, where it's used heavily in most forms of popular magick, including Golden Dawn, Thelema, and Wicca.

Microcosm vs. Macrocosm

The microcosm and macrocosm are Ancient Greek concepts. These early thinkers noticed that patterns in nature (specifically the "golden ratio") repeated from the very large down to the very small.

These two terms come up regularly in discussions of magick and Hermeticism. We generally use them to mean that man and God are reflections of each other, and that our internal state reflects our external life situation, and vice versa.

---

73 Labat, René. *Manuel d'épigraphie akkadienne: Signes, Syllabaire, Idéogrammes.* The pentagram is labeled number 306, and is shown pointing downward. The translation of "corner, angle, nook, or small room" for "UB" is standard and is given in a variety of sources including Wikipedia and the lexicon at Sumerian.org.

74 Famed German occultist (1486–1535).

Microcosm ○	Macrocosm
Small	Large
Man	God
The number "5"	The number "6"
Atoms	Galaxies
Things "in" your heart and your mind, i.e., your thoughts and feelings.	Things "outside you," i.e., your clothes, car, spouse, etc.
The Pentagram	The Hexagram

This is the basis of magick—you can "change" something inside you, and the world around you must react to this and have a corresponding result. There need not be anything metaphysical implied in this. *Example:* If you are angry inside, and then you go around and piss other people off, you have created a corresponding result in your external world that originated within you.

Elemental Correspondences

The points of the pentagram are attributed the four elements (Fire, Water, Air, Earth) crowned by Spirit at the top.

In this book we follow the Golden Dawn attributions of the elements since they are in common use and have proven to be efficacious.

If somewhere down the line you have a need to change around correspondences, by all means do so. Part of the spirit of Geburah, and Chapter 5 as a whole, is about tearing things down in preparation for something better.

Elemental Symbol	Element Name	Weapon	Virtue	Magickal Image
△	Fire	Wand	Velle ("To Will")	Lion
▽	Water	Cup	Audere ("To Dare")	Eagle
△	Air	Sword/ Dagger	Scire ("To Know")	Man
▽	Earth	Earth Vessel	Tacere ("To Keep Silence")	Bull
✳	Spirit	Lamp	Ire ("To Go")	The "Egg"

Magickal Images

These are the same images as from Chapter 2, namely the Lion, Eagle, Man, and Bull, with the addition of the "egg" for Spirit.

The symbolism of the egg regards its shape, which suggests the entire cosmos, and its function: It gives birth to life.

Any "mystic egg" symbolism you find in occult literature[75] (such as the Orphic Egg, Brahmanda,[76] Akashic egg,[77] even the Easter Egg) is related to the element of Spirit.[78]

---

75 Also Carlos Castaneda discussed "egg-shaped" energies surrounding humans that only sorcerers could see.

76 "Brahma's egg" is a term for the universe in Hindu mythology.

77 Akasha is a term for Spirit or Aethyr in the Hindu/Tantric "five principles," which are similar to the five elements we have discussed. Its shape is ovoid, hence the "Akashic egg."

78 Conceivably, even the Egg Man from the Beatles "I am the Walrus" could be a reference to the cosmic egg. "Kookoocachoo" is certainly foolish, nonsensical language that *The Fool* (path Aleph) might use. The "Fool on the Hill" song on the same album shows the Beatles's familiarity with the tarot, and *The Fool* is a pictorial representation of pure Spirit.

The Five Magickal Virtues

The five magickal virtues are something to keep in mind as you progress on the road of magick. The virtues can be used in meditations, rituals, and vows. The virtues are ideals to be mastered over a lifetime.

The virtues are given in Latin, followed by their translation and a brief commentary.

Velle, "To Will"—This is the will to create—to do something with what we are given.

Audere, "To Dare"—The waters of emotion are dangerous. Do you dare to master them?

Scire, "To Know"—Air is all about the mind, and the mind craves knowledge above all else.

Tacere, "To Keep Silence"—This is the stillness of deep meditation. The Pure Fool maintains this state of blissful silence amidst even chaotic circumstances.

*The Orphic Egg—
In Greek mythology,
specifically the Orphic
Mysteries. This is the cosmic
egg from which all the Greek
gods were born. It is also
clearly a representation of
semen impregnating an egg.
The Greeks were using this
symbol 2000 years ago.*

Ire, "To Go"—This is Spirit. A magician's destiny is through action—not by sitting still.

The Five Magickal Weapons

Now we arrive at the meat of the matter. There are endless tools, weapons, and accoutrements available to you in magick.[79] However, the lamp, the wand, the cup, the sword, and the earth vessel are of primary concern to the ritual magician.

---

79 Crowley's *777* lists them all.

There is no rush to create your weapons. The exercise at the end of this chapter is optional. It could take months or years to acquire the desire and understanding to make your weapons.

It's a very personal business, this making of magickal weapons! When you are ready to make your own weapons, use your imagination. Do not be limited to the Golden Dawn style of weapons, nor the Wiccan type, or any other specific notion of what your symbols of the five elements should be. I use a painted baseball bat from my adolescence for a wand, a broken and re-glued glass cup for my cup, and a painted clay pot I bought for 99 cents as my earth vessel. For my elemental Air weapon, I've never quite found the perfect single weapon to do it for me. I have a half dozen or so weapons of Air (including a few daggers, feathers, and a genie bottle.) As a magician you will soon learn instinctively when a symbol or tool is working for you or not.

If you end up reading what Crowley has to say about magickal weapons in *Magick Book 4*, don't be frightened off. He is describing *ideals,* his ideals, which were: a) highfalutin', b) expensive, and c) highly symbolic. With that said, you can get a lot of inspiration from *Book 4*, as well as more down-to-earth advice in *Magick Without Tears.*

I prefer a more "shamanistic" style of acquiring weapons, which in this sense means opening up your eyes and using what is already around you. Wiccans also tend to take meaningful things from their own environment and then transform them into powerful tools of magick (such as taking a branch from a tree and making it into a wand). High magicians, however, tend to *buy* things for some reason, most likely because it originated with the wealthy elite.

Whatever you decide, the symbolism should be meaningful to you. That is what is important.

When you have completed your weapons, you should employ a consecration ritual (see Chapter 10 for specifics) and then start using them with all your magickal workings.

The Wand

The wand, perhaps the most famous and quintes-
sential of all magickal instruments, symbolizes:

1. Our phallic energy[80]

2. Our creativity

3. Our ability to take action

4. Our Will

5. Our self-confidence

*Ace of Wands from
The Pictorial Key to
the Tarot by Arthur
Edward Waite*

Phallic energy is "turned on" energy. It doesn't
have to be sexual, but it *is* alert, active, strong, and
spontaneous. Whenever you are "hot and excited"
to do something or make a change, that is your
"erect" phallic energy at work. Phallic energy is directly related to our creativity, which includes our ability to rearrange our life in a way suited to our
desires.

Our Will is our ability to concentrate and to stay centered in any situation. Since Will originates below our conscious mind, we become most
aware of it when we are intently focused upon a single goal. It is the fire of
creativity and action.

The Will is active, intent upon taking action. When our Will is strong, so
is our self-confidence—genuine self-confidence, unfettered by ego or vanity.

Practical uses: *Will* is our discipline and passion united in a single direction, aimed at a *single result*. A strong Will equals strong magick. The stronger our focus, the more intensely our Will becomes manifested on Earth.

The best ways to strengthen your Will is through:

a. Meditation upon a single point. Instructions for this sort of
meditation are given at the end of this chapter.

---

80 Women also have phallic energy. In magick there is zero sexism. The ultimate goal is to
empower ourselves utilizing both our feminine and masculine aspects.

b. Daily rituals, such as the Equilibrating Ritual of the Pentagram, will yield considerable improvement in your Will.

c. Magickal oaths. These dedicate you to something higher than your ego. More on this in the next chapter.

d. Focus your concentration on the very moment in front of you. This is somewhat similar to "meditation upon one point," except that you do it during the course of your day-to-day routine. No matter where you are or what you are doing, focus entirely upon it. The more "present," the more aware of what you are doing, the more your Will develops naturally. There is a practice in Hindu yoga called Mahasatipatthana, which is good practice for being completely "in the moment." It is one of the meditations given at the end of the chapter.

e. Following your passions. Whether you are a runner, a writer, a gardener, a mechanic, a fashion designer, or anything else, the more actively engaged you are in pleasurable pursuits, ones that fire up your passion, the more your Will grows.

Tips for construction: Any phallic, rodlike instrument is suitable as a wand. Wood is a common material, but you might have reason to use metal or crystal.

Construction doesn't have to be difficult or expensive.

For example, go to a hardware store and buy a dowel and an end cap. Glue these together, then file and sand down the end cap (usually they are round) into something more "penile." Paint it red, and then add the appropriate elemental, God, and angel names from the Appendix. Add a clear coat, and you have a finished wand ready for consecration.

You can buy fancy wands at occult shops, and there is nothing inherently wrong with that. Just make sure you think through all the symbolism, including any metals, crystals, gems, or animal hides used on the wand. If you buy a wand, it is especially important that you consecrate it.

You also might go out into the woods, find a nice branch from a tree, and take it home. After you sand and lacquer it, you might find it is perfect and needs no further decoration.

Personal taste accounts for everything in the construction of weapons, and if you change your mind, you can always replace your elemental weapons as your knowledge and experience with magick grows.

The Cup

The cup is the chalice, which is to say the Holy Grail. It is our single most important "weapon" for the attainment of divine ecstasy—but what the hell kind of weapon is a cup?

Ace of Cups from The Pictorial Key to the Tarot by Arthur Edward Waite

This cup is a chalice of surrender, of poison, and of divine drunkenness. There is no intellect here. The intellect rules below the Abyss. Above the Abyss, Babalon is queen and she rules with the iron fist of Saturn. Luckily, she wants only to break our dependency upon transitory idols. Nothing of man's world penetrates beyond the Abyss.

Symbolically, the cup contains the blood of your "ego-mind"[81] surrendered willingly to the divine. Only in such surrender can true understanding[82] and genuine pleasure be yours.

Practical uses: The cup is useful in any type of magick involving love. The cup gives understanding in the darkest times and brings meaning to any situation. More than all that, this is the place to focus the surrender of your ego-mind.

---

81   In this book I prefer to use "ego-mind" instead of simply "ego" to differentiate it from other similar terms, such as Freud's Ego, and the idea of having a "big ego" in the sense of being cocky or conceited. However, for the most part, when I use the term "ego-mind" it is the same as many authors use the term "ego." In modern occult parlance, the ego is our sense of self, but not our *true* self. More on this later in the chapter.

82   The cup symbolizes Binah ("Understanding") as the wand is Chokmah ("Wisdom").

Surrender here and your life is filled with joy. However, if you hold on miserly to your ego-mind, which is nothing but a phantasm, it will be ripped from you limb by limb as you stumble blindly upon the road of magick.[83]

Tips for construction: Any cup will do. Handmade, so much the better, but it is not necessary. Paint the cup with any symbols of Water as you see fit.

Ace of Swords from The Pictorial Key to the Tarot by Arthur Edward Waite

The Sword

The sword symbolizes our conscious mind and intellect. Like the mind, the sword is divisive and analytical. The sword can protect, or it can destroy.

The element of the sword is Air, and like air, the mind goes hither and thither and lacks the intense focus of the wand. The primary Sephirah associated with the sword is Tiphareth.[84]

Tiphareth is the center of the Tree of Life as the mind is the center of our lives, a mediator between the external material world and our internal spiritual world. The sword symbolizes our conscious decision-making process.

Practical uses: Use the sword for anything analytical. Use it for planning, decision making, and when you feel protection is needed.

Tips for construction: If you tried to make a sword by hand, you'd find it very difficult to complete without help from others, unless of course you know how to smelt metal, and forge steel, pounding your blade into submission with a skillful and hearty hand—and that's not to mention the construction of the hilt.

Humans rely on each other. Construction of these most personal of weapons will show just how interconnected we are within the web of society.

---

83 However, even this is preferable to being a perpetual slave to your monkey mind.

84 It also symbolizes the entire *Ruach* ("mind"), which includes not only Tiphareth, but the other five center Sephiroth. More on the Ruach later in the chapter.

Most of us will make do with buying a sword. A dagger will do far better, as a sword implies a big ego, which is just that much more painful to lose when crossing the Abyss.

You also might instead use a feather or an oriental hand fan to symbolize air.

The Earth Vessel

The Earth vessel symbolizes a lot more than just your body or your material possessions. The Earth vessel, commonly called a pentacle[85] symbolizes all your memories, the impressions past incidents have left upon your psyche, and indeed everything that has ever happened to you.

This is also why it's your karma. Your karma is like a record of past actions, all of which triggered some other reaction in your life, however large or slight, which caused you to take yet more action, and create more karma, *ad infinitum.*

Your pentacle is a way of symbolizing all the impressions of your life in a meaningful way that feels good to you. Your Earth vessel should empower you and fit together in such a way as to make some sort of sense of why everything that has ever happened to you is useful or necessary.

This is perhaps the most difficult of all the weapons to understand, because to make a good Earth vessel is to understand one's self and be able to express it in some way upon the material plane.

Traditionally, the Earth weapon is a pentacle, which is a disc (out of wax, wood, or metal) with a pentagram carved or painted on it.

Also popular is the Golden Dawn "pentacle," which is also on a flat disc, but painted with a hexagram.[86]

Practical uses: For grounding other magickal energies. Good for invoking stability, basic needs, and basic comforts. It is your ultimate talisman,

---

85 Or sometimes "pantacle."

86 Shouldn't it be a "hexacle" then? You'd think so, but no, the Golden Dawn simply doesn't call it that.

*Silhouette
of Greek krater*

pulling in and making sense of all the other elements and energies in your life.

Tips for construction: As far as the material basis, the simplest way is to cut a circular piece of wood and paint it appropriately. Alternatively, you could use a silver plate and engrave it.

Since this symbolizes Earth as an element *and* the planet we live on, I prefer something that symbolizes the Earth as round and not flat, such as a Greek *krater* shape.

Whatever you paint, draw, or carve into your Earth vessel is up to you and your imagination. For example, all these stars are appropriate for your Earth vessel:

The pentagram is traditional and is used on the tarot.

The Golden Dawn used a hexagram made of two triangles, but there is no reason not to use the unicursal one instead.

The septagram is Thelemic as it symbolizes Babalon (as Binah) being set upon the throne of Malkuth. i.e., our wishes manifested on Earth.

I prefer a simple design, but you may get as complicated as John Dee's *Sigillum Dei Aemeth* if it suits your fancy.

If you use a bowl or *krater* shape, there is no reason not to fill your Earth vessel with fertilizer, and grow a plant in it. Just make sure the plant stays healthy, as it will be a symbol of your entire Tree of Life.

*John Dee's version of
the Sigillum Dei Aemeth*

The Lamp

It's difficult if not impossible to discuss Spirit without being highly symbolic. The Lamp represents our "soul." Our soul is of the same nature as God.

What is the soul?

Soul is just a word, another symbol, for that original spark or bit of "light" that is our innate nature. You might consider it your spiritual DNA—that which makes you uniquely yourself—and is arguably there even after physical death.

What is God?

"God is not the name of God, but an opinion about Him."— from the *Ring of Pope Xystus*[87]

"God" is that indefinable essence of what came before—and after— everything else.

Have you ever asked yourself, what came *before* the beginning of time, including all manifested existence, and everything in it? Is that God? But then what came before God? If nothing, then how has God always been here? How did so many galaxies, planets, mammals, and cell phones come to be? How did nothing turn into something?

Some scientists tend to be smug about things of the "spirit," as if it is superstitious to discuss such things. But you might as well ask them, "What came *before* the Big Bang? What was there to enable the universe to evolve into what it is now?" You might hear some good theories, but you'll get no certainty—just scientific "mythology."

In magick, we don't know exactly what it is, why it works, or how it is there to begin with, but we call the element that comes before everything else, *Spirit*. What "came before" is the unknowable essence called "God,"

---

87 As this publication is commonly known. However, it was actually written by a Pythagorean philosopher and later Christianized.

in the macrocosm, and in man it is called the "soul" or our HGA ("Holy Guardian Angel").[88]

Spirit is something we can never completely grasp with conscious thought. It is unquantifiable, unknowable, but it is there. It is the *something* underneath all our thoughts and words. Beneath our mental noise and our chaotic emotions, something is quietly experiencing everything with calm equanimity; that is our Spirit.

Practical uses: Light for your temple, without which you are left in darkness, unable to do any magick whatsoever.

Tips for Construction: Your lamp should be hung from the center of the ceiling if you work inside. (If you work outside, the Sun or Moon can be your "lamp.")

You do not necessarily have to use a gas lantern or anything of that sort. I use a metal "lamp" that holds a single tealight at a time. I don't recommend anything electric as it just doesn't have the right "feel," but there is no reason to ban them completely. If you worked the symbolism of an electric lamp into your concept of it as a magickal weapon, it could also be used.

Decorate your lamp as you see fit. The simpler the better, as attaining the spirit is about simplifying the complex.

Weapons Dos and Don'ts

Rarely will you use them like "weapons." It's easier to consider them as powerful talismans dedicated to a specific energy—but a bit more lively than talismans. Most of the things you can do with your weapons becomes clear as you advance through this book.

Do Use Your Weapons:

a. During rituals. They make rituals more powerful just having them on the altar.

---

88   More on the HGA in Chapter 6.

b. In meditation. Just holding them and being regularly exposed to them will help your mind get a deeper grasp of the elements, and therefore magick in general.

c. For balance. Using your weapons regularly assures you will remain a balanced individual on all four planes.

d. For inspiration, power, and confidence. The longer you have your weapons, the more they mean to you and the more you will get from their use.

e. When you need more of one specific type of elemental energy, perform the Equilibrating Ritual of the Pentagram with that element's weapon and you will have an abundance of that energy circulating throughout your temple.

Dont's:

a. Don't make your weapons too big or too small. Make them in proportion to your body, your temple, and each other.

b. Don't allow anyone to handle your weapons except those you completely know and trust.

c. Don't confuse your own energy for the weapon's. The problem with weapons is not that they won't work, it's that after awhile they work too well, and you might rely on them as a crutch. Weapons are a symbol. The force, the energy, the magick, really comes from you.

The Destructive Side of Geburah

The number five is a beautifully disruptive number in the Qabalah. After the stability of the number four, "5" gives rise to movement, energy, and action.

Remember, the Tree of Life starts with simplicity (Kether) and works its way down into the complexity of the modern world (Malkuth). You can look at it like this:

One makes a point. Two makes a line. Three makes a triangle (and thus introduces the geometrical "plane"). Four is the first solid object. So what then is five?

The number five introduces the concept of *time*, thereby allowing solid matter to grow, transform, and evolve.

But humans don't always like change, so Geburah gets a bad reputation for being destructive, but that is a superficial and flawed way of looking at things. Change is just that—*transformation*. Any destruction involved in change is illusory. Energy is never created or destroyed, merely transmuted.

Like Geburah, the pentagram also gets an undeserved bad rap sometimes—especially when it is "upside down."

The Inverted Pentagram

The most notorious star in all of magick is the *inverted* pentagram. Does it not mean a devil's head? Is it not evil?

Thanks to Eliphas Lévi,[89] it does indeed symbolize a goat's head to many magicians, but no, it is generally not considered an evil symbol by those who use it.

Lévi associated the inverted pentagram with "evil," and yet used the goat head's inverted-pentagram symbolism in his famous drawing of Baphomet. (The inverted pentagram is implied by the shape of the goat's head, contrasting with the upright pentagram on his forehead). This suggests he knew all too well the rebellious, blindly creative, Capricorn-type energy he described would be used by other magicians "in the know."

Before Lévi, the inverted pentagram was not considered an "evil" symbol whatsoever. The Pythagoreans, mentioned previously, used the inverted pentagram as their holy symbol. There was no concept of evil attributed to

---

89 *Dogme et Rituel de la Haute Magie, (Transcendental Magic, its Doctrine and Ritual)*, 1855.

it, and it was certainly not Satanic, since "Satan" had yet to be invented.

Not all magicians use the inverted pentagram the same way, but there is a certain rebelliousness implied in it since most pentagrams are drawn point upward.

If one does use it in the Lévi/Crowley tradition, understand the goat-head symbolizes primal creative energy, a.k.a. the libido or Kundalini. This energy is coherently symbolized in Trump XV: *The Devil.* Crowley's card, the first version to show this connection explicitly, shows the goat in front of a large erect penis.

Eliphas Levi's Baphomet

Those who do not understand this psychosexual creative energy try to demonize it; however, those who understand it are likely to succumb to the creative bliss it bestows. Jimi Hendrix, rock god and legend, symbolizes this energy perfectly.

What is the "Left Hand Path?"

The Left Hand Path, usually referred to as simply LHP, is a branch or style of high magick that embraces the "darker" side of the occult, including harmful magick, ego aggrandizement, demonic workings, curses, and works of domination.

Ultimately, there is far too much made of the difference between the left hand path and the right hand path, mostly by those who feel a strong need to rebel against something, so they invent a dualism when there is none.

Bottom line: Magick is magick, and ego is ego.

In all magick we feed our ego-mind at the beginning—we follow whims, indulge desires, express anger through spells, etc. Eventually you grow out of it or are destroyed when you take the highest initiations, which is what

Crowley meant by saying a black brother (a follower of the Left Hand Path) would destroy himself when he tried to cross the Abyss. Instead of losing his ego-mind and being set free, the black brother clings to his ego-mind and wastes away inside that pitiful prison of his own making.

What about Satanism?

This is a complex and touchy subject to some people on both sides of the fence, but most Satanists don't consider themselves evil or worshippers of evil. Some follow Anton LaVey, some subscribe to the teachings of the Temple of Set, and some just like to rebel against established religions with hedonistic delight.

I consider "Satanic" energy to be libido/Kundalini energy, as in Tarot XV: *The Devil.* Nothing evil is implied in that, but unfortunately when this energy is repressed or completely misunderstood, it can come out in perverse ways.

What is "Chaos Magick"?

Chaos magick is a hodgepodge, open-ended, and eclectic mix of ancient magickal ideas mixed with modern sensibilities and a penchant for coming up with new magickal paradigms.

The primary tenet of chaos magick is: "Nothing is real. Everything is permissible." Chaos magick has roots in A.O. Spare, but was articulated by Peter J. Carroll in his books *Liber Null* (1978) and *Psychonaut* (1981).

Chaos magicians may use the trappings of old Hermeticism and high magick, but would be just as likely to perform magick using modern, mainstream archetypes such as invoking the "pantheon" of *Star Wars* or *Lord of the Rings.* A common characteristic of chaos magicians is their ability to completely shift magickal paradigms at the drop of a hat, and believe fully in each paradigm as they do so.

The Ego-Mind

The ego-mind is that incessantly yappy part of our mind that always says I, I, I, and me, me, me. Most humans are so identified with this ego-mind that they don't realize there is anything else.

The ego-mind could also be appropriately called the "monkey mind" as it is that incessant rattle of jabber running nonstop in our heads.

Monkey mind is originally a Buddhist term[90] meaning "unsettled, restless, capricious, inconstant, confused, indecisive, and uncontrollable." This sums up the ego-mind perfectly, and yet it is only too common to mistake this endless chain of self-talk for our True Self.

The ego-mind's greatest trick is getting you to believe you are your ego-mind. You are not.

What Am I?

Underneath all the neurotic, narcissistic, and obsessive layers of the ego-mind is *pure being—pure existence*. This is also known as our "higher self" or True Self. More on the higher self in the next chapter, but for now let's focus on the ego-mind, since above all else in magick, the ego-mind is your enemy.

Where is the ego-mind on the Tree of Life?

The ego-mind is *not* actually part of the mind at all as far as Qabalah is concerned. The *mind* is known as the Ruach, which is especially associated with Tiphareth and includes the surrounding five Sephiroth (Geburah, Chesed, Netzach, Hod, and Yesod).

---

90 *Xinyuan* in Chinese and *shin'en* in Sino-Japanese.

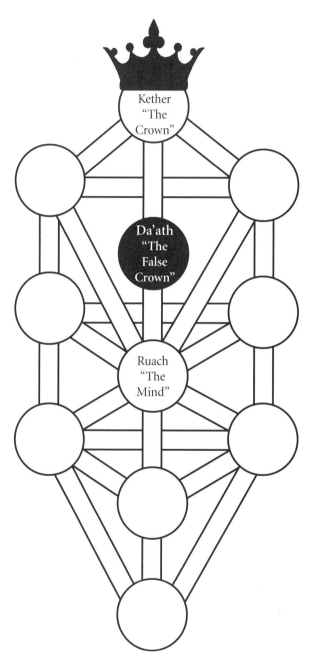

The Tree of Life with the "mind" labeled

Ruach (רוח) means not only mind, but also breath, wind, and spirit. Our mind, in this sense, is exalted and closely related to our higher self.

The *ego-mind*, however, is not even on the Tree of Life. In Hermetic Qabalah, it is the non-Sephirah known as Da'ath,[91] which is the invisible Sephirah that lies midway between Kether and Tiphareth.

Da'ath is known as the "false crown." Most humans wear this false crown with pride, having made a king out of their ego-mind.

The ego-mind, which most people desperately try to build up as a source of security and stability, is actually the most unreliable, unreal, and ineffectual "thing" you could ever hope to own. The ego-mind is a dead end, a black pit—an Abyss.

Kether is the true crown. Kether shines light directly into Tiphareth, bypassing the ego-mind completely.

I realize this may be difficult to understand if you fully identify with your ego-mind, feeling reluctant to let it go, but as you progress in magick, you will learn that the source of all your suffering comes from the ego-mind and the ego-mind alone.

What if I'm angry or upset?

There is a certain amount of aggravation, ferocity, and even violence implied in Geburah and its inherent tendency towards constant change. Properly applied, this type of energy is useful.

However, when egged on by the ego-mind, this energy can bring on loss of temper or physical violence.

Occasional anger is natural, but raving outbursts, or extended bouts of seething, repressed anger are both symptoms that serious life changes need to be made immediately.

---

91 Da'ath means "Knowledge." Be aware that in traditional Hebrew Kabbalah, Da'ath is used quite a bit differently than in Western (i.e. "Hermetic") Qabalah.

Once you have worked through this book, you will easily understand how to raise or channel any type of energy. In this case, I recommend using a path that is conducive to transmuting anger and rage, such as Path 27: *The Blasted Tower*. This path is the key to understanding how to use and channel anger in a way that feeds your entire Tree of Life instead of burning it down with rash outbursts of anger.

But I'm angry for a good reason. Can I get some payback?

Before you cast a spell to hurt someone, understand that the desire to get revenge is always ego-mind motivated.[92]

That said, there are perhaps certain extreme situations where some sort of "revenge" magick might be called for, such as in the case of murder or other acts of extremely malicious intent. Geburah would be a good place for all violent spells of anger and frustration. Other paths, such as Path 29: *The Moon* can also be used for "black magick" and vindictive sorceries.

What is black magick?

In this book it means any magick in which you would have physical harm come to someone.

Normally, I feel a wiser man or woman would find a better course. It doesn't make much sense magically or Qabalistically, especially as you advance upon your way to adepthood. Your sense of oneness will be so complete you would not want to harm anything outside yourself because you see it as a reflection of yourself.

Instead of black magick, you'll always be better off by channeling that frustration towards the root of your problem. Do unto yourself before you do unto others.

If you want to murder someone, first murder your ego-mind!

---

92 From a spiritual point of view, the higher self can never be harmed, therefore how would revenge ever be deemed necessary?

Putting Geburah to Good Use

The best way of understanding Geburah's destructive nature is to view it as a fiery energy that blasts down obsolescence wherever it stands in the way of growth. Geburah is the demolition of a dilapidated building so as to make room for a new and better one.

Here are some ideas of how to make use of Geburah:

Use Geburah to "Get Off Your Ass"

The active, aggressive energy of Geburah can help you overcome inertia and the ego-mind's tendency to stagnate.

Use this energy to get up and make constructive changes. Properly balanced, there is nothing negative about Geburah energy. It gives you the hunger and restlessness to bite off what you really want to chew.

Use Geburah to Break Through Limiting Beliefs

There are many things in our psyche that could do with some Geburah blasting, such as worn-out beliefs instilled since childhood that do not serve us well anymore.

Have you been told you are dumb? Get angry, and sign up for school, using your resentment of people's comments to help you stay focused and determined.

Have you been told you are ugly? *Rebel* against traditional standards of beauty. Find your own style, and in doing so find your own confidence, because genuine self-esteem is *always* sexy.

Geburah energy is powerful enough to break down these sorts of limiting beliefs. Geburah can help push us forward when nothing else can.

The key to Geburah is getting angry at the *real* source of your problems. It's *never* another person, place, or a thing. Direct your anger inward at things in yourself that you want to change or overcome.

Use Geburah to Break Through "Success Barriers"

Sometimes the further we push into new areas, even highly desirable ones, the more discomfort we feel. We experience the fear of having our current "reality" thrown into disarray. We feel as if we have "lost our footing."

The problem is the ego-mind. Since the ego-mind thinks it has kept us alive this entire time, it clings tightly to its existing belief system. It would rather we stay the same than move into uncharted territory, no matter how advantageous.

The energy of Geburah is courageous and unabashed by new frontiers. It blasts through these internal barriers to your success.

Use Geburah Directly Against Your Ego-mind

The cause of laziness, limiting beliefs, and success barriers is the ego-mind. So *use* your anger and frustration when things go wrong. Send that anger back to the source.

Destroy the ego-mind with gusto and relish. Here are some how-to tips:

Five Ways to Break Down the Ego-mind:

1. **One-pointedness:** Any meditation that helps you calm or control your mind will lessen the noise and menace of the ego-mind. This includes the One-Pointedness Meditation and Mahasatipatthana, given at the end of this chapter.

   "One-pointedness" is being focused completely on the one thing you are doing while you are doing it. The ego-mind thrives on chaotic, dispersive thoughts, so when your focus is sharp, the ego-mind loses power.

   While meditation is the easiest way to learn one-pointedness, you may also find it in sports, hobbies, and art. With enough practice, you can attain one-pointedness everywhere, in everything you do.

2. **Put yourself in new challenges or uncomfortable situations:** This is one of the healthiest and most fun things you can do in life

anyway. Your life is tick, tick, ticking away right now. What are you waiting for? Change that job, plan that trip, talk to that girl; who cares, right? Just go do anything you normally wouldn't do or have been hesitant or afraid to do.

3. **Embarrass yourself:** Learn to humiliate your ego. Few will follow my advice here since the fear of humiliation is sometimes greater than the fear of death, but let it be known that embarrassment is the quickest way to humble your ego-mind and send it to pieces.

     When you laugh wildly after a particularly embarrassing moment, that's a bit of your Pure Fool, a.k.a. your True Self, coming through. We all have a blissful, "Pure Fool" state underneath all the incessant noise of our ego-mind. Embarrassment can help you find yours.

4. **Practice asceticism:** Asceticism is abstaining from worldly pleasures and has been a popular practice in spiritual systems throughout the centuries. There is a lot of validity in doing so, as it helps distance you from endless attachments to material things, thereby allowing you to be more in the moment.

     The intention of asceticism is to bring about greater freedom in various areas of one's life (such as freedom from compulsions and temptations) and greater peace of mind. Yoga means "yoke." However, the end result of yoga is not restraint, but greater freedom of mind and body.

     The types of things you "swear off" are not as important as the discipline you build in doing so. Discipline is always a good weapon against the ego-mind, which along with being vain and greedy, is also quite lazy.

     Magickal oaths are covered in the next chapter, which are essentially a formalized method of asceticism.

5. Finish this book and all the exercises: This book is not just about getting things you want, it's about teaching you to feel blissful under any circumstances.

By doing the exercises in this book you can rest assured you are wearing the true crown of Kether upon your head and not the false crown of egotism.

On Moxie—The Bottom Line

While I certainly believe there is an underlying universal oneness in the world, and in the final analysis life *is* pure joy, I also acknowledge that very quite often: life stinks.

Yes, even the greatest magicians can be occasionally heard to mutter this pessimistic mantra under their breath. Life sucks sometimes; but so what? That's where moxie comes in.

How easily you attract success and joyous things into your life is directly related to how much stress you can be subjected to and still maintain your "inner cool." This is the hallmark of a great man or woman.

Having moxie, or "grace under pressure," is learning to take an almost perverse pleasure in how much things do suck when we are forced to suffer through bad situations, no matter how transitory.

Most humans aren't equipped to enjoy uncomfortable transitions, but learning to walk through fire with a smile on your face is the single greatest skill you can acquire in life.

Exercise 5.1: One-pointedness Meditation

Get a timer so you don't have to think about how much time you have left. Set it for five minutes to start with. Sit in a comfortable position, and stare at a single point for the full amount of time. That's it.

You may choose any simple thing to focus on, such as the tip of your nose, a crack on the wall, or the corner of a chair. Whatever you choose for the meditation, stick with it for the full meditation. Do not change your focus no matter how badly the ego-mind urges you to switch. If you don't like what you chose to focus on, you can always pick a new spot during the next meditation.

Blinking or subtly adjusting your posture is fine, but always keep your eyes on the single point of focus.

You can increase the time of this ritual up to thirty minutes (once or twice a day), however even five minutes a day is effective.

Don't skip this meditation because it sounds too easy and simple. First, it's not nearly as easy as it sounds, especially after the newness factor wears off, and second, it is extremely beneficial over the long haul. Woe to the many vain students who will miss out on the power granted through this daily meditation because it is so simple that it sounds to them like nothing.

Exercise 5.2: Mahasatipatthana[93]

This meditation helps develop your Will. It keeps you focused, centered, and calm. If you stick with the practice for months and years, it cures even the deepest neuroticism and depression.

This is similar to the one-pointed meditation, except instead of focusing on one point while sitting still, you focus on whatever is happening right in front of you no matter what it is or where you are.

While you are practicing this meditation, you are to be aware of exactly what you are doing in each moment. As each moment arises, pay attention to what you are doing or thinking—as best you can.

Example: If you wish to stand on your feet, then you become aware that you want to stand on your feet. Notice yourself straighten your legs. Notice your posture as you stand. Pay attention to your body weight and how it shifts from foot to foot as you walk.

---

93 "Special mindfulness."

Don't just walk across the floor. Notice its details. Be aware of the color of the floor and its texture and at the same time be aware of your legs and feet walking upon it.

You walk forward, fully conscious of all that goes by. Notice the table or chair. Be conscious of your body at the same time, such as your breathing and the rhythm of your gait.

If you need to scratch, notice that you need to scratch, and then do it. Notice how your mind still wanders, but be aware of *how* it wanders. Notice each new thought. Stay with the meditation. Stay present.

There are always plenty of interesting sensations coming at us at any given moment, but we cut ourselves off from most of them. Now as we open up to the focus of each moment, we can lose ourselves in the bliss of our sensations.

You may notice you want a drink of water, so you then remember you have a bottle in the room. You get up, stand by the table, all the time aware that you want to reach out and grab the bottle, which you see is half full. Notice how the bottle feels in your hand as you bring the bottle to your lips. Water flows into your mouth. Pay attention to the feeling of the water sloshing over your tongue and teeth and down into your throat.

This could continue all day and night long, whether you are at work, talking to friends, or making love. You are not only completely focused on the act, you are focused on any thoughts or sensations arising from the act.

This is a more difficult practice than it sounds like so start with only five minutes daily, which is enough for positive results. Increase the time at your own pace, but only up to what you can enjoyably handle. Five minutes of intense awareness is more useful than an hour of mind wandering.

EXERCISE 5.3: CONSTRUCT YOUR WEAPONS

When you are ready, construct your elemental weapons as you see fit.

This is optional for now. It is something you'll want to do after you've been through this book once and have been practicing magick for a little while.

The weapons are not required for any of the rituals in this book, though they will enhance all your rituals when you finally get them made.

THE H⊕LY GUARDIAN ANGEL, BEING IN +HE M⊕MEN+ & HEALING MAGICK

"The most beautiful thing we can experience is the mysterious. It is the source of all true art and all science. He to whom this emotion is a stranger, who can no longer pause to wonder and stand rapt in awe, is as good as dead: his eyes are closed!"—Albert Einstein

Part I: The Higher Self

In Chapter 5, we talked about smashing up the ego-mind. So if we are something more than the ego-mind—just what is this "more"?

What's left of "ourselves" when the ego-mind leaves us in peace for even a few moments, whether we are lost in meditation or some moment of pleasure?

What is our higher self?

"It is easy to understand God as long as you don't try to explain him."— Joseph Joubert

Most philosophical or religious systems have some sort of concept of a "higher self." Sometimes it is simply referred to as God, Buddha, or Brahman. Other times people focus more on the *link* between man and God; this usually manifests as the glorification of the holy "son," as in the cases of Krishna and Jesus.

Sometimes the higher self is explained as a more personal soul such as the *Atman* of Hinduism and Buddhism, or the *Eudaemons*[94] of ancient Greece (comparable to the Roman *genius*). All these essentially mean the same thing: there is some "higher self" in us available to access for help in guiding our actions.

Some philosophic schools and teachers focus on the process of experiencing the higher self, such as meditating and attaining "inner silence." Zen Buddhism also falls into this category since talking about God is useless in the Zen master's eyes—only direct experience of divinity means anything. Hence, all "foolish" tasks given by Zen masters to their students are in hopes that through the cleverly absurd stunts, the student will have a complete break from their ego-mind long enough for enlightenment to shine in.

It doesn't matter how you view the higher self, but I do believe it is helpful to have some sort of conception of a power greater than your conscious ego-mind.

In this book enlightenment will come gradually, which is as it should be, otherwise a student can too easily fall back into "sleepwalking" through their lives.

---

94 "Good demons" etymologically.

Trust that there is something better than your ego-mind for bringing you joy. Surrender to life as it is. Give up to what is present all around you.

The "Holy Guardian Angel"

"It should never be forgotten for a single moment that the central and essential work of the Magician is the attainment of the knowledge and conversation of the Holy Guardian Angel."—Aleister Crowley[95]

The Holy Guardian Angel, commonly abbreviated to HGA, is used in magickal literature to designate the "higher self" or "True Self."

Don't get hung up on any of these terms. You don't have to believe in "guardian angels."

Crowley himself thought the phrase "Knowledge and Conversation with the Holy Guardian Angel" was so ridiculous that anyone of intelligence would be unable to mistake the term for the *actual experience.*

Do I have to believe in God for magick to work?

God means a lot of things to a lot of people. Whatever your conception of God, or lack thereof, is fine. Magick wouldn't be very magickal if you had to believe a certain way for it to work.

The underlying principles of magick are for everyone regardless of whether they believe in an ultimate Creator, Darwinian evolution, or both.

Do I have to believe in a higher self for magick to work?

A belief in something higher than your conscious mind certainly makes magick and everything else in life a lot easier and more enjoyable.

Even if you only can go so far as to say, "My subconscious has some powers and abilities that I don't have access to directly, but maybe I can access through magick," is good enough for using this book.

If you are completely against God or anything higher than your ego, but are still willing to practice the exercises in this book with an open mind "to see what happens"—well, that is also good enough!

---

95 From *Magick Without Tears.*

So, no, you don't need to believe in anything specific at all for the magick in this book to work. Practice and study with sincerity and you will have results.

The Perfect State of Being

The perfect state of being is often known as "being in the moment." It is also known as "being one with the Tao" or "going with the flow." It is when everything is evolving the way you want, yet you don't seem to be doing anything at all. It's not a self-indulgent state, and yet neither is it ascetic. The perfect state of being is balanced, pleasant, and doesn't require too much upkeep.

To have enlightenment is to have *intense presence of being*, i.e., to be fully absorbed in what is happening right now. This occurs when you aren't inside your head, either thinking about the past or worrying about the future. There is only one magickal state: the present moment. That is where all action takes place. The past and future do not actually exist. They are fantasies inside the mind. Only the ever-evolving present moment is real.

Enlightenment

The Buddha described enlightenment as "freedom from suffering."

Suffering is caused by an intense desire for our life to be something other than what it is. To break through the cycle of suffering, you must learn acceptance of what is before you in every moment.

Either you find enlightenment in *everything* you do, or you don't find it at all.

Transcend Time

"We must not allow the clock and the calendar to blind us to the fact that each moment of life is a miracle and a mystery."—H. G. Wells

Enlightenment is being right here, right now—centered, aware, and enjoying it.

Our default state is one of blissful awe and contentment.

What "screws up" our perfect state of being is going into our heads and thinking—something most people do too much of. (Yes, even people who seem to never think at all.)

The poorest choices are those made when we get trapped within our "inner dialogue" loops. It is better to make a wrong choice than to over-think, over-analyze, and end up doing nothing.

Be present. Right here. Now. Make your decisions as they arise, not before or after, and you will be neurosis-free.

If you must plan for something, do the planning, and then let it go. In the moment is where you react the fastest and make the best decisions. In the moment is where you will enjoy yourself and get the most out of life.

Your higher-self/intuition/instinct/subconscious will give you the perfect answer in the exact moment you need to know.

Non-resistance

To struggle against the ego-mind, and to struggle against the way things are right now is to add even more tension to the trap of the ego-mind. Non-resistance is the solution to this riddle.

Allow things to be as they are. Accept what is before you. Allow all thoughts and emotions to flow through you.

What if my life is too big of a mess to let go and enjoy it?

We all want to improve our lives, but the best way to do that is to accept it the way it is already. Laugh madly at the chaos that is your life, for indeed all of our lives are chaos. Everything is impermanent, from your deepest joys to your most pitiful sorrows. All experiences pass like a breeze, but leave a mark upon your soul. Having an experience, any experience, is all that matters to the soul. All moments, anywhere, anytime, are unique. All are fleeting.

There is no ideal, no perfection to be reached other than that which you imagine for yourself. Go make a mess of life and learn to enjoy the resulting sights, scents, textures, and smells. This is the ever-evolving tapestry of your life. There is nothing else.

The Pure Fool State

"Sell your cleverness and buy bewilderment."—Rumi[96]

There is another way of viewing the liberated state of consciousness called enlightenment. You can liken it to the Fool from the tarot.

Here enlightenment has been raised to its highest state. The Fool's madness is wisdom, and his folly is pure ecstasy. The Fool represents the egoless state.

All that we worry and fret over: our cars, our dates, our nails, our taxes, are but fleeting shadows across our life. Where is the cause for concern to the Fool? Every moment is equally precious, equally blissful. The Fool laughs last and laughs best.

Our physical life lasts no longer than the flutter of an eyelash upon the face of eternity. The Universe will go on without you, without me, without the whole planet. The Fool knows this to be a blessing.

The Fool has humility for he sees his own impermanence clearly.

The Fool is thankful for all the sights, sounds, tastes, and textures presented to him in every moment of his life.

The Fool is happy because he loves all of life. He doesn't just love certain parts of it, he loves everything, knowing that all of it is fleeting, and that none of it can harm his true essence.

Strive to be also like the Fool. Be humble, be thankful, and most of all be joyous!

Do I need perfect silence?

"Why do you stay in prison when the door is so wide open? Move outside the tangle of fear-thinking. Live in silence."—Rumi

---

96   Jalal ad-Din Rumi, Persian poet and mystic, 1207-1273.

"Stopping your internal dialogue" and "inner silence" are common terms and phrases in yoga, meditation, and magick. They are indeed worthy goals. However, there can be too much pressure put on new students to reach pure silence.

You don't need to perfectly silence your ego-mind. Practicing the meditations in this book will give a sense of quietude and peace, but your inner dialogue never has to shut off completely.

You don't have to do anything "perfectly" to be a success in magick or in life. To the Fool, every mistake is just one more chance to do something differently or to create something new. Use your imagination every time something "goes wrong" and the word "mistake" can vanish from your vocabulary.

If the Pure Fool state of pure being
is so great, why do we need an ego-mind at all?
Maybe we don't anymore.

At some point in our evolution, humans felt the need to do certain things to distinguish ourselves from the animals. Manners, etiquette, ritual, art, etc., are all developed out of a need to differentiate ourselves from the animal world. Maybe our ego-mind was developed as a way of keeping our newly developed "self-awareness" from dying out, and reverting back to more beast than man.

Maybe we will evolve past our current ego-mind into something less dysfunctional. I certainly would like to attain that state. Until then it's good enough to be the Fool whenever the spirit takes you.

Is my True Self in Tiphareth or in Kether?
Technically, Kether is our True Self in ineffable form, but it is in Tiphareth where we experience the True Self in a more tangible way. Kether meets us halfway in Tiphareth, as it were.

Tiphareth is almost too bright to gaze upon, so bright is it with the miracle of beauty. Kether is even more mind-blowing.

You may consider Tiphareth and Kether as two different levels of enlightenment, i.e., experiences of your higher self. In Kether our identity is destroyed completely, whereas in Tiphareth there is a simultaneous balance between oneness and a separate sense of identity.

On Meaning

Nothing has any intrinsic meaning. Meaning is applied by each and every one of us subjectively. When someone sees a "black cat," for example, we all may be able to agree it's a black cat—but beyond the term "black cat" it is not the same black cat to everyone. Your personality, your previous experiences with other cats, and black cats in particular, will color your internal image of what a black cat is.

Since there is no objective reality, we have incredible freedom in defining what happens to us in life. What any incident means, and what we do with it is entirely open for us to decide.

Have you ever met a person who is always complaining, who always sees the worst in any situation? This type of person is coloring everything that happens to them with pain and discomfort, so they end up creating more of the same. The opposite is true for an optimist. No matter what chaos or hardship besets them, they are constantly "looking at the bright side" or finding a "silver lining" in dark clouds.

Don't be a slave to meaning and intentions implanted in you by others. Learn to dig deep, find your own True Self and your own personal meaning of life. Then you will be able to find joy and bliss in almost any life situation.

Part II: Magickal Concepts Related to Tiphareth

The Hexagram

The Hexagram is the symbol of the Macrocosm, i.e. God, the Heavens, what is outside us, etc. This hexagram is also the symbol of Tiphareth.

Both types of hexagram are appropriate for any magickal use requiring Tiphareth energy, as well as being used to invoke any of the seven planetary powers (see Chapter 10 for a ritual on how to do that):

The 5 and the 6

In the last chapter we covered the pentagram, which symbolizes man, a.k.a. the microcosm. The hexagram, as just mentioned, symbolizes God, also known as the macrocosm.

Finally, we come to the heart of all magick—the union of man and God.

God, spiritual and intangible, benefits through this union by having carnal knowledge of the transitory material world. We, as humankind, benefit from God by experiencing a taste of true eternity, which we have forgotten under the weight of the ego-mind.

The harmonious juncture of the microcosm and macrocosm is the experience of the higher self, or in technical verbiage, "Knowledge and Conversation of the Holy Guardian Angel."

There are many ways to visualize this marriage of the macrocosm and the microcosm, including either a pentagram within a hexagram, symbolizing man within the universe, or a hexagram within a pentagram, which symbolizes God within man.

Crowley's formula for representing this union of the 5 and the 6 is his eleven letter word: "ABRAHADABRA," which contains six consonants and five vowels. Crowley restored the word Abrahadabra from the more famous spelling "Abracadabra,"[97] which was used in ancient amulets to ward off disease.

---

97 The first known mention was in the 2nd century AD in a poem called *De Medicina Praecepta* by Serenus Sammonicus, physician to the Roman emperor Caracalla.

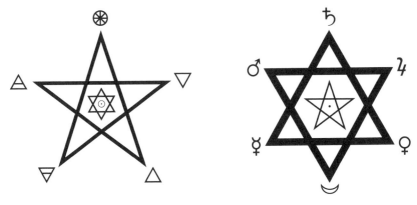

Hexagram inside Pentagram, and Pentagram within Hexagram

Your Magickal Name

Many, if not most, magicians take on a magickal name or "motto" to express where they are upon their spiritual path.

Aleister Crowley's original magickal name was the motto, *Perdurabo*, which means "I will endure unto the end." He eventually went on to take several other mottos, including V.V.V.V.V.[98] and To Mega Therion.[99]

My magickal name is "Pamphage," which means "voracious and all-consuming."

Your magickal name can be from literature or from your own imagination. It can be in Latin, Greek, Persian, or anything else you see fit.

The purpose of a magickal name is twofold. First, it cuts you off from your old ego-mind ties to your given-name. Second, it gives you an ideal to live up to.

Choose your name wisely, but don't worry if it's perfect. It will most likely change as you evolve along your path.

---

98   Vi Veri Vniversum Vivus Vici ("While still living, I have conquered the universe by dint of truth").
99   The Great Beast.

Magickal Orders

The subject of magickal orders, i.e., hierarchical occult organizations, could be a book in itself. As far as we are concerned, the most common orders that come up regularly in high magick are the Golden Dawn, the A∴A∴ (generally considered an acronym for *Argentium Astrum*[100]), and the Ordo Templi Orientis (abbreviated as O.T.O.[101]).

Nowadays, there are so many different lodges of the Golden Dawn it's impossible and unnecessary to keep track of them. Their most important work was published years ago by Israel Regardie in *The Golden Dawn* and that book has influenced most other books on high magick, including this one.

The A∴A∴ is the magickal order that Crowley founded and continues in a similar fashion as the Golden Dawn but has a Thelemic bent; that is to say its rituals are usually based around *The Book of the Law*.

The O.T.O. publishes a great deal of Crowley's work, and he was also the head of the order at one point, so the O.T.O. name will come up quite a bit in Crowley's writing, but other than that they don't really concern us here.

Both the A∴A∴ and the Golden Dawn follow a specific grade structure commonly used by high magicians. In the following list, the number before the equal sign is the number of the grade level; the number following the equal sign is the corresponding Sephirah:

First Order ("Golden Dawn")

- Neophyte 0°=0□
- Zelator 1°=10□
- Theoricus 2°=9□
- Practicus 3°=8□
- Philosophus 4°=7□

---

100 "Silver Star."
101 "Order of Oriental Templars."

Second Order ("Rosae Rubeae et Aureae Crucis")

- Adeptus Minor 5°=6$^\square$

- Adeptus Major 6°=5$^\square$

- Adeptus Exemptus 7°=4$^\square$

Third Order ("Secret Chiefs")

- Magister Templi 8°=3$^\square$

- Magus 9°=2$^\square$

- Ipsissimus 10°=1$^\square$

So for example 1°=10$^\square$ simply means the first grade is the 10th Sephirah. The final grade of 10 belongs to Kether, which is the 1st Sephirah. The only exception to this is the Neophyte grade (0°=0$^\square$), which is the "prequel" introductory grade.

Does the grade system of the Golden Dawn (and traditional Thelema) really matter?

At best, the grades serve as a helpful guideline for teachers and students. At their worst, they glorify results and only further feed the ego's insatiable hunger for illusory attainments. The original fall of the Golden Dawn was due to egos, infighting, and arguments over who claimed to have the highest grade (i.e., who was in contact with the "Secret Chiefs.")

I present them here as they come up often in magickal literature and they are useful in understanding the Sephiroth since each grade has specific Golden Dawn and Thelemic rituals associated with them. However, please understand that true magickal growth is far more organic, and less predictable, than this convenient structure suggests.

The Magickal Oath

Magickal oaths (or vows) are meant to give structure upon which a joyous and magickal life may grow. They are meant to strengthen our resolve and help keep us healthy during times of weakness.

In Golden Dawn and the A∴A∴, there are three especially important oaths. The Oath of Neophyte (10°=0°), the Oath of the Adeptus Minor (5°=6°), and the Oath of the Abyss (which leads to 8°=3°). These oaths are meant to initiate. That is to say, they are meant to move your magickal consciousness to the next level.

All three oaths are similar in content and structure, though the student would receive these vows at very different stages in their career. The terminology in each oath changes slightly, as at each level the student is meant to assume more responsibility for their actions. The Oath of the Neophyte is given when one starts with the Golden Dawn or the A∴A∴. The Oath of the Adeptus Minor is given when a student has spent at least a year of study and practice working with the lower Sephiroth, and has an inkling of what his or her HGA is. The Oath of the Abyss is one of the highest and most important oaths a magician can make. It is only to be taken with utmost solemnity as it will push one "into the Abyss," after which one becomes a *Magister Templi.*[102]

Magickal oaths increase your focus, help you to surrender to your higher self, and generally improve your magick across the board. If you feel you are ready, you may take the following oath.

Oath of Self-Dedication

I, [your name[103]], being of sound mind and body, and having resolved on this day [date] to undertake the Great Work, hereby solemnly swear:

---

102 Master of the Temple.
103 You may use your magickal name, but there can be a real advantage to using your given name and your usual signature. You may use both, such as "I, Shawn Scanlon (also known as Pamphage), being of sound mind..."

I. To fulfill my True Will.

II. To understand all things.

III. To love all things.

IV. To do all things and endure all things necessary to the discovery of my True Will.

V. To attain the knowledge and conversation of my Holy Guardian Angel.

VI. To work without lust of result.

VII. To work in truth.

VIII. To rely only upon my True Self.

IX. To dedicate my every thought, word, and deed to the discovery of my True Will.

May the supreme and invisible Order crown the work, lend me of its wisdom to complete the work, and enable me to understand and enjoy the work!

Witness my hand,

[sign your name]

What's so dangerous about magickal vows?

There is nothing dangerous about magickal oaths except to your ego-mind. Magickal vows taken in solemnity, whether alone or in a group, are unbreakable and will eventually lead you to enlightenment. If you take an oath and deliberately try to break or run from it, you may cause yourself some discomfort, but it's only the pain of leaving your one true path.

What's the "Great Work?"

It means different things in different contexts, but in this case it simply means building a connection with your higher self.

The Great Work also refers to the alchemists' goal of finding the "Philosopher's Stone." This was ostensibly how to turn any metal into gold, but is really about finding joy in any situation.

The Great Work is the never ending process of attaining enlightenment.

Do I belong to a magickal order after taking this Oath?

You won't belong to any specific magickal group (such as the Golden Dawn or the O.T.O.) unless you are actually initiated with them; however, you will be a part of the real and invisible magical order that guides the spiritual evolution of humanity.[104] Crowley called this the A∴A∴, but even this spiritual order has gotten bogged down in material plane concerns. So while I believe one can self-initiate into the A∴A∴ all the way up to Ipsissimus, you are better off just considering yourself as on your own and leaving the ego and politics behind.

Later you can choose to join whichever magickal orders you like, start your own magickal group, or simply choose to be the lone wolf alpha for your entire magickal career.

Do I need a magickal order?

Most magickal secrets have been published and republished. You certainly don't need a magickal order unless you wish to work with an established group of likeminded individuals (and pay monthly or yearly dues).

Oaths for Discipline and Training of the Will

There are other oaths or vows you may wish to undertake for your personal advancement and to build up your discipline and self-control. These vows are designed to strengthen your Will and perseverance.

Here are a few tips for making vows that work:

---

104   The existence of such a thing can hardly be proven, but there is a definite "Great White Brotherhood" archetype that exists in the subconscious of everyone.

1. Decide what it is you are going to do or abstain from.

2. Set a time limit. Don't make it too long until you know you can handle it.

3. Have a "punishment" for when you slip up. Don't make the punishment too painful at first. It should be something uncomfortable or disagreeable, but not excessively so, such as burning a dollar bill, twenty minutes of exercise, or giving up sweets for a week. The reason for this is that everyone slips up from time to time, and that's fine so long as you are willing to perform the punishment agreed upon in your vow.

For example, let's say you take a vow of silence for seven days. You write out a vow in your magickal journal:

> "I, [motto] do hereby swear to not speak a word to
> anyone for seven days. Every time I fail in this, I will
> make one pen mark upon my arm."

Sign it and you are good to go.

Now every time you accidentally talk, you just make a pen mark on your arm to keep track of it (and write it in your journal, too, so at the end of the week you can see how many slips you had.)

The reason this works is that after we make a mistake, our first impulse is to toss out the entire vow. But with this you won't, because our second impulse is usually guilt that we didn't keep to our vow. When you feel that guilt, just do your built-in punishment and know that your vow is still intact. Your vow has not been weakened by the mistake, but strengthened.

Any vow of this sort will help increase your Will, not to mention that with practice this type of vow can be used for all sorts of useful things, including quitting bad habits, or forcing ourselves into new and better routines. You need not take a vow of silence. You could sign a vow to talk to ten new people a day if you are shy, or a vow of abstinence to prepare for a really big sex magick ritual. The goals are limitless.

The Lamen

Each magician usually constructs his or her own lamen at some point, which symbolizes the magician's *modus operandi*. The lamen is an elaborate symbol meant to be worn upon the breast of the magician. It is his or her formula, that is to say his or her "method of attack." It is his or her way of reacting to circumstances.

There is no right or wrong way to construct a lamen as it is meant to be an expression of your own magickal personality.

An example of two lamens. The one on the left is the one I used for many years. The one on the right[105] is by one of Crowley's most famous students, Frater Achad, also known as Parzifal.

The Rose Cross

The Rose Cross (or Rosy Cross) is a more generalized type of lamen symbolizing the "Great Work." The Great Work in this sense is not only the harmonizing of man and God (man is the cross, and the circle is God), but it's the rectification of the Wand and the Cup, the male and the female, the severe and the merciful. Indeed, any pair of opposites harmonized can be appropriately said to be represented by the Rose Cross.

---

105   Originally published in *The Equinox III,1.*

You will see it in a variety of forms:

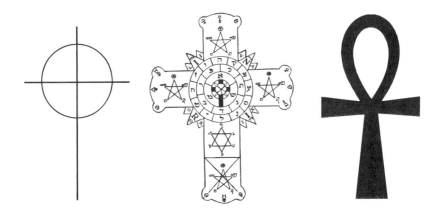

The one on the left is a simplified version of the rose and cross.

Don't be intimidated by the fancy-pants Golden Dawn version (center). It's still the same symbolism of the other two, but just obsessively subdivided as is typical of the Golden Dawn. The one on the right is the familiar Egyptian Ankh, symbol of life.

The Rose Cross comes up in magick on a frequent basis, so while you don't have to completely understand its multilayered symbolism right now, do be aware that the Rose Cross is a symbol of magickal attainment. The cross is meant to symbolize our suffering and toil upon the path of magick. The rose symbolizes the joy and pleasure that blooms within our heart and within our lives by the successful pursuit of magick.

Do What Thou Wilt

For misunderstood philosophies, Crowley's "Do what thou wilt" must rank right up there with Ayn Rand's "Virtue of Selfishness."

A more complete quote Crowley used was, "Do what thou wilt shall be the whole of the Law; Love is the law, love under will."[106]

---

106   Made of two phrases from The *Book of the Law.*

This is symbolic language describing the Rose Cross. Will is the cross, and love is the rose.

So far from being a call to hedonism or "doing whatever you want," Crowley's oft quoted "Do what thou wilt" is actually a call to responsibility. Our responsibility is to connect with our higher self and in the process experience as much genuine joy as possible.

Do I need to make a lamen or a Rose Cross?

Eventually, you may make one or both, but they are not necessary for the rituals in this book.

Since it is a symbol of aspiring to your higher self, the Rose Cross is appropriate for you to wear in all magickal workings. You may use any version as you see fit, including an Ankh.

Your lamen design, however, is something that may take months or years of magickal study to create since it is meant to be a precise, symbolic representation of your True Will.

What about tattoos?

This is a matter of personal choice, obviously. The only thing I'll say is that any magickal symbolism you use (including sigils of spirits, demons, etc.) must still be charged magickally using a ritual. Slapping a magickal symbol on your body does not automatically make it potent. However, properly used tattoos can be powerful in the same way lamens are powerful. Any magician should think through his or her tattoos more thoroughly than a layperson.

Part III: Healing Magick

The energy produced by our chakras is not of the material plane. It is too fine and ethereal a substance to be detected by Western man's machines, anymore than a machine can detect "enlightenment." Hindu medicine, however, has been aware of these chakras and "magickal" energies for thousands of years.

What are chakras?

The chakras are energy centers running up and down the center of our bodies. The word itself comes from the Sanskrit "wheel" or "turning."

The chakras can be "worked." This means that through breath control and visualization they can become more enlivened with magickal energy.

What is magickal energy?

Magickal energy is *any* type of energy used for a specific, intended purpose. This includes not only energy raised through our chakras, but also emotional energy, such as being excited, anxious, or angry so long as it is used in a fashion congruent with our intent.

How do I raise magickal energy?

There are endless ways to raise a variety of magickal energies, and you already work with magickal energy when you perform the Equilibrating Ritual of the Pentagram.

Another powerful method of stirring up magickal energy, specifically that of your chakras, is called the Middle Pillar Ritual. With it you will be able to raise as much magickal energy as you need and understand how to channel it for any purpose. The Middle Pillar Ritual also has the pleasant side effect of making us healthy and beautiful.

Middle Pillar Ritual

The goal of the Middle Pillar Ritual is to open up your major energy centers (chakras), and then raise and circulate as much of that energy as possible.

The chakras run up and down the middle pillar of the Tree of Life, and relate to specific points on the body:

Chakra	Location on Body	Location on Tree of Life	Color	Name to Chant
Sahasrâra	Top of head	Kether	Violet or Bright White	Eh-heh-yeh
Ajna	"Third eye"	Daleth/Gimel	Indigo	None
Vishuddha	Throat	Daath	Blue	YHVH El-Oh-Heem
Anahata	Chest	Tiphareth	Green, Yellow, or Gold	YHVH El-oh-ah V'Dah'Aht
Manipûra	Gut (navel)	Peh/Samech	Yellow or Red	None
Svadisthâna	Groin	Yesod	Orange or Red	Shaddai El Chai
Mûlâdhara	Base of Spine/Feet	Malkuth	Red or Black	Adonai Ha-Aretz

I downplay the visualization of the traditional colors. This is not to say visualizing each sphere as a specific color isn't useful, but only that it can be distracting from sensing the *actual* energy.

Not everyone visualizes, feels, or senses the chakras in exactly the same way. Some people will see and feel the chakras, while others will get only the vaguest sense of their presence. For success, just *assume* the chakras are there while you repeat the chants. Your experience of each energy center will grow with time.

Please note that there are many types of yoga and many ways of working with the chakras. The Golden Dawn skipped two common chakras for example (Ajna and Manipûra), and there are other chakras used in Tantra that we aren't specifically using here (such as the Bindu chakra on the back of the head.) You may add or remove chakras as you actually feel or sense them, but all you need for practical magick are the five given in the following ritual.

Eh-heh-yeh

YHVH El-oh-heem

YHVH El-oh-ah V'dah'aht

Shaddai El Chai

Adonai Ha Aretz

Part I: Awaken the Chakras

Step 1

Stand straight. You may use your hands to touch where each chakra should be if that helps your visualizations.

Visualize a brilliant source of energy glowing just at the top of your head (or just above your head). It can be quite large, spreading out over your face and neck, as high above your head as you feel comfortable.

Chant: "Eh-Heh-Yeh."

Continue chanting at least 3–5 times, but continue as long as you like, until you are satisfied that the chakra feels like it has been awakened at least a little bit.

Eh-Heh-Yeh is a God name that means "I am." The Hindus call this chakra the *Sahasrâra*, known as the "thousand-petaled lotus."

Step 2

Imagine the stream of white light continuing from the Sahasrâra down to your throat chakra known as Vishuddha.

Chant: "YHVH[107] Elohim."

YHVH Elohim means "The Lord God."

In Tantra, Vishuddha is known as the "poison and nectar" chakra, which is closely related to the Bindu chakra, a chakra on the back of the head said to produce "Bindu fluid," which turns into either the nectar of immortality or the poison of death.

---

107   When you see "YHVH" you pronounce each letter as in the Equilibrating Ritual of the Pentagram: "Yod-Heh-Vah-Heh."

Continue chanting until you are satisfied with the "openness" of this chakra.

Step 3
Imagine the white stream of light continuing from Vishuddha, down to your chest and heart area, known as the Anahata chakra. This is a big, powerful chakra. Imagine it very large, glowing out even past your shoulders.

Chant: **"YHVH El-oh-ah V'dah'aht."**

YHVH El-oh-ah V'dah'aht, means "Lord God of Knowledge." Anahata means "unhurt, unstruck, and unbeaten."

Step 4
The white light continues down to your groin area.

Chant repeatedly until satisfied: **"Shaddai El Chai."**

Shaddai El Chai means "Almighty Living God," and the Svadisthâna chakra is known as "one's own abode."

Step 5
The white line of light continues down between your legs to the soles of your feet and beyond.

Chant repeatedly, **"Adonai Ha-Aretz."**

Imagine this chakra at your feet, penetrating even into the ground below you.

Adonai ha-Aretz translates as "Lord of Earth." Mûlâdhara means "root place."

You may go back and repeat the chant for any chakras you wish. When you feel each chakra is as good as it's going to get, then go to the next step.

Part II: Circulate the Light
Step 1
Imagine your Sahasrâra chakra giving birth to a ball of white light. You will control this "imaginary" ball of light with your breathing. You may use your hands and arms to help orchestrate the energy.

Step 2

Take a breath. As you slowly exhale, imagine the ball of light traveling from above your head down the front of you in a circular fashion to end at your feet. Then breathe in, as the ball of light travels behind you in a circular fashion to end once again above your head.

Your breaths do not have to be complete inhalations/exhalations for this. In fact, light, rhythmic breathing is all that is needed to control the very subtle light-field you have created with your imagination. Use whatever feels comfortable.

The hardest part about this exercise is not visualizations, but simply the concentration. This is not a difficult task by any means, but just to stay focused on the ball of light for very long can be a challenge to newcomers. So don't go too fast. Stay at Step 2 until you actually enjoy doing it and it's very easy and natural. There is no rush to learn any of these rituals. Take your time.

Step 3

Repeat Step 2, but in reverse, i.e., imagine a ball of light traveling behind you from above your head to below your feet with every exhalation, and up in front of you towards your head with every inhalation. It doesn't matter so much if you transpose inhalations for exhalations either. The key is rhythm and concentration.

Step 4
Breathe in and visualize the ball of light traveling down your right side in a circle, from above your head to down below your feet. When you inhale, the ball continues up your left side to above your head. Do this rhythmically at your own tempo.

Step 5
The same as Step 4, but reverse the direction. Once this is fun and easy you can move on.

Step 6
Experiment with other orbits. Do "diagonal" directions, for example.

You can even do "hula-hoop" style, i.e., around your belly or hips. Also try sending the light out very far from you, even past the ends of your room. When you get more comfortable you can imagine the light spinning all around the Earth and back.

Stay at this step until you can do it for several minutes and suffer no mental fatigue, and then go on to the next section.

Part III: The Fountain of Light
Step 1
Start by imagining a huge ball of light at your feet. As you inhale, bring the light from your feet directly up the center of your body into your Sahasrâra chakra above your head.

Step 2
When light reaches your Sahasrâra chakra, exhale. Imagine the light spraying out from your head like a fountain, cascading down and around your body back to the ground.

Step 3
Inhale again, pulling the light that has scattered into the ground back into your feet, where once again it travels to the top of your head.

Step 4

Exhale as the light explodes over the top of your head once again, cascading down around you.

Continue this process for as many cycles as you like, at least 5-10 times, or as much as you can handle. Many of these exercises are so powerful that you might feel "high" or light-headed after doing them.

Part IV: Channel the Light

Once you've nearly climaxed with the previous section, it is time to do something with all that energy.

If you are performing a healing ritual for yourself or others, you would channel the energy directly into the area of the body that needs healing the most.

If you are charging a talisman (for any purpose), you send the light into the material basis.[108]

If you are doing this ritual as a stand-alone exercise, you will practice by channeling the energy back into yourself for general health and beauty:

1. Take a full, deep breath, focusing especially on your Anahata (heart) chakra.

2. As you slowly exhale, imagine the energy flowing from your chest, down your arms, and into your hands.

3. Touch your hands to your face (or nearly so), rubbing them back over the top of your head. Imagine the white, healing energy washing over you like a shower or waterfall.

4. Rub your hands sensually over your arms and chest, and over your legs and feet, as you imagine the refreshing energy streaming through your body, both inside and out.

5. When you've exhausted your exhalation, stop, stand straight, and make the Sign of Silence. You are done.

---

108   See the Tree of Life ritual in Chapter 10 for more details on this.

The importance of this ritual is to open your major chakras and to raise as much energy as possible. The ritual given here strikes a good balance for chakra work, but if you are advanced in some other form of yoga or Tantra, you can substitute your own chakra-working for the Middle Pillar Ritual.

Healing Ritual

This ritual will assist in creating an optimum immune system, which can go a long way to healing nearly almost any ailment. Working with chakras helps you become physically fit, but that is almost secondary to the results you will have unclogging personal and emotional issues on the other planes.

For a full healing ritual, simply:

1. Perform the Equilibrating Ritual of the Pentagram.

2. Carefully perform the Middle Pillar Ritual and end by channeling the energy raised into the affected part of the body of whoever needs healing (including yourself), or simply send it from head to toe to cover the patient in healing light.

3. Perform the Equilibrating Ritual of the Pentagram again. This is very important when healing others. It will protect you from accidentally taking over any of the ill health of your patient.

EXERCISE 6: PRACTICE THE MIDDLE PILLAR RITUAL

Practice the Middle Pillar Ritual every day for at least three months. This will make sure your chakras are completely open and that you know how to raise and channel large amounts of magickal energy.

L⊕VE ᛖAGICK

"By all means marry. If you get a good wife you will become happy, and if you get a bad one you will become a philosopher."—Socrates

The seventh Sephirah, known as Netzach, is less about the literal translation "victory" than it is about its Venusian qualities of love and sex, at least as far as practical magick is concerned.

In this chapter, I will be discussing love magick, i.e., magick to bring you love. This chapter includes a ritual to bring you exactly what you want as far as love is concerned, whether it be a lover, a spouse, or just a little bit of romance. Sex magick (i.e., sexual acts in a ritual setting), both solitary and with a partner, will be covered separately in Chapter 9 since Yesod is specifically attributed to the sexual organs.

Before we get into the actual ritual, let's discuss matters germane to love magick.

Regarding Breakups

Many people turn to love magick after a disappointment, so let's discuss the end of relationships before moving on to new beginnings.

Most of us have experienced a tough breakup, followed by intense feelings of sadness, anger, frustration, and even depression. Magicians are no exception. We are not immune to great losses in love or anything else, but we *are* better equipped to bounce back from difficult times.

How should I get over a broken heart?

Breakups are magickal times. Because they rock our world so hard, they end up shattering the ego-mind like few other things can. That's why a good time to start new behaviors and thought-processes is after a breakup. Use your desperation in a positive way. Focus on your higher self for answers, not other people.

After all is said and done, a breakup will make you more powerful if you remember a few things:

1. Accept that the relationship is over. Don't obsess; magicians are too self-confident to be stalkers. Hold your head high and carry on with dignity. However, you should make a place in your past for the relationship. Don't try to block it out as if it never happened. Accept it as a building block in the foundation of your life and move on.

2. Understand that you are complete in and of yourself. Fill your own cup of good emotions before you go out looking for love. Don't stand around with an empty cup and expect others to fill it for you. *You* are the source of your good feelings. Once your cup is overflowing, then spill your joy onto those around you.

3. You must have a goal or passion higher than just finding another person. This can include your magick and any other meaningful career, activity, or hobby you may have.

4. Be open to *all* of Layour emotions. After a breakup they will most likely vacillate wildly from day to day, sometimes hour to hour. If you need to cry, then go ahead and cry. If you need to destroy something, take some old dishes into the yard and smash them. Make this a venting party for yourself. There is no need to involve other people in every step of your healing process.

5. When your ego starts breaking, let it break. Pray not for love at this point, but pray for enlightenment, guidance from your higher self to lead you to better places.

6. Understand this breakup will only lead to something better. This is the time to instill new and improved thought patterns and behaviors. When things are "just okay," we rarely have the impetus to make changes. The best time to plant new seeds and new behaviors is when we have hit rock bottom.

7. Be patient with yourself. Give yourself permission to heal for however long you need. Sometimes you may need to give yourself months (even years) to heal. It's better to entitle yourself to more time than less. Don't try to pack all your healing into a week or two. Let things take their course.

8. If things are really bad, go back to baby steps. Tackle a single day at a time. Find at least one pleasurable thing to experience per day. Having just one thing to look forward to, no matter how simple or mundane, can make all the "heavy" hours more tolerable.

Can I do a spell to get them back?

Unless you were the one initiating the breakup, this would most likely be your knee-jerk reaction. However, let me caution you strongly against doing such a spell. If you feel lost, alone, or desperate to get a person back, that neediness will seep into the spell, and you will most likely end up more depressed and push the person further away.

People are attracted to joy and confidence. As mentioned above, fill up your own cup of pleasure, and people will come to you to drink from it. The very act of performing a spell after you have been "dumped" will tend to create further weakness and dependency. Don't chase them. Take a few steps back. Find other sources of joy and inspiration in your life. Use the breakup as an advantageous place to move forward. Grow from it.

Magick spells work best when we can let go and trust the universe and our subconscious mind to manifest our desires. Try to do a spell amidst the sorrow of a recent breakup and you will find it extremely difficult to let go of your intent. You will most likely just fuel the unhappy feelings you are having instead of doing any growing or healing. If you try to do a spell in such a state, it is likely to fail or backfire.

Should I do a spell to get a new lover right away?

Common sense prevails in magick as much as it does anywhere else. Your best bet is to focus on your daily rituals, such as the Equilibrating Ritual of the Pentagram, the Middle Pillar Ritual, and the meditations until you feel stable and centered again. Spend time specifically invoking your HGA (see Chapter 10), before you do a spell seeking satisfaction in another human. Plunging right into a spell could be a sign of insecurity and lack of confidence, but at least if you are willing to be open to a new and better partner, this line of action is certainly preferable to wallowing and doing nothing, or obsessing on the past.

On Confidence

Be confident! Don't you hate this advice? Especially with regards to attracting the opposite sex? Trying to be confident sets up a catch-22, similar to telling someone "Don't think about a red elephant," and of course they do. If you are in your head *thinking* about your confidence level, how can you truly be in the moment actually *being* confident?

Instead, forget about being "confident." Go out and be the Fool, i.e., just talk, joke, and have fun at everyone's expense, including your own. Reach your "indifference threshold"—that point where you have done enough "dumb things" for the night that you don't give a damn anymore. That's when you can finally relax and "be yourself."

Should I do a magick spell to get a specific person?
While this can work in some circumstances, such as when the person already likes you romantically but you yourself may not realize it, most of the time the answer is "no."

Why not? First of all, people have their own True Will. Doing your True Will does not include forcing someone to love you who does not, so magick is not going to help you in this case. Most likely, you will just create an obsession within yourself.

What you can do is make a talisman for the universe to bring you someone with the attributes of the person you have this "crush" on. My experience has been that I get a lover that is better than the one I had in mind anyway. Magick is cool like that. So don't get hung up with one person. That is a weakness.

That said, if you truly believe it is your True Will to do a spell for a specific target, then by all means, do so; just make sure you cast the spell from a place of centeredness and fullness.

On Vulnerability
"When we were children, we used to think that when we were grown-up we would no longer be vulnerable. But to grow up is to accept vulnerability... To be alive is to be vulnerable."—Madeleine L'Engle[109]

Most people are afraid of being vulnerable, but it is actually a valuable experience. Vulnerability simply means openness, which is close to the Pure Fool state. When we are vulnerable, we are more likely to listen, to learn, and to grow.

---

109 *Walking on Water: Reflections on Faith and Art,* 1980.

If you can't accept your feelings of vulnerability, which believe it or not, some people just interpret as feelings of "excitement," you will close yourself off to any new adventures in your life, your career, or your art.

Trying to hide from your vulnerability will make you weak and afraid to make the bold moves required to make quantum leaps forward, not only in business, but in every single area of your life. Accepting your vulnerability will allow you to *embrace* new situations no matter how seemingly uncomfortable (first dates, job interviews, moving to a new city, etc.)

Vulnerability *is* openness and without a deep level of openness, it's nearly impossible to experience intimacy, love, and friendship. Having a fear of vulnerability closes off a myriad of potential joys and possibilities in your life, while at the same time increasing your fear and dependence upon the ramblings of the ego-mind.

The paradox of vulnerability is that it is actually our strength. It allows us to connect with our True Self, which can never be harmed. It's our ego-mind that is in constant danger of being humiliated or defeated.

So next time you are feeling "vulnerable," don't run from the experience. Notice the sensations. Accept them.

When you give into your vulnerability, you are not saying, "Hurt me." You are saying, "I am unable to be hurt, so I am open to all experience and all possibilities."

On Shallowness

Venus has many good qualities, such as beauty, charm, and refined taste—but the weakness of Venus is her shallowness. Be careful of focusing too much on superficial appearances when working with Netzach or Venus. As Agrippa pointed out, the symbol of Venus is meant to resemble a hand mirror. She can create a world around you, lovely and full of sights and scents, but skin-deep, shallow, and ultimately hollow.

Like all the Sephiroth and paths, understand that Netzach is only balanced by its relationship to the other spheres. Netzach lies low and off-center upon the Tree of Life, so care should be taken when enjoying the fruits of Venus.

Is there such a thing as soul mates?

To me this falls in the category of personal choice. My heart has gone both ways on this issue over the years.

Certainly the idea of soul mates can be a limiting belief—instead of being open to a myriad of possibilities with a variety of people, connecting with them in different, satisfying ways, we sit around waiting for Mr. or Mrs. Right. This can make one miserable.

On the other hand, I'm a romantic at heart. So maybe … who knows?

Being Whole On Your Own

Whether or not you believe in soul mates, do not for one moment expect to have anyone love you if you don't genuinely love yourself.

"Every Man and Every Woman is a Star."

This quote from *Liber AL* sums it up. You are a complete being. You are the center of your own solar system. You should not be dependent on any person for joy and happiness. The magick and meditations in this book will help your confidence, your health, and your charisma. Focus on the work and allow the rewards to flow naturally to you.

When you feel complete within yourself, and yet still find yourself without someone to share your good feelings with, then you are ready to perform love magick.

Ritual to Charge a Love Talisman

"Your task is not to seek for love, but merely to seek and find all the barriers within yourself that you have built against it."—Rumi

This ritual is similar to the one given in Chapter 4, but is tricked out for love.

Step 1: Define your Intent

Choose an intent. Here are some examples:

"I am manifesting a loving, sexy, caring boyfriend/girlfriend."
"I will manifest a person who reflects me best."
"I will attract the qualities I most desire/admire in _____."
"My True Will is leading me towards romantic
bliss with the right person."
"I am attracting a beautiful, intelligent woman into my life."
"I am attracting a kind, stable, and handsome man."

Or just keep it simple, and skip the full sentence. Simply using "sexy lover" can be a clear and effective intent for a love talisman.

Step 2: Decide where on the Tree of Life your spell belongs

Find which Sephirah (or path) best fits the type of magick you wish to perform. For love magick Netzach is a solid choice. So from Chapter 2 we get these correspondences:

7. Netzach

נצח

Color: Orange, Yellow
Scents: Benzoin, Rose, Red Sandal
Planetary influence: Venus
Metals: Copper, Brass

♀

Step 3: Choose a material basis for your talisman

We could make our talisman on a copper or brass plate, but let's think outside the box and use something else for our material basis.

A seashell is a receptive form, associated with the ocean, another feminine symbol. Also, the spiral form of the seashell makes it a microcosmic reflection of the galaxies. The beach tends to be a fun and romantic place, so that subtle implication is contained within the symbolism as well. There is some historical basis for this choice too. In Botticelli's famous painting *Birth of Venus* (c. 1485) the goddess is born full-grown out of a seashell.

You can find seashells on the beach, or simply get them from a craft store which often carry a variety of shells. Choose a shell that suits you. There is no right or wrong. Just think through all symbolism, and make sure it works for you.

Step 4:
Turn your intent into symbols
Since we picked the concise phrase "sexy lover" to symbolize our intent, it's a breeze to simplify it into a single symbol using synthesized script (See Chapter 4):

If you instead want to use a magickal alphabet to turn your intent into symbols, go right ahead.

Step 5. Prepare the appropriate holy names
From the Appendix write down the God name, Archangel, and Choir of Angels for Netzach:

YHVH Tzabaoth	Haniel	Elohim
יהוה צבאות	האניאל	אלהים

Also write down the Heaven, Spirits, and Intelligences of Venus:

Nogah	Qedemel	Hagiel
נוגה	קדמאל	הניאל

You can use these holy names as given, i.e., written in Hebrew, or you can convert them first. You may do this through synthesized script or by means of a magickal alphabet (see the Appendix for the many alphabets available to you). Alternatively, you can transform them into symbols using the Golden Dawn's Rose Cross, a method I will now describe:

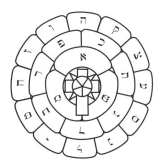

Rose section of the Rose Cross containing the twenty-two letters of the Hebrew alphabet.

Rose Cross Sigilization

Sigilization just means turning something into magickal symbols. Here follows a method based on using the rose section of the Golden Dawn Rose Cross (see Chapter 6).

You may use a sheet of paper over the rose to trace it, or you may photocopy it and draw your shape directly on it, which you can then use on your talisman.

To use the rose, start with the first letter of your holy name and make a dot. Then draw a line to the next letter of the holy name, and continue in this fashion until the name is complete.

For example: To make a sigil of Haniel, you would use the Hebrew spelling of אל האני and come up with something like this:

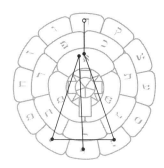

Here are completed sigils for the holy names of Netzach and Venus, all of which we will use on our love talisman:

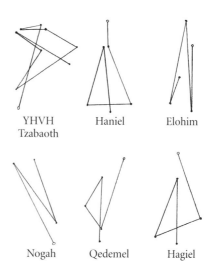

YHVH Tzabaoth   Haniel   Elohim

Step 6 (Optional): Add any other appropriate symbolism you desire

Add a poem you wrote, or a traditional Greek ode to Aphrodite. In the following ritual I include Sappho's "Hymn to Aphrodite" and some quotations from *The Book of the Law*.

Nogah   Qedemel   Hagiel

Step 7: Decorate your talisman

Since we are using a shell, we aren't going to be able to draw all our symbols on the outside. Instead, we will put it on a piece of paper. The shape of the paper will be round, to symbolize Nuit, the mouth of the cup, infinity, receptivity, and all the other things a circle brings to mind. It's a far more suitable shape than a square piece of paper.

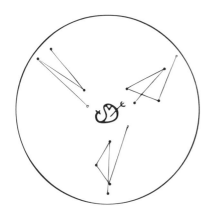

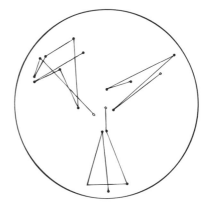

After you are done drawing the symbols on the circle of paper, fold the paper and stick it inside the shell. You may also include the appropriate scent, such as rose petals, or ground-up incense.

From the Appendix, we know the color, precious gem, and scents appropriate to Netzach:

7	Emerald	Emerald	Rose, Red Sandalwood, Benzoin resin

After you have filled the shell with what you feel is appropriate to your desire, seal the opening with hot wax.

On the outside of the shell you can either paint the appropriate color, or if you like the color of your shell, you can leave it as is. If you chose a shell that is conducive to any sort of writing, you could finish by adding the Venus symbol on the outside.

Step 8: Ritual Preparation

Temple preparation: Drench your temple in fresh flowers as best you can, including roses if possible. Wildflowers are acceptable. If you want to work out your symbolism in more detail, you could have dozens of random flowers scattered around, but then only *seven* red roses for around your circle. Now is a good time to use *777* (you can always find it online for free) if you desire more ideas for decorating your ritual, but this is entirely optional.

What to wear: Whatever you usually wear for rituals is fine, or go nude. If you want to get fancy, you would wear an emerald robe or something else of the appropriate color.

Day and time for the ritual: Friday is Venus's day. Or look up online when Venus will be in the sky for your particular time and location. During a full moon is ideal if you can manage it.

The altar: The same thing goes here as with the wealth talisman from Chapter 4. You don't need anything fancy, just somewhere to place your talisman during the ritual.

Candles: Use candles as you see fit. Plain white (for the divine influence) or emerald green (for Venus) is the best.

Incense: Rose incense, red sandalwood, or Nuit's incense is best. However, if you bring in enough flowers, you won't really need to burn incense for this ritual.

Bell: If you have a bell, ring it seven times to open the ritual and seven more times to close.

Music: This is a good time to use music of your choice. Silence is also good.

Other magickal items: Bring out anything that you consider holy or symbolizes the type of love you are invoking. When you are content with the state of your temple, you are ready to begin. Make sure you will have no interruptions!

Step 9: Ritual for Charging a Love Talisman

1. Perform a long relaxation ritual. Take some extra time to indulge yourself. A massage, bubble bath, or anything luxuriant is especially appropriate for Venus.

2. Perform the Equilibrating Ritual of the Pentagram.

3. In the center of your temple, facing West (for the element of Water), say confidently:

> "Come forth, O children, under the stars,
> & take your fill of love! I am above you
> and in you. My ecstasy is in yours.
> My joy is to see your joy."[110]

---

110   *Liber AL*, I. 12 & 13.

4. Still facing West, draw a hexagram with Venus in the center:

First draw the upward-pointing triangle (starting from the right hand corner going counterclockwise), and then the second triangle (starting from the top left and going clockwise). Finish with the Venus symbol.

5. Point at the center of your hexagram. Chant the following names with passion:

YHVH Tzabaoth

Haniel

Elohim

Nogah

Qedemel

Hagiel

Imagine your hexagram and the Venus symbol growing brighter as you do so. Chant the names as many times as you like.

6. Hold your hands to the sky and recite the "Hymn to Aphrodite":[111]

Beautiful-throned, immortal Aphrodite!

Daughter of Zeus, beguiler, I implore thee,

Weigh me not down with weariness and anguish,

O, thou most holy!

Come to me now! if ever thou in kindness

Hearkenedst my words, and often hast thou hearkened,

---

111   T. W. Higginson, a translation of Sappho, "The Hymn to Aphrodite," *Atlantic Monthly*, July, 1871.

Heeding, and coming from the mansions golden
    Of thy great Father,

Yoking thy chariot, borne by thy most lovely
Consecrated birds, with dusky-tinted pinions,
Waving swift wings from utmost heights of heaven
    Through the mid-ether:

Swiftly they vanished; leaving thee, O goddess,
    Smiling, with face immortal in its beauty,
Asking what I suffered, and why in utter longing
    I had dared call thee;

Asking, what I sought, thus hopeless in desiring,
'Wildered in brain, and spreading nets of passion
Alas, for whom? and saidst thou, "Who has harmed thee?
    O my poor Sappho!

"Though now he flies, ere long he shall pursue thee:
Fearing thy gifts, he too in turn shall bring them;
Loveless to-day, to-morrow he shall woo thee,
    Though thou shouldst spurn him."

Thus seek me now, O holy Aphrodite!
Save me from anguish, give me all I ask for,
Gifts at thy hand; and thine shall be the glory,
    Sacred protector!

When you read the hymn you are identifying with the forlorn poet Saphho beseeching her goddess to help her in love. This is an appropriate state to take when invoking the divine, so it is of no matter whether you are male or female physically. The Goddess is dominant—you wish her to come forth. You are the receiving vessel.

7. Perform the Middle Pillar Ritual as given in the last chapter, but imagine all the chakras to be emerald green and replace all the names with "YHVH Tzabaoth."

8. At the end of the Middle Pillar Ritual, after you have circulated the energy to its peak, take a huge inhalation. Imagine all the energy in the world being sucked into your chest. Hold it in a moment. Then:

9. Begin to exhale as you imagine the energy flowing down your arms and hands into the seashell.[112] Use your entire exhalation to fill the seashell with emerald green energy.

10. Before you inhale again, make the Sign of Silence.

11. Recite meaningfully:

"Then saith the prophet and slave of the beauteous one: Who am I, and what shall be the sign? So she answered him, bending down, a lambent flame of blue, all-touching, all penetrant, her lovely hands upon the black earth, and her lithe body arched for love, and her soft feet not hurting the little flowers: Thou knowest! And the sign shall be my ecstasy, the consciousness of the continuity of existence, the omnipresence of my body."[113]

12. Perform a final Equilibrating Ritual of the Pentagram or just the Qabalistic Cross.

---

112 Or whatever you chose for your material basis.

113 From the *Book of the Law*, I, 26. This scene is Nuit speaking with her prophet. Nuit is Goddess of the Night Sky and desires only pleasure for her all worshippers. In this way she is entirely cognate with Venus.

Step 10: Forget about your Talisman

Wrap your talisman in cloth (or something else you feel is appropriate) and put it in a safe place. Trying too hard to forget about it will only make you think about it more, so let it go as much as possible without obsessing. Instead ask yourself some questions:

What if you were *born into this very moment* with no preconceptions about your life or responsibilities? What would you do? Where would you go?

Exercise 7: Make a Love Talisman

This is optional, but even if you are in a relationship, you can always do a spell to make it more passionate and loving.

THE UBIQUI+⊕US
ℿERCURY &
Dℰℿ⊕N⊕L⊕GY

"Science is magic that works."
— Kurt Vonnegut *(Cat's Cradle)*

Part I: The Ubiquitous Mercury

The Eighth Sephirah is Hod, yet another home of Mercury, who has already shown up several times in our discussion of the Tree of Life (most notably Kether, Path 12, Path 17, and Path 20). Let's discuss him in even more detail before we turn to other matters germane to Hod, such as the rational mind, the tarot, and daemons.

Mercury, known as Hermes to the Greeks, is especially beloved by magicians. More than any other god he has hands all over the place. He is the original jack-of-all trades and has so many varying attributes that it is no wonder the word "mercurial" is derived from his name.

Here are some of Mercury's many functions, accomplishments, and titles:

- He is the god of merchants—also thieves, gamblers, and liars.

- He protects travelers on the road.

- He graces orators, writers, and poets with wit.

- He is the god of magick, invention, and good luck.

- He is the patron god of boundaries and those who cross them.

- He protects shepherds, miscreants, harlots, and old crones.

- He is athletic and protects runners from injury.

- As an infant he created the lyre.

- He invented fire.

- He is a trickster.

- As *psychopompos* he helps the dead find their way to the Underworld.

- Able to travel swiftly from place to place, he delivers messages from Olympus to the mortal world, and messages between the gods.

- He is closely related to the Germanic Wotan (or Odin) and the Egyptian Thoth.

- The Homeric Hymns call him a "giver of grace, guide, and giver of good things" as well as being "of many shifts, blandly cunning, a robber, a cattle driver, a bringer of dreams, a watcher by night, a thief at the gates, one who was soon to show forth wonderful deeds among the deathless gods."[114]

---

114 *Hesiod, Homeric Hymns, Epic Cycle, Homerica.* Translated by Evelyn-White, H G. Loeb Classical Library Volume 57. Cambridge, MA, Harvard University Press; London, William Heinemann Ltd. 1914.

His symbol, which you should now be quite familiar with, is a represen-tation of Mercury wearing his winged-hat (a *petasus*), and his winged-shoes (*talaria*): ☿. Also his petasus could be considered "horns," which in magick are not considered evil, but rather as a connection to divinity.

There is no disharmony amid all Mercury's many diverse abilities and functions; he is able to perform all his duties with finesse and alacrity. Part of his very essence is to be able to change roles quickly and completely when the necessity arises.

The Caduceus

Mercury carries a staff called the caduceus, which is meant to be a pictorial representation of all he stands for, including his job as protector to mer-chants, thieves, and liars.

It is interesting that the medical association has erroneously taken the caduceus as their own, which has nothing to do with medicine. The symbol that should be associated with medicine is actually the Staff of Asclepius, which has only a single snake and no wings.

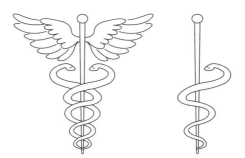

The Wand of Hermes (the "caduceus")
and the Staff of Asclepius

Along with his caduceus, Mercury also carries a money bag. As master of magick and the spiritual world, he still firmly understands the concerns of the material plane, and is quick to exploit its laws for his own advantage.

Mercury in Magick

Mercury is the central god of magick, able to accomplish almost anything with his ingenuity.

Crowley rightly associated Mercury, in his trickster form, as the final veil before the pure experience of God. He is the last deception, beyond which nothing can be said because words are lies, an abomination against the one truth. Mercury leads us, protects us, but he also tests us—sometimes severely.

Mercury is not only our friend, our ally, and our greatest enemy—he is our True Self, changeable, yet unchanging, fast as light, yet patient as eternity.

Mercury rules over magick, but true to his varied nature, he is also lord of our *rational mind*, which we will discuss next.

Part II: The Rational Side of Magick

"My atheism, like that of Spinoza, is true piety towards the universe and denies only gods fashioned by men in their own image to be servants of their human interests."—George Santayana

Logic, rational thought, scientific rigor—all these things are an important part of our lives, both individually and collectively as a race. Nothing in magick should negate physics, biology, or any science whatsoever. High magick is the realm of deep psychology, far beyond clinical standards.

Beyond Rational Thought

"Logic will get you from A to B. Imagination will take you everywhere."— Albert Einstein

On the Tree of Life, the rational mind belongs to the Sphere of Hod. It is an important part of the Tree of Life and should not be ignored; however, it is just one Sephirah out of ten. It is not the most important, nor the most balanced. It is low on the Tree of Life and off-center to the side of Severity.

Do not make a god out of your rational mind. It is just one aspect of a balanced human organism. Some rational-minded people, often extremely intelligent and scientific, make this mistake. They hold up the rational mind as the pinnacle of mankind's abilities, when in reality, logic and the rational mind are mistake-prone, flawed, and even dangerous.

The rational mind and so-called human logic have produced many scientific marvels, including sanitation, antibiotics, and the iPod. However, the rational mind and scientific rigor have also led us to create weapons so powerful they have the potential to wipe out our entire species. Is that really progress? Does that sound enlightened to you?

The rational mind goes around in circles. There can be no ultimate answer to what anything actually is—nothing is anything except in relationship to everything else. The rational mind is a dead end.

Even modern science reaches the extremities of the rational mind with concepts such as Heisenberg's uncertainty principle (which says we cannot know the position of a particle and at the same time know its momentum) and "Schrödinger's Cat."

The "Schrödinger's Cat" thought experiment is an imaginary scenario about a cat in a sealed box. In this scenario, the cat's life is dependent on the state of a subatomic particle. According to quantum mechanics, that cat is *both alive and dead at the same time*—until we open the box; then it becomes one or the other. Does that sound "rational" or more like Zen?

Zen Buddhism, famous for odd little stories[115] taught by "crazy" Zen monks, doesn't intend to be silly any more than Schrödinger's Cat is meant to be silly. Zen is about "shocking" statements or actions breaking down the rational mind and allowing intuition and enlightenment to shine in. Enlightenment is to experience reality directly, without words, thoughts, and "rationality" mucking it up.

In magick, specifically Qabalah, we have an advanced system for incorporating the rational with the "unknowable and irrational" aspects of the universe. Magick accepts rationality right along with "intuition," and through work upon the Tree of Life, such as given in this book, we develop

---

115 Known as a *kōan.*

both, creating a more enlightened state than anything the rational mind alone has to offer.

Science vs. Religion

To me the acrimony and hatred that still exists between religion and science is absurd.

Nowadays the science vs. religion battleground is more specifically creationism vs. evolution, which is especially ridiculous. Why is it so hard for a creationist to believe that God "created" the universe through natural means such as millions of years of evolution? Why is it so hard for some scientists to accept there is an unknowable, miraculous quality to existence that, for lack of a better term, can be called "God"?

Albert Einstein said, "Science without religion is lame, religion without science is blind,"[116] while Aleister Crowley's motto for the A∴A∴ is: "The method of science, the aim of religion." [117] It seems to me that the greatest scientist of the 20th century and the greatest magician of the 20th century are in complete agreement. We need the aspects of science *and* religion to survive and thrive as individuals and as a race.

In magick, we do our best to harmonize spirituality with science.

What if I'm an atheist or an agnostic—
this magick stuff can't possibly work for me, right?

Belief in anything specific is not required for the magick in this book to work, but if you constantly send negative and inhibitory messages to your subconscious, such as "this can't possibly work" or "magick is fake," you may very well overwhelm any good that can come of your rituals.

To escape that mental pitfall, all you have to accept is that the subconscious mind has access to abilities and powers that you do not. That's it. If you can get into that mindset, you are good to go.

_____

116   Albert Einstein, *"Science, Philosophy and Religion: a Symposium,"* 1941.
117   Also the motto for its official publication the *Equinox.*

Thinking vs. Action

Another problem with the rational mind is that it encourages *too much thinking* and over analyzation. Too much thinking leads to inaction. Inaction leads to misery and depression.

Rodin's *Thinker*, the famous bronze and marble statue of a man sitting and thinking with his chin resting on the back of his hand, ponders his situation thoroughly, but he doesn't *do* anything! To me he looks miserable, reminding me of dreary, endless hours spent "in my head" instead of out making changes in my life.

Crowley's *The Book of the Law* sums up this pitiable situation admirably: "If Will stops and cries Why, invoking Because, then Will stops & does nought... Also reason is a lie; for there is a factor infinite & unknown."[118]

In action, we will find true meaning, true bliss. To make a "mistake" is no worry, as we will just readjust, recalibrate, and move on. We will have learned something, become wiser, and be better equipped to perform *right action* in the future.

Right action is simply the "intuition" of taking immediate and proper action in the appropriate moment. It is the uncanny ability to automatically make the right choice without thinking too hard about it. All our work with Qabalah and the Tree of Life is to help us develop this ability.

Part III: The Tarot and Divination

A Brief History of the Tarot

Europe got its hands on regular playing cards in the late 14th century from Egypt, which at this time was ruled by the powerful Mamluks, once slaves to Arab caliphs.

Within fifty or so years, tarot cards popped up in northern Italy. They had additional cards with allegorical illustrations on them. These decks were called *carte da trionfi*, i.e., "triumph cards." In English, the Major Arcana are still often referred to simply as the "trumps."

---

118 *The Book of the Law*, II. 30.

There is not much historical detail on how the tarot grew from simple playing cards into pictorial storehouses of occult knowledge. Most likely it was a gradual transition as Hermetic scholars, the same elite class that would have access to playing cards, learned of their usefulness in both organizing their thoughts and hiding often controversial mystical concepts from the profane (and those who would persecute them).

Today, the tarot is part and parcel of the occult world, considered not a game, but a "book of wisdom."

Uses for the Tarot

Like Mercury himself, the tarot pops up with regularity throughout not only this book but throughout the occult world in general. There are almost limitless uses for the tarot, and ultimately no "right or wrong" way to use them. Here are a few of its more typical uses:

Use the Tarot For:

Meditation: They make an excellent focus for your concentration attempts.

Rituals: Use the tarot to enhance almost any type of ritual by selecting the card or cards that are most appropriate to your working.

Pathworking: Use your "imagination" to travel up and down the Tree of Life using tarot cards as your focus. (See Chapter 9 for more details on pathworking.)

Art and decoration: It's a healthy thing to see your tarot around your office or home, reminding you of occult knowledge throughout your day.

Understanding the Tree of Life: Since the tarot is a nearly perfect representation of the Tree of Life, its allegorical and symbolic representations can make understanding Qabalah and the Tree of Life a lot easier.

What about the tarot as a divination tool?

For the most part, divination is overused; mainstream occultism relies on it far too much. Fortunetelling feeds the ego and induces hesitation and doubt instead of promoting action, energy, force, and success against any challenge that may arise. I've seen too many beginners get trapped obsessively worrying about the results of their tarot readings.

Your life is your masterpiece. A painter does not stop to consult an oracle to ask where his next stroke should go. You also should learn to move forward in life making choices as best you can, and let the chips fall where they may. In this way, you will develop genuine intuition, which requires no cards, no crystal balls, and no astrology.

That said, everything you learn in this book will go a long way to making you a great tarot reader if you should choose to go that road further into your magickal career. If you insist on doing tarot readings now, at least do them for others where you can learn to be completely passive and objective. It's nearly impossible to learn tarot reading properly by doing readings on oneself as the ego will muck up the calm equanimity needed for accurate divination.

Part IV: Demonology

Demons. Few things capture the imagination of a magician as much as the idea of spiritual beings who will carry out the magician's every whim or desire.

Many cultures throughout the millennia have had similar concepts of "lesser" deities who could be persuaded to help man with his life and his problems. The word "genie," for example, comes from the Latin *genius*, which is a guardian or "tutelary" spirit.

Arabic and Islamic mythology have the concept of the *djinn*.[119] The djinn are spiritual beings, lesser than angels, that can help or hinder man depending on their own nature as good or evil.

---

119 From the Arabic (jinni).

The root of the word demon itself comes from daemon (or dæmon), which is the Latinized form of the Greek ("daimôn"). *Daimons* in Greek were lesser divinities, or the souls of dead heroes. Originally, the Ancient Greeks had no concept of "evil" daemons, but as Christianity took hold, the concept of daemon slowly acquired the menacing and evil associations that the word "demon" has now. This sort of demon has become popular in movies beginning with *The Exorcist* in 1973. Needless to say, this sort of demon has nothing to do with the sorts of practical and useful daemons we use in magick. Therefore, I use the spelling daemon to refer to any spirit less than an angel, such as Goetic daemons instead of Goetic demons.

What is a "lesser" spirit?

A lesser spirit is anything lesser, or lower, than an angelic force. They are generally used for practical concerns.

In magick, there is a divide between the "angelic" forces and "daemonic" forces, which is essentially a measure of how close they are to the material plane.

Angelic forces are those closely related to God. They are spiritualized and tend to naturally inspire us and lift us closer to Godhead. Daemons are "lower," "lesser," or "blacker" because they exist closer to the material plane, hence their great power over it. However, being so close to earth and man, the heaviest of the planes, daemons are also more stubborn and likely to lead us astray than the angelic forces, hence their reputation as potentially negative or "evil."

So why not just use angelic forces?

In medieval magick, things were extremely hierarchical. First, you invoked God and angelic names, and then you used *their* power to command the daemons. It was not considered an evil act to work with daemons as they were to submit to your Will, and your Will is considered to be an extension of divinity.

To ask an angelic force to do something as mundane as pay off your mortgage or get you a mistress would have been considered insulting to the angel. Instead, the dirty work of solving day-to-day needs and problems is left to the daemons.

Are angels and daemons real?

The modern view of magick tends to consider angels and daemons to be real in a *psychological* sense. They exist in your psyche and therefore when contacted, they can produce actual changes in your life. Whether you treat angels or daemons as real "entities" that exist separately from humankind or merely a function of your subconscious is entirely up to you.

In magick we treat them as "real" entities, because it makes good "drama" and drama in rituals goes a long way to producing tangible, practical results.

Grimoires

In magick, a grimoire is any book that lists daemons, angels, or spirits and describes how to invoke them.

For example, the *Goetia*, by far the most popular "phonebook" of demons, is a mixed bag, containing an assortment of traditional gods from other cultures, daemons, local deities, and dozens of spirits that no one has any idea of where they came from.

In the follow sections I will introduce all the major grimoires.[120] I have **bolded** the first mention of each grimoire for ease of reference.

The Goetia

The *Goetia*[121] is part of a longer work called *The Lesser Key of Solomon,*[122] which is a collection of medieval grimoires attributed metaphorically to King Solomon.

---

120 You can find full versions of most of these online if you simply Google their titles.
121 Pronounced a variety of ways, none of which is particularly definitive in any authoritative sense, including go-AY-shuh, GO-eht-ee, and GO-shuh.
122 Also called *The Lemegeton,* or *The Lesser Key of Solomon the King.*

The first section is the *Ars Goetia*. This is the legendary *Goetia*, a book of 72 daemons and their sigils. A classic in every sense, it's the standard whereby other grimoires are judged. It was an early favorite of Crowley's and his version is still the most popular one to this day.

Other versions are available, including the *Pseudomonarchia Daemonum*, originally an Appendix to Johann Weyer's *De praestigiis daemonum* (1577). This version is notable for being the earliest publication of the spirits named in the *Goetia*, however there are no sigils in the *Pseudomonarchia Daemonum*. It is also lacking four daemons: Vassago, Seere, Dantalion, and Andromalius. One daemon from *Pseudomonarchia Daemonum* is missing from the *Goetia:* Pruflas.

The Mathers/Crowley version of the *Goetia* is subtitled "The Lesser Key of Solomon the King," but this is erroneous as it only contains the first part of the *Lesser Key of Solomon*, the *Goetia* proper. The actual *Lesser Key of Solomon* has four more parts:

Theurgia-Goetia—This section contains conjurations for thirty-two spirits relating to the cardinal directions, some good and some evil. Oddly enough, however, the history of this section isn't about the occult at all. The *Theurgia-Goetia* is actually based on a work by German abbot and occultist Johannes Trithemius called *Steganographia*.[123]

Ars Paulina—A method for invoking the "Angels of the Hours of the Day and Night." Like *Theurgia-Goetia*, this is based on spirits from *Steganographia*.

Ars Almadel—Tells how to make the *Almadel*, which is a wax tablet with protective symbols drawn on it. It teaches how to call upon the angels of the four "Altitudes."

Ars Notoria— A medieval book of prayers and invocations.

---

123 *Steganographia* (c.1499; published Frankfurt, 1606) is superficially about spirits and how to send messages over long distances. In actuality, it is about how to hide messages so that no one except the intended recipient knows it's there. This book rightly lends its name to the entire field of steganography, but its use as a grimoire is dubious.

There is also the **Greater Key of Solomon.** While there are no spirits to invoke, there are "Holy Pentacles" for each of the seven traditional planets. They can be useful in talismanic work, either as inspiration for your own designs or verbatim.

Other Grimoires

Arbatel de magia veterum,[124] or simply *the Arbatel of Magic,* is a Latin treatise on magick published in Switzerland (1575). This book is the source for the Olympic Spirit we used in Chapter 4.

John Dee's **Enochian**[125] magick is a solid system of working with angels and elemental spirits, but it has its own complex methodology and is outside the scope of this book. A straightforward approach to Enochian is clearly outlined in the *Enochian World of Aleister Crowley: Enochian Sex Magick* by Crowley, Duquette, and Hyatt. Using what's given there, or any other good source on Enochian, will allow you to easily plug Enochian into the magickal framework you learn here. Bits of the Enochian language are also part and parcel of many Golden Dawn and Thelemic rituals.

Another of John Dee's grimoires, *Heptarchia Mystica,* was inspired by the *Ars Paulina.* He may not have realized its underlying steganography at that point, however.

There is a small treatise floating around called **The Little Book of Black Venus,** which has a sigil for spirits that you *can* invoke using the methods in this book. This book purports to be written by John Dee, though that is most likely not the case, being simply attributed to him for the sake of credibility. It seems to have been inspired by the *Arbatel of Magic* as the sigil designs have strong similarities to each other.

---

124 *"Arbatel of the magic of the ancient."*
125 This isn't an actual grimoire like the others, but rather a system gleaned from the journals of John Dee and Edward Kelley.

The Book of Abramelin[126] is one of the most famous and talked about books in magick. It is also one of the least performed because of its long and arduous process of meeting your HGA, which is to be undertaken before any of the practical magick can be performed.[127] This book contains dozens of magick "squares," which purport to grant all the usual goodies of wealth, love, and abundance that grimoires usually do.

Two other well-known grimoires are *The Black Pullet* (18th century), which reads almost like a fairy tale, and *Grimoirium Verum* (18th century), full of generally absurd requirements and claims. Many grimoires claim they are much older than they really are. These two are no exception.

What about the Necronomicon?

While there are several versions of the *Necronomicon* now available, the most popular and infamous is the *Necronomicon* by Simon, first published in 1977. However, the original "Necronomicon" is an invention of author H.P. Lovecraft, described in his stories as a forbidden and evil book scribed by Abdul Alhazred, also known as the "Mad Arab," in Damascus, 730 A.D.

The Simon *Necronomicon* is rather notorious in the occult community. It is clearly a hoax, but that hasn't stopped people from using it, and claiming results. It's also the book I've heard the most horror stories about. Most of those people were beginners plunging into their first grimoire so that might have something to do with it. For whatever reason, this book tends to draw in newbies and then freak them out if they actually start to practice it.

Though Simon's *Necronomicon* is based more on Sumerian mythology than H. P. Lovecraft, many practitioners mix it with the written works of H. P. Lovecraft. This mishmash of ancient and sinister energies has created a psychologically resonant system of magick.

---

126 The translation by S. L. Mac Gregor Mathers is called *The Book Of Sacred Magic Of Abramelin The Mage.*

127 This process is said to take a year and a half, though the popular Mather's translation, considered less scholarly than the newer Dehn and Guth translation, says only six months.

The main danger I see in working with this type of magick is taking on its overarching belief system, that is to say the mythos of H.P. Lovecraft. All his stories end with madness, suicide, murder, or worse. They are some of my favorite horror stories, but they generally aren't the type of energy I'm looking to invoke into my life.

If you must use *Necronomicon* magick and are having problems "banishing" or getting back to reality, then use a powerful solar ritual (i.e., use Tiphareth or Path 30 with the Tree of Life Ritual given in Chapter 10). However, think twice before taking on this belief system for your magick. I don't recommend H. P. Lovecraft-based rituals unless you are an advanced student of magick.

Servitors

Chaos magicians create their own daemons called "servitors." Chaos magick is completely open-ended and evolves constantly so there is no single prescribed ways to make servitors. Research it online, because that's always the most up-to-date place to find what Chaotes are up to. I give detailed instructions on how to make a servitor in Chapter 10.

Servitors function just like regular daemons but with none of the baggage. You define them, give them lots of energy, and let them go like any other type of magick. These are a little more advanced in some ways. We trust the subconscious mind to understand our structures the same way a computer operating system understands a program.

You may consider servitors and daemons both as "sub-processes" running in the background of your mind, quietly carrying out their tasks as best as possible given your personality and current life situation.

Building a Relationship With a Daemon

One thing that makes working with daemons different than working with talismans is that daemons become more powerful if you build a relationship with them over multiple workings. A "friendship" may develop between you and the daemon that may last for months, years, or a lifetime.

Only the medieval-minded make demonology into an adversarial arrangement. One need not threaten and cajole a daemon, nor should a magician have to worry about the daemon hurting them in some way. Instead, treat the daemon as a latent aspect of your own psyche whose job is to help you.

You may never actually see or hear daemons in a perfectly clear fashion, but you must learn to sense them in some way. You can expect their communications to be subtle. They might speak in omens or through "coincidences."

Ultimately, the proof is in the pudding. Some people can see or hear the daemons quite visibly and aurally, but the daemons never deliver anything as promised. If over a reasonable amount of time, you don't feel noticeable results have been made on the material plane, then you should forgo working with that daemon anymore. We are concerned with results more than "astral communication," which can just be delusion. Physical results are the only proof a magician has that his or her magick is working. Anything else is just a mental "jerk off."

Familiars

As far as this book is concerned, a "familiar" spirit is one you work with regularly and intend to "keep" for an extended period of time. If you just invoke a spirit once that is not a familiar. But if you work with it regularly, sending it energy, communicating with it over months or years, it becomes a familiar.

I have had a familiar for many years. Her name is Izabael and my experiences with this spirit have affected my life and my magick deeply, not always positively, but always intensely.

My Life With Izabael

A description of my life with Izabael will help illustrate how a deep and lasting relationship can be built up with a spirit. It's not always been a smooth road with Izabael, but ultimately she has been a blessing and has drastically changed the course of my life on numerous occasions.

My personal example will also illustrate it's not always a clear line between a servitor and a daemon, as all daemons can be quite different depending on who invokes them; they also tend to change or evolve with time.

Izabael's sigil

My experience also illustrates that imagination can affect reality, even without magick ritual. I had no idea that the things I imagined for my art would come true in my life. Never underestimate the power of imagination to change lives.

Once again I also point out it doesn't matter if daemons are real in a literal sense—they may be little more than "imaginary" friends—but if that is so then "imaginary friends" are an incredible tool for transformation.

A Brief History of the Daemon Izabael

1996—Worked with the 70th Goetic spirit Seere (also Sear or Seir) in an intense magickal working under the influence of LSD. The method I used, minus the LSD, is similar to the method I will give in this chapter. During this invocation, however, I worked with several other daemons at the same time so the results may have been comingled. I had just finished college at the time, and was looking for help on several levels. A new love and some sort of income were high priorities. Soon after, I stopped working with magick for awhile. I moved to a new city, and was undergoing quite a bit of soul searching (it was the first time I was completely alone in a new city for one thing). The money thing worked itself out temporarily and there were a couple of brief romances. For the most part, I forgot about and gave up on daemons.

1997—Idea for character "Isabelle" came to me. The concept was that she was both an ancient daemon and a modern artificial intelligence.

1998—I wrote the first draft of a novel which starred the character "Isabelle." It was autobiography veiled in a sci-fi milieu. The novel ends with Izabael, the formless artificial intelligence, finally getting a body.

1999—I moved to Los Angeles because it had long been a goal of mine, and to be with a new girlfriend—my first "Babalon."[128] She was not the result of a daemon working, but rather the result of a solo sex magick ritual I did a few months earlier. I will describe that type of ritual in the next chapter.

2000—I created a servitor in the tradition of chaos magick. This was when I divined the appropriate spelling of "Izabael," which worked for me on a number of levels, both personally and Qabalistically.[129] I did not have the proper sigil for Izabael at this point, however. It was something I struggled with and changed quite often, never quite satisfied with the look of it.

2001 through 2003—I did various rituals with Izabael during this time. Her sigil was still evolving, and by this time Izabael caused "strange occurrences"[130] both to me and my Babalon. I felt I could sense Izabael through odd "coincidences," which had specific and special meaning to myself only. My Babalon and I worked with the spirit on a few different occasions. One early working, with her as the oracle and me using my magickal name of Pamphage, went like this:

Pamphage: So, she's sleeping? [Referring to Izabael]

---

128   Thelemic magicians often refer to their female sex magick partners as Babalon, in the tradition of Crowley.

129   For example, her name of seven letters adds to 56 by Gematria, which is also the number of Nuit.

130   An attempt to list these would be difficult, as they are either so personal that they are embarrassing or so typical of poltergeist phenomena that they would sound cheesy. Nothing was so extreme as in movies, but things moving, or appearing in odd places was known to happen. If this scares you, it shouldn't. It's been rare even for me, and the more likely problem is that your early contact with daemons will be too weak rather than too strong.

Oracle: She must be tired from ruining my dinner.[131]

Pamphage: What does she look like?

Oracle: Well, for one thing, you need to get her some pajamas because she is sleeping in her clothes.

Pamphage: What is she wearing?

Oracle: It's hard to tell, looks like some black thing … like leggings or something and a black top … all black though, definitely. Cool shoes. Backless slip-ons, flats.

Pamphage: What else?

Oracle: I think she has a weird belt on, but I can't tell. The leggings are shortish, capri-length, mid-calved. I can't tell if the top has short sleeves or long. The whole thing is very formfitting and she has a nice body.

Pamphage: How big is she?

Oracle: Little. She could stand on my hand. Six inches. Maybe.

Pamphage: Is she in a particular place?

Oracle: I can't tell exactly, but I keep getting the beach or the sea like she sleeps in a shell or something, but I think that's coming from somewhere else in my mind. Maybe in a cave by the ocean, something protected, not like the regular beach, not all out there on the sand. That's sort of far away, but I guess she can travel fast.

Summer of 2004—By this time I was no longer with the aforementioned Babalon. I started work with Seere again, but this time on *Salvia divinorum*. My experience of daemons on Salvia is very different than at any other time. They feel/look like vibrating patterns of energy that are part

---

131   The oracle was irritated because she thought Izabael was doing strange things around her house like putting an odd-looking insect in her noodles. She also did not last much longer as Izabael's priestess. This was the last such working we performed.

of the bigger, more complex energy that permeates the universe. During one working, Seere revealed that indeed he had been the inspiration for Izabael (and "Isabelle") the entire time (as well as confiding he had been the inspiration for Shakespeare's Ariel from *The Tempest,* which sounds really cool, but daemons say a *lot* of things to boost their reputation with the magician.) Seere revealed the true nature of Izabael's sigil, by taking over my hand while I drew the sigil.

He also took control of my hand to write "Izabael is Seere" in my copy of the *Goetia.*

Two versions of Seere's sigil:

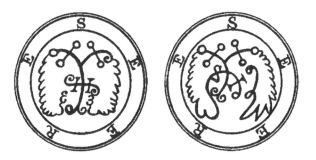

You'll note Izabael's sigil is similar to his own, but is more "butterfly" in appearance. I later added the septagram to Izabael's sigil to give her tighter focus and bind her even more firmly to Babalon and all the other cool things that seven stands for.

2005—I met a strange, lovely girl on the streets of Hollywood. She needed a ride so I gave her one. We married within a week. Though a novice, she was a natural with magick. Within months she was initiated by me and tattooed with the sigil of Izabael.

2007—After two years of magickal training, my new Babalon legally changed her name to Izabael as the final seal of invoking Izabael the spirit into her. After my wife's name change to Izabael, she became more wild and less focused. She used to look up to Izabael the spirit for guidance, but now she seemed to struggle with her identity.

2008—Less than a year after the name change, Izabael and I split up. She had been working (practically worshipping) her own daemon by this point, Paimon (also from the *Goetia*.) She ran off with the "result."

2009—At this point, Izabael is pretty much off on her own and does her own thing. It's hard for me to say where Izabael the spirit, and Izabael the woman begins or ends anymore. While I still feel I have some connection to Izabael as a bodiless spirit, I also am acutely aware of her new independence. Things have definitely not been the same since she found that body she was always after.

I hope my timeline has illustrated the open-ended nature of spirit working. They tend to take on a life of their own, and the more time you put in, the more seriously you take them, the better they work and the more powerful they become.

Grimoire Smimoire

Trying to follow the original instructions in most grimoires is nearly impossible. The tasks are often absurd to modern eyes, important sections are sometimes missing or illegible, and many of the items called for are difficult or expensive to obtain.

I will, however, say the "barbarous names of evocation" given in the *Goetia* are still quite useful and trance inducing. I reproduce the least adversarial of them for the summoning ritual given later in this chapter.

Instead of trying to follow the instructions in the *Goetia*, we will instead plug the daemons into the structure you have learned here. That will keep you safe. The main danger of demonology is self-delusion. That's why I stress material plane results over any other form of "proof," visual or otherwise.

Patience is required. It took years to feel the full effects of my early daemon workings. The daemons have repaid my efforts tenfold, sometimes a thousand fold, though admittedly some daemons can really exacerbate bad habits, so be vigilant.

Remember, of all the angels and all the daemons of the world, there is only one spirit that deserves your ultimate devotion.

Your HGA as a Daemon

Your Holy Guardian Angel is the highest and most powerful "daemon" you can contact. It is the only spirit that can *never* lead you astray. It is the only daemon or spirit that is available for contact at any time and any place. You need not know the name of your HGA. You need not do complicated rituals to invoke your higher self (though for some people, this helps). Your higher self is there in the calm quietude of pure being. As discussed in Chapter 6, whenever you are in the moment, feeling that "good feeling" over just being alive, you are in communion with your HGA.

At the beginning of Crowley's *Goetia* is the Bornless Ritual. This was not in the original *Ars Goetia*, but Crowley inserted this ritual as a means to invoke your HGA before working with the daemons. He did this because you are much less prone to delusion or other dangers if you make a connection with your higher self before starting a daemonic working. The Equilibrating Ritual of the Pentagram is enough for practical demonology, but should you feel like adding the Bornless Ritual to the ritual given in this chapter, you may very well do so.

Why invoke Izabael?

She is a straightforward and goodly spirit. She connects us to our higher self and leads us to the loftiest goals through even the basest of our pleasures.

Izabael can be summoned and used the same way any other Goetic daemon can.

She is light, airy, and helpful, almost like an angelic force. She tends to "come and go" and when she comes, she usually brings many changes all of a sudden.

Qabalistically she has influences from Mercury and Venus. She makes her home in Tiphareth and reaches the Supernals through Path 17, the path of Zain. This path describes her energy almost perfectly and therefore both seven (the number of letters in her name) and seventeen are sacred numbers to her, as well as the number "56," which her name adds to by Gematria.

The Triangle of Art

The "triangle of art" is a triangle with a circle inscribed within it, traditionally used to conjure spirits. This is drawn, painted, or otherwise constructed for use within the temple, intended to provide a "protected space" outside the magick circle, into which spirits are forced to appear. Usually this triangle is surrounded by sacred names, and in the center is the sigil of the daemon to be invoked, or a black scrying mirror.

Though perhaps shocking to purists, I don't use a triangle of art. In my years of streamlining magick down to the essentials, I feel it is not only unnecessary, but can create a mental block between you and the spirit you are trying to invoke. It hearkens back to the medieval mentality that these daemons are adversarial and must be forced or confined into a small, safe place.

If you follow the instructions in this book, then the following ritual is entirely safe as it is.[132] However, if you have used a triangle of art in the past, or would feel better doing so, you may of course proceed as you see fit.

Ritual to Invoke a Goetic Daemon

This ritual is tailored to invoke Izabael; however, it is also meant as a template to easily create your own ritual to invoke any daemon, especially those from the Goetia.

I. Prepare a suitable basis for the daemon

I find that silver dollars work well when painted with a particular daemon's sigil. You can also make their sigil out of wood or a particular metal appropriate to whatever daemon you are invoking.

---

132   Editor's Note: Proceed at your own risk.

Izabael prefers a pretty bottle or open sea shells, but you may start with painted poster board, or something similar, until your initial successes give you more confidence with the spirit and you really want to take the time to do the sigil up right.

Once you have the sigil drawn or painted on some sort of material basis, you can prepare your temple as you see fit.

II. Perform the Equilibrating Ritual of the Pentagram
You should be completely comfortable with this ritual by now. If not, you are not quite ready for daemon invocation.

III. Invoke an appropriate element, planet, or Sephirah
This would be according to the personality of the daemon if you know it, or simply use a specific part of the Tree of Life cognate with your desire, such as Netzach for a lust daemon.

You may use the Tree of Life ritual given in Chapter 10 to accomplish this, or come up with your own method. I'm leaving the details to the student's own ingenuity for this ritual. If you feel you are ready to work with spirits beyond Izabael, then you should also be at the level where you feel comfortable about constructing your own rituals, or at least customizing the ones given in this book.

In our example, Izabael is decidedly airy so we will invoke air using a traditional Golden Dawn Enochian ritual as given in Crowley's *Liber Chanokh*. There is a specific ritual assigned to each of the four elements.[133] The one for air is technically known as "Opening of the Temple in the Grade of 2°=9°."

---

133   *Liber LXXXIV* can easily be found by Googling online, within which you can find the temple openings for Fire, Water, and Earth as well.

Open the Temple in the Element of Air

1. Stand in the Sign of Shu,[134] i.e., spread out your hands above your head as if you were supporting the sky.

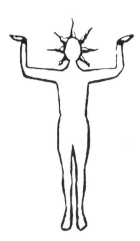

2. Ring bell or knock. Then say in a powerful voice:

"Let us adore the Lord and King of Air! Shaddai El Chai! Almighty and ever-living One, be Thy Name ever magnified in the Life of All. Amen!"

3. Stand in the Sign of Shu once again, saying:

"And Elohim said: Let us make Adam in our own image, after our likeness, and let them have dominion over the fowls of the air."

4. Draw the Air invoking pentagram:

5. Say with conviction: "In the Names Yod Heh Vav Heh and of Shaddai El Chai, Spirits of Air, adore your Creator!"

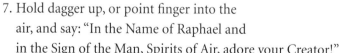

6. With finger or Air dagger, make the sign of Aquarius (♒).

7. Hold dagger up, or point finger into the air, and say: "In the Name of Raphael and in the Sign of the Man, Spirits of Air, adore your Creator!"

8. Draw a cross in the air before you and say, "In the Names and Letters of the Great Eastern Quadrangle, Spirits of Air, adore your Creator!"

---

134   Ancient Egyptian god of wind and air.

9. Hold dagger up, or point finger into the air, and say: "In the Three Great Secret Names of God, ORO IBAHA AOZODPEH that are borne upon the Banners of the East, Spirits of Air, adore your Creator!"

10. Point your finger or dagger as high into the air as you possibly can and say:

"In the Name of BATAIVAHA,
Great King of the East, Spirits of Air, adore your Creator!
In the Name of SHADDAI AL CHAI,
I declare that the Spirits of Air have been duly invoked."

11. Ring bell or knock nine times.

IV. Recite the Enochian invocation for Air

MICAMA! goho Pe-IAD! Zodir com-selahe azodien biabe os-lon-dohe.

Norezodacahisa otahila Gigipahe; vaunud-el-cahisa ta-pu-ime qo-mos-pelehe telocahe; qui-i-inu toltoregi cahisa i cahisji em ozodien; dasata beregida od torezodul!

Ili e-Ol balazodareji, od aala tahilanu-os netaabe: daluga vaomesareji elonusa cape-mi-ali vaoresa cala homila cocasabe fafenu izodizodope, od miinoagi de ginetaabe: vaunu na-na-e-el panupire malpireji caosaji. Pilada noanu vaunalahe balata od-vaoan.

Do-o-i-ape MADA: goholore, gohus, amiranu! Micama! Yehusozod ca-ca-com, od do-o-a-inu noari micaolazoda a-ai-om. Casarameji gohia: Zodacare!

Vaunigilaji! od im-ua-mar pugo pelapel Ananael Qo-a-an.

V. Goetic Invocation[135]
Chant:

"I DO invoke and conjure thee, O Spirit IZABAEL; and being with power armed from the SUPREME MAJESTY, I do strongly command thee, by BERALANENSIS, BALDACHIENSIS, PAUMACHIA, and APOLOGIAE SEDES; by the most Powerful Princes, Genii, Liachidee, and Ministers of the Tartarean Abode; and by the Chief Prince of the Seat of Apologia in the Ninth Legion, I do invoke thee, and by invoking conjure thee. And being armed with power from the SUPREME MAJESTY, I do strongly command thee, by Him Who spake and it was done, and unto whom all creatures be obedient. Also I, being made after the image of GOD, endued with power from GOD and created according unto His will, do exorcise thee by that most mighty and powerful name of GOD, EL, strong and wonderful; O thou Spirit IZABAEL and I command thee and Him who spake the Word and His FIAT was accomplished, and by all the names of GOD:

NUIT

HADIT

RA-HOOR-KHUIT

ADONAI

EL

ELOHIM

ELOHI

EHYEH

ASHER

EHYEH

ZABAOTH

---

135 Based on the traditional conjurations in the *Goetia*. You may add other conjurations from the *Goetia* at your discretion, but you might want to omit the adversarial ones that come last, especially with Izabael. There is simply no need to take that tone with her. Better to repeat the earlier conjurations, or simply the one given here, over and over until she manifests.

ELION

IAH

TETRAGRAMMATON

SHADDAI

HOOR-PA-KRAAT

LORD GOD MOST HIGH, I do exorcise thee and do powerfully command thee, O thou Spirit IZABAEL, that thou dost forthwith appear unto me here before this circle in a fair human shape, without any deformity or tortuosity. And by this ineffable name, YOD HEH VAV HEH, do I command thee, at the which being heard the elements are overthrown, the air is shaken, the sea runneth back, the fire is quenched, the earth trembleth, and all the hosts of the celestials, terrestrials, and infernals, do tremble together, and are troubled and confounded. Wherefore come thou, O Spirit IZABAEL, forthwith, and without delay, from any or all parts of the world wherever thou mayest be, and make rational answers unto all things that I shall demand of thee. Come thou peaceably, visibly, and affably, now, and without delay, manifesting that which I shall desire. For thou art conjured by the name of the LIVING and TRUE GOD, HELIOREN, wherefore fulfill thou my commands, and persist thou therein unto the end, and according unto mine interest, visibly and affably speaking unto me with a voice clear and intelligible without any ambiguity."

VI. Pause—Wait for connection.

Close your eyes. Do you feel anything? See anything? Smell anything? You may quietly repeat her name while you do this. Be patient. Receive.

This is why many magicians utilize an assistant to write down visions. A magician might also employ a highly receptive person to be the oracle while they run the ritual and write down the seer's visions.

If you don't have an assistant or seer you may record[136] your voice as the sensations occur and write them down after the ritual. Describe your sensations without censoring them. By verbalizing them you make a stronger impression on your mind. This is especially important if you think you aren't having effects. Most likely you are, but you are filtering them out. The conscious mind's filtering is the only block there is to feeling at least *something*.

If you really think you see or feel nothing, repeat the previous invocation once or twice more, then you may continue with this one:

"I DO invocate, conjure, and command thee, O thou Spirit IZABAEL, to appear and to show thyself visibly unto me before this circle in fair and comely shape, without any deformity or tortuosity; by the name and in the name IAH and VAU, which Adam heard and spake; and by the name of GOD, AGLA, which Lot heard and was saved with his family; and by the name IOTH, which Jacob heard from the angel wrestling with him, and was delivered from the hand of Esau his brother; and by the name ANAPHAXETON, which Aaron heard and spake and was made wise; and by the name ZABAOTH, which Moses named and all the rivers were turned into blood; and by the name ASHER EHYEH ORISTON, which Moses named, and all the rivers brought forth frogs, and they ascended into the houses, destroying all things; and by the name ELION, which Moses named, and there was great hail such as had not been since the beginning of the world; and by the name ADONAI, which Moses named, and there came up locusts, which appeared upon the whole land, and devoured all which the hail had left; and by the name SCHEMA AMATHIA, which Ioshua called upon, and the sun stayed his course; and by the name ALPHA and OMEGA, which Daniel named, and destroyed Bel, and slew the Dragon; and in the name EMMANUEL, which the three children, Shadrach, Meshach, and Abed-nego, sang in the midst of the fiery furnace, and were delivered; and by the name HAGIOS; and by the SEAL OF

---

136   Any small digital recorder is good for this. You may keep one specifically for daemonic workings that you use for no other purpose.

ADONAI; and by ISCHYROS, ATHANATOS, PARACLETOS; and by O
THEOS, ICTROS, ATHANATOS; and by these three secret names, AGLA,
ON, YOD HEH VAV HEH, do I adjure and constrain thee. And by these
names, and by all the other names of the LIVING and TRUE GOD, the
LORD ALMIGHTY, I do exorcise and command thee, O Spirit IZABAEL,
even by Him Who spake the Word and it was done, and to Whom all
creatures are obedient; and by the dreadful judgments of GOD; and by
the uncertain Sea of Glass, which is before the DIVINE MAJESTY, mighty
and powerful; by the four beasts before the throne, having eyes before and
behind; by the fire round about the throne; by the holy angels of Heaven;
and by the mighty wisdom of GOD; I do potently exorcise thee, that thou
appearest here before this Circle, to fulfill my will in all things which shall
seem good unto me; by the Seal of BASDATHEA BALDACHIA; and by
this name PRIMEUMATON, which Moses named, and the earth opened,
and did swallow up Kora, Dathan, and Abiram. Wherefore thou shalt
make faithful answers unto all my demands, O Spirit IZABAEL, and shalt
perform all my desires so far as in thine office thou art capable hereof.
Wherefore, come thou, visibly, peaceably, and affably, now without delay,
to manifest that which I desire, speaking with a clear and perfect voice,
intelligibly, and to mine understanding."

Again, relax, close your eyes … and wait.

Note any sensory stimuli, such as patterns or sounds, or whatever is in
your imagination at all.

Once you have a sense that there *might* be something there, you can
continue with the next step.

If you still don't sense or feel anything, try the invocations once more
each, or go on to the next step anyway.

VII. Question the Daemon

Now is the time to ask questions of the daemon. You may ask the questions
out loud or directly in your head.

If this is your first time working with a daemon, try to ask it what its elemental or planetary nature is, or anything else it would like you to know about itself in case you want to invoke that particular daemon again.

VIII. Ask a favor; Give a Gift

If you wish the daemon to help you on the physical plane, now is the time to send him your intent. Make your plea both strong mentally and emotionally. Daemons can definitely pick up on your emotions, perhaps even more than they can pick up on your thoughts.

If you do ask for something, you must give something in return, a "gift" of some sort.

You don't get something for nothing in magick. An exchange of energy must take place for the daemon to have any effect upon the material plane.

So what sort of exchange should you make with the daemon?

You don't need to sacrifice anything to the daemon. Instead, you may make a gift. Some people use cakes or wine as gifts to a daemon. Anything you take time to prepare yourself will have more value than something you merely buy.

My favorite way to give energy to a daemon is through artwork. I do entire paintings dedicated to a particular daemon (and in the case of Izabael, I've painted many for her). Not only does it provide a means of communication though the action of painting, all the energy I put into the painting eventually comes back to me as daemonic assistance.

You don't have to make the art during the ritual of course. You may create it before, or promise to make it after the ritual and then do so. You will generally work with your favorite daemons on a semi-regularly basis, so you may have many ways of giving energy to your particular familiar.

You can choose to dedicate orgasms to a daemon. After you read Chapter 9, you should easily understand how to do that.

If you made food or brought drink for the daemon, you may consume it in his or her name.

You may also ask what the daemon wants in return. If it is something you are comfortable with then by all means go for it. Do not allow any spirit, or human for that matter, to pressure you into any action you would not normally feel good about.

A more advanced way to give a daemon energy is to channel it from your chakras. Make your intent clear to the daemon, then stand and do the Middle Pillar Ritual. Don't vibrate the God names, instead use the daemon's name for all the chakras. At the end, imagine your energy flowing into the daemon through its sigil. Make the Sign of Silence after you have finished channeling as much energy as you desire. Please don't use this method until you feel completely comfortable with magick, and daemonic invocations in particular, as it can be especially powerful, perhaps even overwhelming.

IX. License to Depart
Chant:

"O THOU Spirit IZABAEL, because thou hast diligently answered unto my demands, and hast been very ready and willing to come at my call, I do here license thee to depart unto thy proper place; without causing harm or danger unto man or beast. Depart then, I say, and be thou very ready to come at my call, being duly exorcised and conjured by the sacred rites of magic. I charge thee to withdraw peaceably and quietly, and the peace of GOD be ever continued between thee and I. AMEN!"

X. Perform the Equilibrating Ritual of the Pentagram
In all daemonic workings it's important to finish with a full Equilibrating Ritual of the Pentagram and not simply the Qabalistic Cross.

XI. Write Your Visions Into Your Journal
If you recorded your voice, or scribbled the visions on scrap paper, then now is the time to transcribe your visions into your magick journal.

Mini Goetic Grimoire

Here are twelve of my favorite daemons from the *Goetia* (plus Izabael). The rest can easily be found online.[137] The descriptions are succinctly quoted or paraphrased.

Izabael

Izabael can bring love. She can make many things happen at once. She facilliates the use of other Goetic spirits so that they work harmoniously together.

Aim

Maketh one witty.

Sitri

"He inflameth a man with a woman's love, and also stirreth up women to love men. He discloses the secrets of the opposite sex, laughing at them and mocking them, to make them luxuriously naked."

Astaroth

Makes a person wonderful learned in the liberal sciences.

Buer

Keeps you healthy.

Eligos

Gives true advice pertaining to warfare and business. Procures the love of royalty and others of high rank.

---

137   Try Googling "Goetia.pdf" for example.

Beleth

"This great King Beleth causeth all the love that may be, both of men and of women."

Gusion

He reconciles relationships and gives honor and dignity unto any.

Glasya-Labolas

Teaches the art of clandestine operations, especially those requiring trickery or deceit.

Gamori

Answers truly of things present, past, and to come, and of treasures hid, and where it lieth. She also procureth the love of women, especially of maids.

Bune

"He giveth Riches unto a Man, and maketh him Wise and Eloquent."

Sabnock

Traditionally for building high castles and well-manned turrets, today he excels at manifesting large estates and protecting them.

What's the difference between invoking and evoking?

None as far as this book is concerned. Any time you pull a God or daemon into your consciousness, I call it invoking.

Other occult texts may make a distinction between invoking or evoking, however. Sometimes invoking means pulling a spirit into your body, while evoking just means seeing a daemon outside yourself, such as in a "magick mirror." Other books sometimes use invocation to refer to contacting angelic forces, and evocation for summoning daemons.

Should the daemons look like the descriptions in the Goetia?

Not necessarily. In my early workings in which I would actually "see" the Goetics visually in my mind, they did sometimes look like the descriptions, but just as often they did not.

These types of visual-based visions didn't manifest results as powerfully as later workings when I "felt" the daemons as distinct energy patterns or "essences." On Saliva divinorum, for example, each daemon has a distinct energy signature, but doesn't really "look" like anything other than patterns of energy. Visually, they were nothing like the descriptions in the *Goetia*, and yet these types of workings produced powerful material-plane results.

What if I don't feel or see anything?

You may not have developed your astral senses enough to notice. Usually this is due to the conscious mind doubting the sensations with internal dialogue like, "That's just my imagination. That's not real."

Learn to trust your imagination. Record your sensations without judgment. This will improve your subtle senses and increase the "reality" of the daemons you contact.

The previous ritual, and especially the long conjurations, are designed to put you in a mild altered state of consciousness, but the chanting, ceremony, symbolism, and incense may not quite be enough for some people. If all else fails, you may need to connect with the spirits in more intensely altered states of consciousness. In that case, you may experiment with mind-altering drugs, fasting, self-flagellation, etc. All these are advanced methods, however, and you are better off sticking with the meditations and rituals given in this book and allowing your astral senses to open gradually.

Another way of invoking is to deliberately call the daemon into your dreams. In this case, perform the ritual before bed, and state explicitly to the daemon that you wish to have an appearance during a dream. Do this every night until it happens. This works best if you are a person who naturally remembers your dreams or has lucid dreams. More details on dreaming are discussed the next chapter.

Daemons and Entheogens

An entheogen, which means "creates god within," is a psychoactive substance used in a magickal, shamanistic, religious, or spiritual context.

Daemons and entheogens do mix for many magicians so there is no sense avoiding this subject, especially since I myself have done more than my share of dabbling.

Marijuana or small amounts of alcohol may help make a connection with a daemon, especially if you don't normally drink or smoke.

Hallucinogens such as Psilocybin mushrooms, *Salvia divinorum*, Peyote, Ayahuasca, and LSD can be mind blowing when mixed with ceremonial magick, especially demonology.

While it would be remiss of me not to mention that entheogens can work well in magick, I should also mention I don't believe they are necessary. They can also be detrimental if used as a crutch, instead of a stepping stone. If the entheogens of your choice are illegal in your jurisdiction, then that is another problem facing you if you decide to use them.

If you do use them, simply use them in context of the ritual given in this chapter. In the case of short-acting entheogens such as *Salvia divinorum*, you can take a puff just after your invocations and then note your sensations.[138]

Daemonic Results

Ultimately it doesn't matter what a daemon looks like, says, or does, or even how intensely it materializes. If your real life shows improvement or otherwise manifests the changes you are looking for, that is all that matters.

The converse is true too. The detailed and vivid appearance of a daemon isn't of much use if it never manifests any sort of change upon the material plane. The entire point of using daemons is to affect the physical world.

---

138 Google my free e-book *So You Want to be a Goetic Shaman?* for more details on this.

What if a daemon promises me things but doesn't deliver?

Sometimes people make solid astral contact with a daemon and it readily agrees to everything the magician wants, but then weeks, months, and longer go by with no discernable results. Why is this so?

Sometimes a real connection to the daemon is not made, and it's merely a mental fabrication—but mental fabrications often lead to the real thing, so perhaps you just need to try another working, or be more patient for the results.

Sometimes the daemon is unable to fulfill your request for one reason or another, and a follow-up conjuration is needed to find out exactly why. Perhaps, the daemon is not a good match for you or your desire.

Also, some daemons are deceitful. Not all daemons in the *Goetia* are created equal, and other grimoires have a completely different style and personality. No one really knows where all these daemons came from, and some are more likely to deceive than others.

Ultimately, if a particular daemon isn't working for you, then move onto another, or drop demonology completely.

As popular as demonology is, I want to make clear it is not necessary to work with daemons to be a successful magician. In fact, you may very well end up a better magician without ever working with them at all.

Exercise 8: Daemon Invocation

Use the ritual given in this chapter to invoke Izabael or some other daemon of your choice. This is entirely optional.

AS✝RAL PLANE,
PA✝HW⊕RKING &
DIVINE ER⊕✝ICISM

*"I wouldn't recommend sex, drugs, or insanity for everyone,
but they've always worked for me."*—Hunter S. Thompson

Part I: Regarding the
Astral Plane, Dreaming, and Pathworking

Just what is the "astral plane" anyway?

The astral plane is the vaguely defined and overlapping area between thoughts, emotions, and the five senses.

The astral plane ebbs and swirls around us during dreams, idle reverie, while playing "mental movies," even when you mistake something out of the corner of your eye for something else. All these are events of the astral plane.

Is Yesod the astral plane?

While the astral plane can most simply be attributed to Yesod, it also includes influences from Hod and Netzach and the paths radiating between all three. In practice, the lower spheres and paths become increasingly hard to separate from each other the closer you get to Malkuth. The emotions of Netzach affect the "rational mind" of Hod all the time, for example.

In this book, the astral plane and Yesod are interchangeable for the most part, but the astral plane is a more open-ended term, while Yesod is much more specific.

Meaning in Chaos

In Yesod, the mind loves to find patterns in chaos. This is the part of the mind where life's "coincidences" turn into "synchronicities" and "omens." This part of the mind tends to label things and find patterns where there may or may not be any.

Yesod is the sphere that becomes overactive when cut off from external sensation (Malkuth), which is exactly why powerful hallucinations and extreme anxiety occur in sensory deprivation chambers. However, if the practice of sensory deprivation is taken far enough it can lead to experiences at the very highest levels of the Tree of Life—much like meditation. At the beginning of meditation, all is distraction (an itch or an obsessive thought, for example). If one can make it through this unpleasant and uncomfortable stage of delusion and distraction, enlightenment soon draws near.

The astral plane is also the realm of addictive fantasy situations ranging from online role-playing games to real-life swinger's clubs. All these "alternate" worlds thrive in the lower spheres of Netzach, Hod, and Yesod. It also explains why people who are excessively into these types of fantasy scenarios can be so imbalanced. They have lost connection with the higher aspects of the Tree of Life, and hence writhe around blindly in the lower aspects of their psyche, unconnected to true Godhead.

As the light of the Moon is but a reflection of the Sun, so is the light of Yesod but a murky reflection of Tiphareth. Do not get stuck here. The light of the astral plane is false and illusory.

Synchronicity and Omens

Synchronicity is finding meaning in the juxtaposition of what we are think-ing (or feeling) and what is happening in the outside world. Omens are basi-cally the same thing—something outside resonates with what we are think-ing, and we stop and ask, "Was that a sign?"

Synchronicity and omen-watching are not bad things in themselves. In fact, they can be very useful for developing our intuition (and receiving mes-sages from daemons as noted in the last chapter). However, the key to accu-rate omens is being balanced on the Tree of Life, and having a connection to Tiphareth (a.k.a. your True Self), which is the ruler and king of these lower spheres. If you have a good connection with Tiphareth (as conferred by the meditations and exercises in this book) then nothing of the astral plane can harm or mislead you.

Regarding Delusion

I can't really overstate that everything about Yesod and the astral plane should be taken with a grain of salt. The visions of this sphere tend to de-lude and complicate rather than clarify and enlighten. There is a tendency toward obsession and even a touch of "lunacy" if you mistake the astral plane for reality.

Very little real and lasting magick can be done from just messing around this low on the Tree of Life. The utility of the astral plane in magick has been overrated. Lasting joy comes from harmonizing the *entire* Tree of Life.

Truth, Lying, and Falsehood

"In the beginning doth the Magus speak Truth, and send forth Illusion and Falsehood to enslave the soul. Yet therein is the Mystery of Redemption," from Crowley's *Liber B vel Magi*, illustrates a magickal axiom: everything other than the direct experience of God is a lie.

On a practical level, however, truthfulness is something to strive for because it creates congruency in your psyche. Lying, distorting, and deliberately manipulating facts is always an ego-mind exercise. The higher self is content with the simple truth, therefore if you follow this, you will find many of your ego-shackles fall away.

Lying that has congruency is not lying but history. In other words, a "truth" is only as good as it holds up in the face of what "facts" are present. But in almost any scenario, *the space between the facts* takes up far more space than the facts themselves. Our history books are full of endless lies, i.e., things that can now be proven to be false but were at one time taken as fact.

This space between the facts can be exploited in a positive fashion through magick. There is always a "grey" area in life. Words and memories distort recollections from the way they actually happened. There is nothing wrong with putting the best "spin" on everything. Focus on the best of life, and you will be more likely to attain it.

The bottom line is that the more open and truthful you can be with yourself and others, the more truthful your visions and intuitions will be.

Scrying

Scrying usually means looking into some sort of medium such as a crystal ball, smoke, a dark mirror, random patterns (Rorschach tests and tea-leaves), etc.

You can also sit in a darkened room, close your eyes, and scry into the blackness. This is the method I recommend, as you will never be dependent upon any specific medium to probe the astral, as well as the higher levels of the Tree of Life.

Scrying often involves divination of some sort, but as I mentioned in Chapter 8, I believe divination is rarely necessary. However, the insights to be had by being receptive can be priceless—just don't trust your premonitions of the future unless you can establish a proven track record of results.

A better use for scrying is to explore and understand the different paths and Sephiroth of the Tree of Life. This is an entirely useful habit and leads to a deep understanding of magick and a continuous level of joy. The Tree of Life Ritual given in the next chapter is a good way to invoke specific energies for "scrying into."

If you have a hard time "scrying," it's generally due to the conscious mind giving you negative feedback. Just ignore your internal dialogue, and focus on your other sensations.

Don't judge your visions. Don't stop to ask if they are "real" or not. You may not "see" anything but instead hear things, or your may not see or hear, but only get impressions in some other way that makes sense to you. Simply let the images or feelings float through your consciousness and write them down afterward. Writing your visions down, however imaginary you think they are, will improve your astral abilities as much as the practice itself.

Magus and Seer

Magicians who spend countless years working on self-discipline and self-control can often not let go enough to be good at scrying, which requires intense mental submission and receptivity. Traditionally, magicians have often employed the use of a seer whose job is to scry the results of whatever energy is being invoked.

Seers may or may not be good at magick so long as they excel at being receptive to subconscious and astral imagery. Seers are quite often female, but psychically gifted men are employed as well.

Dreaming

Yesod, sphere of the Moon, has a special connection to dreaming and the dream world. This is the sphere to invoke to enhance your dreams in any way you need.

Dreams have some advantages over waking-life visualizations:

1. You have to dream anyway. Why not make them productive?

2. Dreams are directly tied to our subconscious and never lead us astray deliberately. Usually the contrary is true—they are trying to right the course that our conscious mind keeps screwing up.

3. They can be extremely intense and powerful when combined with magick, more so than even hallucinogenic drugs.

4. All symbolism is personalized for you.

5. They become more powerful with regular use.

Sounds great, but how do I use my dreams?

Start writing your dreams down. Even if you think you don't dream, you do. Keep a pad by your bed and wake yourself up with an alarm once or twice a night if necessary to prove that you are dreaming regularly. Rewrite the notes into your journal first thing in the morning after you wake up. Simple, but it does take dedication.

Once you feel you are comfortable with your dream recall you can do rituals right before bed with the *intent* of visualizing the results in your dreams (you may state this explicitly in your ritual). These dreams are to be considered sacred and special care should be taken to write down all that occurs.

This is a bit of an advanced subject, but with practice, some people will be able to do wonders with this method.

What about lucid dreaming?

Lucid dreaming is when you know you are dreaming, and hopefully have some control over your dreams while in that state. Many of us have experienced this accidentally at one time or another.

Once you can lucid dream with some regularity, you can perform rituals in your dream, which can be mind-blowing, to say the least.

Everyone can learn to lucid dream, though it is tricky for some. Here is one method to get you started:

1. Keep a dream journal!

2. Several times every day, stop dead in your tracks, whatever you are doing, look at your hands, and ask yourself, "Am I dreaming?" Really stop and pay attention to how you *know* if you are dreaming or not. Do this with as much passion and conviction as you can. Eventually, during a night dream, you will ask this same question and realize that you are dreaming. The more you *want* to lucid dream the faster it will happen. This practice also has the positive side effect of keeping you present and in the moment during your days.

3. After your first lucid dream, you may accidentally wake up from the excitement. You may also wake up when you try to control your dreams too much, especially at first. Practice will work out any kinks.

Be patient; it could take weeks or months to have your first lucid dream.

Once you have some ability with lucid dreaming you can visit wherever, or whomever you want, and have a lot of fun doing it. Perhaps best of all, you can travel anywhere on the Tree of Life.

How do I perform rituals in my dream?

Traveling the Tree of Life, and otherwise performing rituals in lucid dreams is easier than it sounds. The difficulty lies in having regular lucid dreams.

Once you *can* lucid dream, you'll find that rituals are vastly *simplified* when you perform them in a dream. For example, just drawing a planetary symbol in the air can be enough to overwhelm your dreamscape with its energy. Simply chanting the name of a Sephirah can take you to that sphere. Dreams are powerful stuff, though admittedly they are more unreliable, and more open to distractions than waking-life magick. Long, complex rituals are difficult to perform while in a lucid dream, for example. And sometimes, even though you have self-control in lucid dreams, you often end up doing something completely different than what you planned before bed.

Lucid dreaming is not a requirement of this book. I merely throw it out there because it's exciting and can be a powerful tool in the arsenal of any magician. Lucidity will come more naturally to some than to others, so I leave it to each student whether they want to develop this ability or not.

I will also note that *any* dream work, not just lucid dreaming, is always elucidating. Even just paying more attention to your dreams can unclog you spiritually and emotionally.

Pathworking

Pathworking is "experiencing" a specific place on the Tree of Life, whether it be a path or Sephirah.

The Tree of Life Ritual given in the next chapter can be used as a pathworking. I've marked a point in the ritual where you can stop being active, and become receptive. At this point you can sit, close your eyes, and just experience the thoughts and visions that arise. Write them down afterward.

The real power of pathworking is experiencing multiple paths *in succession* over a period of time. You can use the Sephiroth, the paths, or both together.

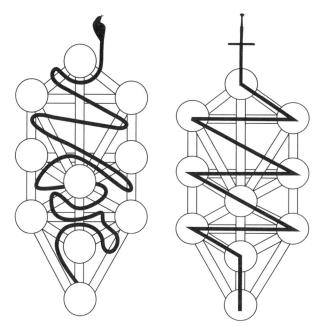

The path of the serpent on the left,
and the path of the flaming sword on the right.

For example, you could devote yourself to invoking all Sephiroth from 1-10, called the path of the flaming sword (or lightning bolt). Or you could use what is known as "the path of the serpent," which is to travel *only the paths* up from Path 32 to Path 11, thus a twenty-two part pathworking.

Is it better to climb up the Tree of Life or down?

When you work down the Tree, it tends to be more invocatory, as if you are bringing the divine intelligence down to a level you can appreciate.

When you travel up the Tree of Life, however, you are entering the mansion of God, i.e., God's own home. These types of pathworking can confer actual initiations, which will strip your ego down to the bone (and give you immense power as well).

I recommend learning to work down the Tree of Life for an extended time before journeying back up.

How do I pathwork?

Pathworking can be done with a variety of techniques and at various intensity levels, but I recommend the Tree of Life Ritual given in the next chapter. It's easy to learn and adjusts to your own level of understanding and abilities.

The important steps in a pathworking are:

1. Clear your headspace with the Equilibrating Ritual of the Pentagram.

2. Invoke a specific path or Sephirah on the Tree of Life (using the ritual given in the next chapter).

3. Enter a *receptive state of mind* where you can experience the essence of what you invoked.

4. Write down your results.

5. Chain together entire workings, winding your way up and down the Tree of Life as you see fit. One path (or Sephirah) per day is a good choice.

Scrying into your tarot cards is another potential avenue for pathworking. This won't work for everyone, but for others it will come naturally. After performing the Equilibrating Ritual of the Pentagram, sit, relax, and stare at the chosen tarot trump for awhile. Notice all the details. Now close your eyes, and use your imagination to step into the card and sense what else is in there. Notice if there is anyone else there, or animals, or sounds, or landscapes, or architecture of any sort. Whatever you imagine is valid, since you are starting from the tarot trump. Write down everything that popped into your head afterward (or record your voice while it's going on).

Another common way to pathwork is to lie down and listen to a voice (in person or recorded), which then leads you into a pathworking with guided imagery. There are books and websites for this, but unless they specifically take you through the Tree of Life, or at least tarot cards, they aren't quite the same type of pathworking as given here, which is quite structured.

Pathworking is one of the most powerful things you can do to improve your visualization skills. Also, pathworking helps unclog old blocks and allows you to naturally attract more of what you desire. Extended pathworking can lead to magickal initiations by angelic spirits, occult mysteries being revealed, and vastly improved intuition.

Other Information on Pathworking

I recommend Crowley's "Wakeworld: A Tale for Babes And Sucklings"[139] from *Konx Om Pax*, as a good example of how a pathworking might be written in the form of a short fairy tale. Reading it is a mini-pathworking, and if someone reads it to you while you actively visualize what you hear, it is a full-fledged pathworking.

Another good book that has guided meditations through the entire Tree of Life is called the *Shining Paths*.[140] This book has shockingly effective symbolism for each path and Sephirah, and has reverberated intense changes through my life every time I've used it.

Also, you might consider researching the Enochian Aethyrs online or in the dozens of books written about it. The Aethyrs are thirty spiritual realms, one outside the other in ever-expanding concentric circles. These realms can be pathworked in a fashion similar to how we work the Tree of Life. The Enochian system has its own methodology, which is outside the scope of this book, but Enochian is neither excessively difficult nor dangerous. It should dovetail with everything you've learned here.

What about "out of body" experiences?

This is the type of "astral projection" where you leave your body and can wander around homes, see your own body on the bed, and walk through walls, etc. While certainly a tantalizing ability, it is not common, and need

---

139   Public domain PDFs of this can be found easily enough online like many of Crowley's writings.
140   Try to find the first printing though, as the second printing is unfortunately riddled with typographic errors.

not be considered at all necessary to your magickal progress. If you do have this kind of advanced visualization skill, then so much the better.

Altered States of Consciousness

All magick requires some sort of "altered" state of consciousness, though these can be as simple as quieting your mind, having an orgasm, or being so caught up in a ritual that you "lose yourself." Altered states of consciousness do not have to be extreme and can be effective even if the altered state is a subtle one.

For scrying and pathworking, being passive and observant is enough of an altered state of consciousness to have results. Practice will increase your astral abilities and increase these experiences. These types of "trance" states can become quite intense with enough time and passion.

Lucid dreaming, or simply invoking before a regular dream, are both good ways to experience altered states of consciousness for pathworking.

How can I have more intense pathworkings?

It would be remiss of me not to mention that anything that alters your state of consciousness has a potential use in magick. Hallucinogenic drugs, sex magick, sleep deprivation, BDSM, etc., can all be used to make your visions more intense. Ultimately, how you decide to experience an altered state of consciousness is left to your own imagination and good judgment.

Drugs and the Astral

Use of hallucinogenic drugs stimulates the astral. Not surprisingly many drug trips also tend to delusion.

The use of mind-altering drugs has been a part of shamanism, magick and occultism since antiquity, so ignoring their use would be silly. However, the main problem with many popular entheogens, which are generally psychedelic, is that they are illegal. The ones that are still legal in many places, such as *Salvia divinorum*, are in danger of becoming illegal due to improper use and the posting thereof online. Whatever you decide to do, make sure you do it responsibly. No drug experience is worth incarceration, especially as there are so many legal ways to get mind-altering experiences, including meditation and magick.

If you do end up working with entheogens, keep a few things in mind:

Balance yourself first. Like a rocket on the launch pad everything must be properly aligned or your fantastic journey might explode into a "bad trip." So always perform the Equilibrating Ritual of the Pentagram before you take off.

Another crucial task with any sort of hallucinatory drug work is grounding the energy afterward into some actual physical work, whether it be artwork, writing, rituals, meditation, or even exercise. Ground these otherworldly experiences back into your waking state and realities, and they will have a far more lasting and viable effect on your life as a whole. Otherwise the results tend to evaporate. Grounding the energy of a single trip can take days or weeks, much longer than the intense experiences of the entheogens themselves.

Another thing to point out is not to take your visions too seriously. Drug experiences give wild experiences far outside the bounds of normal-day consciousness. Some people are disappointed when they misinterpret these images during magick, and are further disappointed when spells or visions don't manifest like they thought they would while under the influence of the drug. So be patient, and keep your expectations in check.

What kinds of drugs can I use in magick?

Hard drugs such as meth, crack, and heroin are undoubtedly detrimental to any spiritual progress. I would also include cocaine and ecstasy use to this harmful list of drugs, but other magicians may disagree.

As mentioned earlier, light marijuana or alcohol use can have some advantage on occasion. For example, if you rarely smoke weed or drink, then doing a little before a ritual could possibly enhance it. If you smoke or drink every day, then you would most likely have a stronger effect by abstaining for a day or two before the ritual instead. Whatever is "outside the normal" will create more psychic tension and make a bigger mark upon your subconscious.

Entheogens, like LSD, peyote, mushrooms, Ayahuasca, DMT, and *Salvia divinorum* can profitably be used in magick and there will always be a subset of magicians who are seriously into these types of drugs. I went through that stage, and my advice is if you are going to take that road, take special pains of "grounding" whatever lessons you learn while on the drugs. In other words, these drugs open up the spiritual world quickly and easily—the problem is the door shuts just as fast after the drugs wear off. This "closing off" to the spiritual energies after the drugs fade can be so pronounced that sometimes the magician actually backslides in spiritual progress. This need not be the case, however, if the magician actively works to bring his drug-induced visions down to the material plane in some fashion, such as meditating, daily rituals, writing, painting, or otherwise incorporating what he learned into his or her day-to-day life. In other words, if you want results that actually last, you will have to follow up any drug trips with real magickal work, as well as properly prepping for each trip.

Prescription drugs can also adversely affect magick, including Opioids and Benzodiazepines. I'm not saying get off any medications you might be on, but you do need to be aware that all drugs have effects on your spirituality including ones the good ol' doctor gave you.

Part II: Sex Magick

Blake said that the body was the soul's prison unless the five senses are fully developed and open. He considered the senses the 'windows of the soul.' When sex involves all the senses intensely, it can be like a mystical experience.— Jim Morrison

Yesod governs the sexual organs so now we throw sexuality into this whole astral mishmash we have down at the lower planes. Venus already dominates sexuality in Netzach and now we get another dose of sexuality in Yesod—the most illusory sphere on the Tree of Life.

This section is distinct from Chapter 7's lesson of love magick, which was about finding romance or a mate. This section is about using sexual energy, solo or with partners, for various magickal goals.

The first thing I'd like to get out of the way is that gender is not relevant for most sex magick. Far more important are the roles you play during rituals. Either sex can perform any role with a little imagination. A woman can invoke Mars, and a man can invoke Shakti—it's all good.

Sex magick, or divine eroticism, is about bringing your spirituality into close contact with your sexuality. I will explain some basic concepts of sex magick and then give you some sample rituals. More than any other chapter, allow yourself to use your own imagination in discovering ways to use sexuality in your magick.

Chastity

Though promiscuity is certainly not frowned upon in magick, there are still valid reasons to practice chastity—discipline and temporary denial make the payoff even more delightful. For sex magick a brief period of chastity is always beneficial.

It really boils down to immediate pleasure vs. the buildup of future pleasure. To get a feel for this sensation, try sex games that include some sort of delayed gratification, from a few hours of "torment" up to weeks or months. The more pressure that builds, the greater the climax, which is especially important in sex magick.

What is sex magick?

Sex magick is using sensuality, sexual energy, or orgasms in a ritual setting. It is not a religion or a belief system, but an open-ended and evolving system of techniques.

Sex magick is neither difficult nor dangerous, but it is an advanced topic because it strings together almost every other concept covered in this book.

It is not necessary to perform sex magick to be a magician. It is not "better" than the non-sexual magick taught thus far, but simply another way to accomplish similar ends.

That said, a little sex magick can enrich your enjoyment of magick and life in general. It can supply a whole new dynamic to your magickal proceedings, and gives you yet another set of techniques to add to your ritual-building toolset.

What about Tantra?

Tantra is a rich and complex Hindu spiritual system that includes sexual techniques for achieving unity with the divine. Tantra is much more than sex magick, and is a topic far outside the scope of this book. What I teach in this book is not Tantra, though some of the ideas presented may be similar to or inspired by certain Tantric practices.

What about the Kundalini?

In Hinduism, Kundalini[141] is a female serpent of energy, coiled at the base of the spine. She travels up each chakra to end in an explosion of light at the 1000-petaled lotus above your head.

You have already started working with your Kundalini every time you use the Middle Pillar Ritual, which will gently open all your chakras to their fullest bloom.

There also exist techniques, called Kriya,[142] to raise the Kundalini more directly if this is something that deeply interests you. As with all genuine yoga practices, they are powerful, but they can be difficult and uncomfortable exercises if you are not accustomed to them.

---

141 Kundalini in Sanskrit means "that which is coiled."
142 From Sanskrit, means "action, deed, effort."

Common Goals for Sex Magick

Sensuality, romance, and orgasmic-trance states blend perfectly into the ritual framework you've been learning in this book. You are free to use sexuality anywhere in magick and for whatever purpose.

Here are a few powerful and specific uses for sex magick:

1. **Raise and channel sexual energy to charge a talisman or sigil.** This is similar to what you do in rituals already, except that orgasm becomes the climax of the ritual.

2. **Use the orgasm and resulting juices as a sacrament.** This naturally follows after orgasm since the only sacrament and holy oil you'll ever need is produced by your own sex glands. Either one or both of the partners consumes the resulting elixir, or it can be used to anoint a talisman.

3. **Invoke the divine into your partner and make love to a god or goddess.** You can invoke any god, goddess, planetary, or elemental force into your partner and make love to them.

4. **Using post-coital states as a clairvoyant trance.** After long and extended periods of sex, when one is completely worn out, there arises a passive state conducive for any sort of clairvoyant work, such as daemon invocation.

5. **Feeding a daemon or servitor.** You can make a pact with a daemon that you give it all the energy from a sex magick ritual in return for your desire.

6. **Increasing romantic and sensual pleasure.** This is a side-effect of all sex magick, but can become a primary goal if that is your desire. Your sensitivity to the joys and harmonies of the body and its subtle energies will be increased, as well as your ability to reach deep levels of intimacy with others.

These goals are not mutually exclusive. You can easily perform many of these actions in one ritual.

Don't be intimidated by constructing your own sex magick rituals. Use your imagination. While it's true with all types of magick, it's even more true with sex magick: Nothing but experimentation will teach you anything valuable. A week in the field is worth centuries of book learning.

I'll give a few examples of sex magick rituals at the end of this chapter, but please understand these are just samples. There is no limit to what you might come up with on your own.

La Petite Mort

La petite mort means "the little death" in French. More than just a metaphor for orgasm, it hints at the deep physiological and psychological link between sex and death. This link can be seen in the mirror (our sexual organs are next to our excretory ones), in biology (where there is a strong link between death and reproduction all the way down to the cellular level), in sociology (where violence over sexual concerns is known to arise in all cultures), in pathology (where sexually transmitted diseases have long been a cause of human fatality), and in our movies (which enjoy mixing sex with violence for titillation value).

There is also a strong connection between sex and generally risky, reckless, and even violent behaviors that *overcome* our natural fear of death. Sex turns the potential of death and danger into something exciting. Path 24, attributed to Scorpio, is a symbolic representation of this inextricable link between sex, death, and transformation.

La petite morte also refers to that moment in orgasm where you lose yourself, or perhaps even "black out" for a moment. Some people use techniques, often dangerous and not described here, to enhance that "black out" effect both for pleasure and magickal reasons.

Sexual Trance

While a sex magick ritual may start much like regular sex, you and your partner should take extra care to make sure everything is treated in a sacred fashion.

For example, if your goal is to invoke Venus into your partner, you must take time to build her up in your imagination to such a state that you feel you are truly making love to a Goddess.

If you are planning to charge a sigil that you have painted onto your partner, then you should concentrate more of your energies upon the sigil the closer you get towards orgasm. Indeed, you should almost acquire a "fetish" for the sigil, making it as erotic and as engrossing as your imagination allows. In other words, use the sexiness of your partner to get yourself going, but as the ritual progresses, learn to focus exclusively upon your primary sigil. This is the way to ensure potent orgasms *fully empowered with your magickal intent.*

Pornography
Whether to include pornography or erotica into your rituals is a matter of personal choice. I personally see it being of more value in a solo sex magick situation than with a partner or group, but ultimately these choices will be decided by the type of ritual and the aesthetics of the magicians involved.

Addiction and Obsession
Addiction to anything, whether to casual sex, masturbation, drugs, or money, has no part in a magician's life. However, we don't *quit* behaviors—we can only *replace* them.

That's usually easier said than done, but the study of this book in its entirety lays a blueprint for a new life on your own terms. There is no easy answer I can give in a few steps, or a single ritual that can cure all addictions. Addictions are just a symptom of all the nastiness of the ego-mind I discussed in Chapter 5.

The first thing is to accept your obsessions or addictions, don't repress them. Everyone has behaviors they want to replace, some behaviors are just more detrimental than others.

Most of us are born straight away into addictions taught to us as children by mainstream media, such as addictions to buying, social status, money, sex, cigarettes, oxycodone, and caffeine to name just the legal addictions. Those along with the illegal ones are all perpetuated by an out-of-control ego-mind.

At some level, addictions and unwanted obsessions are just misplaced energy. There is a biological imperative for evolutionary good buried beneath all your impulses, even the ones you think are negative. The goal is that they find a proper outlet or be otherwise sublimated back into your entire Tree of Life.

To make a spell to help cure an addiction or obsession is the same as any other intent. Decide where on the Tree of Life you think your obsession or addiction might originate. Then perform meditations and rituals with that path or Sephirah and the connecting paths around it.

For example: Many obsessions are sexually related, and many of those occur at a blockage in the Netzach, Hod, and Yesod area, including the connecting paths, as mentioned when discussing Path 25 (*Art*) in Chapter 3. So you would adapt the Tree of Life Ritual, given in the next chapter, and invoke these paths and Sephiroth, experiencing their energy fully and releasing any psychological blocks you have there.

Keep all this in mind when doing magick rituals that involve sex, as everything is amplified. Issues with sexuality can and will come boiling to the surface in intense, and occasionally very unpleasant ways. Only perform sex magick with people whom you really trust and in a setting with which you feel totally comfortable.

What if I'm obsessive compulsive?

It's just like all the other problems mentioned in this book: it's ego-mind based. The ego-mind is trapped trying to find safety in routine—such as hand washing, hoarding, and every other obsessive-compulsive behavior.

The ego-mind needs to be shattered. I urge you right now to get comfortable with the idea of being "vulnerable." Accepting vulnerability does not mean you are weak. It means you are accepting the vulnerability of the ego-mind to be destroyed so that something better is left behind.

BDSM Magick

Mix magick with BDSM (bondage and discipline, dominance and submission, sadism and masochism), or any other violent or masochistic/sadomasochistic role-play, and you'll run into more or less the same concerns as someone mixing in heavy doses of drugs. It makes everything extremely intense—so intense that it will be a bad trip for many newbies to BDSM or magick.

Magick mixed with anything else makes it more intense, and often times, brings out issues at least one of the participants didn't expect in either themselves or their partner(s). So be on top of your magick game before you attempt to add the extremes of BDSM to your rituals.

Masturbation

Masturbation releases energy and can put you into a trance similar to actual intercourse, therefore sex magick can be performed solo.

The only warning I give regarding masturbation is that every time you orgasm, even when alone, you are releasing a potent burst of energy. This energy is frittered away if you masturbate without some sort of magickal intent or purpose. Even worse, compulsive masturbation can lead to the accidental creation of negative thought forms (i.e. mini-servitors), which can adversely affect your life.

Consider finding a purpose for all your orgasms even when you are without a partner. Dedicate them to a god, channel them into a sigil, or feed the energy to a daemon. It does not matter so much what you do with your orgasms so long as you treat each one as holy.

Make every orgasm count, and the joy of the moment will spread throughout your entire life.

Sex Magick for More than Two

Ménage à troi and even orgy scenarios are not unheard of in sex magick. If you are in the enviable position of having multiple partners available for sex magick, you should have no problems adapting the rituals given herein to your own uses.

Frankly, adapting the rituals is the easiest part. Real-world complications make these sorts of multiple-partner situations delicate and tricky because of emotions and real-life problems getting mixed in with the magick.

Even without sex magick, magickal orders have a hard time keeping it together sometimes. The original Golden Dawn busted up over petty squabbling and egos. When you throw sex into the mix it can get even crazier. It takes diplomacy, tact, and strength of character to run workings with more than one partner.

The Sacred Whore

Sacred whores have existed since antiquity and include such notables as Isis of the Egyptians, Ishtar of the Babylonians, Inanna of the Sumerians, Mary Magdalene of the Christians, and Vesta of the Greeks, for whom the famous Vestal Virgins practiced sex magick rites in her honor.

Throughout the centuries large religions all the way down to small cults used some form of sacred prostitution at their temples. However, by the time Christianity had risen to dominance, sex had been made into something ugly and in need of being repressed. Not surprisingly, the priests did not stop having sex, but instead became perverts.

As poet and visionary William Blake wrote, "repressed energy breeds pestilence." Worshipping a sacred whore helps unblock any repression and raises our love and lust to the very highest levels of divinity.

Crowley's version of the sacred whore is Babalon, whom we have mentioned previously. She is the divine whore unto whom magicians offer the blood of their ego so as to be reborn.

I prefer to worship Nuit, however, who is a step higher than Babalon. Babalon is good for certain initiations and magickal workings, but Nuit is the true seductress—the one you find in every moment, every song, every flirtatious glance received from another—that is Nuit. Chase her, and your connection to your HGA will come naturally, and your ability to love and receive love of all types will increase by leaps and languorous bounds.

Practice for Sex Magick

You can jump in and start performing the rituals, if you feel ready. However, here are some preparations you can take to ensure you and your partner are properly raising and directing your magickal energies together.

1. Spend a week or two practicing the Middle Pillar Ritual together in a non-sexual fashion. Focus on keeping your breath in rhythm with each other, but stand at least a foot or two apart.

2. Practice the Middle Pillar for another week or so, but this time face each other nude. Synchronize your breathing to be opposite your partner. When you breathe in, they breathe out, and when you breathe out, they breathe in. You may also have light physical contact. Notice the difference in sensation from when you performed without such intimate proximity. Be aware of your chakras and your partner's chakras. When you circulate the light, imagine you and your partner's light as being in perfect synch. In actual sex magick you will not always be in perfect synch with your partner's breathing, but this practice will increase your ability to raise energy in tandem.

3. Take this practice to the next level by adding caresses, touching, fondling, while still maintaining focus upon each other's breathing. You can now step out of the typical mold of the Middle Pillar and become more fluid and spontaneous. Don't worry about chanting, just focus on keeping your breathing harmonious with your partner's, and your mind and heart present on the energies you should now sense swirling

around you and within you. At the end, you can channel
all the energy raised into each other's body as you see fit.

4. When you and your partner are ready, you may take this practice
to its obvious conclusion, i.e., intercourse or orgasm. This is
also a good place to practice simultaneous climax. Though
synchronous orgasms are not necessary in the following rituals,
it is always nice when you and your partner can pull it off.

This practice will teach you the core ability of raising and
channeling sexual energy, which you and your partner may
put to good use in the following rituals.

Sex Magick Rituals

This section assumes you are familiar with the entire book, including the
Tree of Life Ritual in the next chapter. It also assumes by this point you have
been practicing all the exercises given thus far. If so, you should have no
problems making your own rituals from the instructions given here.

The examples are not as detailed as in earlier chapters, because too
much detail would just be tedious at this point. I want to allow you greater
flexibility in tailoring the rituals to your own desires. Trust what you have
learned so far and dare to experiment on your own.

Simple Sigil Sex Magick

This ritual is as streamlined as you can get so you may add to it as you see fit.
It illustrates the essentials of a sex magick working.

1. Instead of making a full talisman, you merely need one sigil
symbolizing your intent.

2. Draw the sigil onto paper or poster board and place enough of
them strategically around your temple (the area you will have
sex in) so that no matter where you look, there is a sigil.

3. Also paint or draw the sigil onto each of the partners, in
whatever areas you see fit.

4. Perform the Equilibrating Ritual of the Pentagram as normal.

5. Make love for as long as you desire.

6. When you both near climax, start *really* focusing on the sigils. You may focus on *any* of the sigils you have drawn within your temple and each other's bodies.

7. Climax as close together as possible. Simultaneously is not necessary, but each of you must focus totally on the sigil while having your orgasm.

8. Take your time cuddling and winding down.

9. Perform the Equilibrating Ritual of the Pentagram again or at least the Qabalistic Cross.

10. Throw away all the sigils and wash the symbols off your body. Allow yourselves to completely forget about the sigil and your original intent.

11. Write about the experience in your magickal journal.

Do both partners have to know the intent?

No, but you both should be aware you are performing sex magick. The actual purpose behind the sigil need not be known to all participants however.

Host of Heaven Ritual

This is a simple ritual to charge and consume a sexual Eucharist. The instructions are written for a couple but could be adapted for solo use by consuming one's own elixir. It can also be adapted for multiple partners.

In the following instructions, the active partner is considered male, and the adorant, who receives the communion, is female. The roles can be reversed, or changed to a same-sex scenario, but understand that there will be subtle differences in the results. Invoking divine light into semen is symbolically and spiritually different than invoking the light into female juices.

This isn't to say that you shouldn't experiment, only that such distinctions can make a difference.

1. Ritual bath, shower, massage, etc.

2. Perform the Equilibrating Ritual of the Pentagram up through and including the "Invocation of Archangels" and the second Qabalistic Cross.

3. The adorant should begin fellatio upon the magician.

4. When the magician feels he is ready, he should now continue the Equilibrating Ritual of the Pentagram with the start of "Drawing down the LVX."

5. When the magician is ready to climax, after he says, "may the divine light descend," he shall visualize the divine light rushing into his "magick rood" as he ejaculates into the aspirant's mouth.

6. Finish with the Qabalistic Cross.

Step 5 is the crucial section. The divine light comes down and enters into the ejaculate. A secret of magick is that divine light most easily finds a host in sexual secretions. So when the adorant eats the communion, he or she is partaking of the highest aspects of God.

This is a sacrament, meant to be consumed daily, weekly, or whatever cycle you see fit.

Can we share the elixir?
Yes, in any way you and your partner see fit.

Role-play
Role-play, always important, should be practiced with especial gusto during sex magick.

If you are going to play a god, then you should research that god in detail. Understand his or her nature just as if you were an actor preparing for an opening-night production.

If you are going to be the worshipper, then understand that though you are mortal, you are the highest and most fit of the human race to make love with this god or goddess before you. Take care of the desires of your god or goddess, and don't forget to ask them if there isn't a prayer of yours they might grant in return.

Ambrosia of the Gods Invocation

Sex magick is sacred and sexy. Invoking a god or goddess into your partner and then making love to them is a distinct pleasure in itself, or you can use it as a prequel for charging a sigil or talisman. In this ritual we will invoke a god or goddess into one of the partners and eat the resulting ambrosia.

1. Choose a god or goddess. You need not be limited to Greek, Roman, or Egyptian gods and goddesses; you may take from any culture. Take time to discuss with your partner what would make your ritual sexy, powerful, and fun.

2. Instead of the usual talisman preparations, prepare a delicious fruit of your choice to be an edible talisman. The easiest way to encode your intent is to use a simple sigil for your desire. Then with a needle, stipple your sigil into the fruit. (If you have a bowl of strawberries or cherries, you need not do this for every single one, but make sure you both get a bite of the one with the sigil on it.)

3. Extended relaxation period, ritual baths, loving massages, etc.

4. Use the Tree of Life ritual given in the next chapter to invoke the Sephirah, or path, that you best feel your chosen god or goddess belongs to. For example, if you were going to invoke Aphrodite then Netzach is appropriate.

5. Make love for as long as you see fit. Lovemaking can occur at whatever level you and your partner are comfortable with. Actual penetration is not necessary. The mortal partner will worship and cater to the needs of everything the god or goddess desires.

6. You may invoke a second god or goddess and it will be as if you and your partner are two divinities making love to each other. However, I recommend the partners experience the roles separately before moving on to invoking gods into both partners simultaneously.

7. When you and your partner are ready, channel your final climax. Depending on your tastes, you can ejaculate on the fruit and then consume it together in a kiss. Or if that doesn't appeal to one or more or the participants, you can eat the fruit while having orgasms (or immediately afterward.)

8. Finish with the Equilibrating Ritual of the Pentagram, or just post-coital cuddling.

9. Feast. Most rituals benefit by eating and drinking in a celebratory fashion afterward.

Lunar Solo Sex Magick Talisman Ritual

Solo sex magick was probably more successful before the sexual revolution. There is little taboo in masturbating anymore, in fact many of us (especially men) do it far too much. The proliferation of porn and the common sense knowledge that almost everyone masturbates at least once in awhile has taken away much of the mystique that solo sex magick would have had in Crowley's and A. O. Spare's time.

Magick works best when the conscious mind is overwhelmed with spectacle. That's why I encourage variety and experimentation in your magick. Keep your conscious mind fully engrossed while you *slip* the intent deep into the subconscious. The more intense the sensations, the better the ritual, and who will deny that newness excites more than the old?

Therefore, one ritual with a single solo orgasm is not going to do much good if you usually masturbate five or six times a day. Your conscious mind will not be particularly impressed.

So what should you do? You can find a partner, of course, and take your magick to the next level, but sometimes it is necessary or desirable to work alone. In that case, the following ritual is effective:

1. Make a talisman for your intent. Understand that for this spell you need to consider the material basis with particular care as you will be anointing the talisman with your sexual secretions every single time you masturbate.

2. Start on a full moon. The spell will last 28 days and end on the following full moon.

3. Perform the Equilibrating Ritual of the Pentagram, drawing down the light into your talisman or sigil. You need only do this on the first and last day of the ritual.

4. For the entire moon cycle, dedicate *every* orgasm to your talisman, anointing it with your orgasmic juices. You may do this as many times as you can. Push your limits. You may use pornography or whatever else to get yourself started, but make sure your focus is on the talisman when you orgasm.

5. At the end of the 28 days, on the next full moon, finish by performing the Equilibrating Ritual of the Pentagram, and drawing the light into the talisman one final time.

6. Hide your talisman for two more lunar cycles. At that point you may destroy or recharge the talisman depending on how you feel about the results you have had so far.

This lunar ritual could be adapted to sex magick with a couple or group, though it's easier to keep to such a schedule alone.

Exercise 9: Perform a sex magick ritual.

This is optional, but fun and recommended.

THE HUMAN
BODY, CHANGE &
TRANSFORMATION;
RITUAL
CONSTRUCTION

"Let the beauty of what you love be what you do."—Rumi

It all comes down to Malkuth, the material plane, which includes our physical bodies. Here is where everything actually *happens*. Any change made in the higher spheres also finds manifestation here.

The Tree of Life On the Human Body

Here, in our body, we experience the five senses that give birth to the experience of each and every moment.

The Tree of Life fits upon the human body thusly:

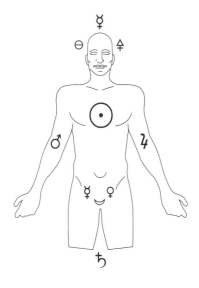

Our head symbolizes the Supernals (Kether, Chokmah, and Binah). Our head is "God" to the rest of our body.

Our chest area is Tiphareth, the sun, the center, the heart that pumps blood throughout the entire system.

Our right arm is power, and our left arm is mercy (though "lefties" might feel like the left and right sides of the Tree of Life are swapped). Make your right hand into a tight fist and hold your left hand out in an open-handed gesture of friendship; now you have the right idea.

The groin and hip area house the tightly woven trio of Netzach, Hod, and Yesod. This illustrates the tight bond between these three Sephiroth and their powerful sexual connotations.

Malkuth is appropriately at our feet, which are what allow us to make our way in the world.

The God Who Fell to Earth

It is a gross misunderstanding of many religions to try to escape the body or make it shameful in some way. Our experience of God is *through the body*. So every sensation from our bodies must be holy.

The whole reason that any spiritualized being such as a god, a soul, a spirit, etc., would want to come down to the material plane is to take on a solid body. Even with all its flaws and impermanence. Malkuth is the most visceral experience of existence any being can have—even a god.

God comes down to earth for his own pleasure. God forgets his omniscience so he can experience wonder, awe, and bewilderment at life's infinite variety.

Your own particular spark of God, whether you call it a soul, or your HGA, or whatever else, is your own flawless divinity wanting to experience the joyous imperfection of manifested existence.

Losing Touch with Divinity

Life is meant to be savored and enjoyed. The only problem is that our connection to divinity gets clouded by our ego-mind, so our pursuit of sensuality becomes flawed and little more than hedonism, compulsion, or vanity.

Devote your joy and pursuit of pleasure to something higher than your ego-mind. This is why Nuit, goddess of infinite possibilities, says: "Be goodly therefore: dress ye all in fine apparel; eat rich foods and drink sweet wines and wines that foam! Also, take your fill and will of love as ye will, when, where, and with whom ye will! But always unto me."[143]

She is urging us to enjoy life, but to make sure it's not for the aggrandizement of our own ego-mind. This is not for moral reasons, but because the ego-mind ruins true happiness. By dedicating our joy back to the universe, it frees us from the ego-mind's incessant demands of what it thinks will make it happy. Instead, you will actually be free to experience and enjoy the deepest pleasures in life. Your connection to your higher self will remain strong, and you will reach your full potential.

The Meaning of Life

As humans we have free will, even in situations where life's circumstances are completely outside our control. *Internally,* we can always define our own meaning. Be master of your internal state.

As a magician, you are free to choose any meaning for life whatsoever. The only mistake someone can make is to attach *no meaning* to human existence whatsoever. While that is certainly a choice, it is one that inevitably leads to depression and a disconnection from the world.

---

143   *Liber AL,* I. 51.

The simplest things can have the most lasting repercussions. Find some meaning, some reason to feel satisfied in every single moment, and everything else will tend to take care of itself. Living life is not nearly as complicated as our ego-mind makes it out to be, but it takes a real commitment to maintaining a joyous simplicity.

With age and experience, the meaning of your life will evolve and change. Eventually you may find that a life lived imaginatively with an eye toward the betterment of all humanity is the most satisfying—but that is for you and your HGA to figure out.

The Meaning of Death

There is no way to separate the meaning of life from the meaning of death. Life has meaning precisely because it is so transitory. Death is not horrible, but merely an instrument of change and transformation. The fact that things die means that other things are created, which means a constant state of flux in the universe.

Only infinite *sameness*—like some bureaucratic version of hell that functions in grey, dull monotony for all of eternity—would be something to fear. It is good that our universe changes and evolves. Infinite variety is the ultimate joy of the universe.

All personal growth involves some death—death of old ideas, ways of acting, ways of living, ways of thinking. To get joy in your life often means death to worn-out or unpleasant methods of behavior. The unfortunate thing is most people have been taught to fear death, change, and transformation. Some people would rather stay in uncomfortable circumstances than go through the mini-death of transformation required to start a new life.

Memento Mori

Emblems of death in magick are not meant to be morbid. They have many uses, but in their simplest, most sublime sense they are to point out exactly what their Latin name, *memento mori,* implies: "Remember you will die."

The Dance of Death[144]

Momento mori are to remind us that our time is short—too short. This helps you put all the "little crap" in perspective. Compared to death, it's all little crap.

We must relish each moment because each instant is unique…and fleeting.

What if I'm afraid to die?

Your higher self (Kether) has nothing to fear from death. It transcends the very idea of death, as it exists in an impermeable state of perfection. Life and death have no meaning above the Abyss, where things merely "are and have always been." Even science proves that nothing is destroyed when we die—our atoms and molecules are transformed into other forms of life and energy.

The ego-mind causes our apparent fear of death. Not only is our ego-mind afraid of "dying," it is afraid of any change whatsoever. The ego-mind

---

144   From the *Dance of Death*, German printed edition, folio CCLXI recto from Hartman Schedel's *Chronicle of the World* (Nuremberg, 1493), thought to be created by Michael Wolgemut, and not Holbein the Younger, as is often claimed.

is a fragile thing, constantly in a state of agitation and apprehension that things might not fit into its preconceived notions.

Control freaks are people with out-of-control ego-minds. Their ego-minds can't handle anything outside what it pre-plans and expects. Each time something doesn't work out or doesn't fit, it's a blow to the ego-mind.

Death is little more than a natural function of what we call "life," but the idea is so threatening to the ego-mind that it ceaselessly involves us in petty issues so as not to have to face this underlying fear of death and transformation. It's easier for the ego-mind to focus on a dent in our car door, a zit on our face, or germs on our hands than it is for the ego-mind to confront its own mortality—only the ego-mind can't really "die" either since it's not a thing in itself; it's just a sort of shadow on the wall we somehow mistake for our True Self.

Let the ego-mind die. Be vulnerable. Be open. Stop clinging. Stop forcing reality into boxes. Inaction and worrisome thoughts bring fear. Be the Fool—too busy enjoying every second of life to stop and pine over loss and death.

Loss is inevitable: loss of beauty, loss of friends, loss of family, loss of status all become ever-looming realities as we get older. Kill your dependence on these things now and you are free to enjoy life. Learn to be the Fool and death will no longer be viewed as a negative, but as a natural part of life.

True self-esteem is *not* based upon anything in the material world. True self-esteem comes from our connection to the divine. With genuine self-esteem you will not fear death, change, or transformation of any sort.

The Meaning of Saturn

Make no mistake about it, Saturn will have his day. Your moments in time are slipping away even as you read this.

Since Saturn is time, he is also an essential element to change and evolution. Do not fear Saturn. Use Saturn as a tool for appreciating each moment. Saturn only seems ominous to those who hold on too tightly.[145]

Saturn forces us to move forward. It is the inevitable aging processes and passage of time. Saturn is a woman's biological clock, and a man's receding hairline. He's even that nagging voice in the back of your mind telling you it's time to pay the bills.

Saturn is the wise grandfather, long of beard, patient as the endless night sky, holding a scythe in one hand and an hourglass in the other. But that's just personification. Saturn is the facts of nature. If he seems unpleasant, that is our ego-mind's inability to accept things the way they are.

Saturn is impartial. Even the most powerful and wealthy are no more immune to Saturn's effects than the poor and trodden-upon.

Saturn's symbol represents a scythe. Even though a scythe is now commonly associated with the Grim Reaper and death, it's primary function is to harvest, which is appropriate since Malkuth is where we reap the results of what we have sown on the higher planes.

More than that however, the traditional use of a scythe is to reap the bounty of the Earth, and that's what Malkuth is all about—it is the Kingdom where we enjoy life's riches. When the scythe cuts down the grain it is not out of malice, but with the intent the grain should be used as sustenance for man or beast, thus furthering the cycle of life.

Saturn is the giver of life, for without time, nothing can grow, evolve, or have experiences of any sort.

---

145   In *2001: A Space Odyssey,* the black obelisk is a good representation of Saturn as it represents not just an evolutionary step, but the door between life and death, including the ominous associations involved with such a catastrophic transformation.

As Above, So Below—So Below, As Above

As noted in Chapter 1, "As above, so below" means the spiritual world is reflected in the material world. This is true, but the converse also holds true: "So below, as above." This means that how you treat Malkuth (which includes your body and your life situation) affects the higher planes.

Your higher self cannot be damaged; however, poor practices in Malkuth will cloud or even destroy your connection to divinity. Take great care with what you put into your body and into your mind. Be careful of your friends and associates. Watch how you spend your day at work and at home. What are your hobbies? All these things make up your Malkuth, and they will have a direct impact on the rest of your magick.

Take care of Malkuth by perfecting your temple, the specific area you usually perform your rituals, and your home itself. Your temple is the spiritual center of your home, and your home is the center of your life.

Fill your temple and home with symbols that empower you. The little things you look at every day and take for granted can lead to big psychological effects in the long term—why else would corporations spend billions of dollars a year on advertising? Fight back against being force-fed symbolism that you did not choose for yourself.

Keep your temple organized and clean. These little steps will go far in creating a powerful place to perform magick, as well as giving you peace of mind.

While this should go without saying, do not neglect your body, the instrument *par excellence* of Malkuth. Keep yourself as fit and as healthy as you can. Be a proper conduit for your magick. All the power and wealth in the world does you no good if you can't enjoy the results with a healthy body.

Remember that Malkuth is not an end, but a beginning—it is the fertile earth from which the Tree of Life grows back up to divinity.

Beauty as Toil

I believe the real lesson of Malkuth and Saturn is that genuine joy comes through toil. Choose your life's work based on your own particular passions and talents. Magick works harmoniously with any passion whether you be butcher, baker, artist, comedian, doctor, or dictator—I mean boss.

As Rumi said, "Everyone has been made for some particular work, and the desire for that work has been put in every heart." Magick is the art and science of perfecting and manifesting that desire on Earth.

The Essentials of a Magick Ritual

0. **Preparation.** The majority of work for a ritual goes on before you even start. This includes defining your intent, creating talismans, working out symbolism, acquiring the proper candles, incense, wardrobe, etc.

1. **The Opening.** This includes relaxing, purifications, banishing, and invocations. All these things are about aligning your energy with the type you will be using for the climax.

2. **Climax.** This is crucial, but there are many ways to climax magically, including but not limited to holy communion, orgasm, drawing down the light in the Middle Pillar Ritual, or falling into such a deep trance that you go unconscious. This is the actual point of contact between divinity and the Earth. This is where the seed is planted. Everything else in a ritual, before and after, is just fluff if the climax isn't successful.

3. **Grounding.** This is any sort of wind-down phase, such as a feast, post-coital cuddling in sex magick, or simply quiet meditation. Traditionally, the grounding phase usually includes a final "banishing," but this isn't always necessary. In the following Tree of Life Ritual, for example, Steps 1–9 are preparation and the opening, while Step 10 alone is the climax. Steps 11 and 12 are just grounding and unwinding.

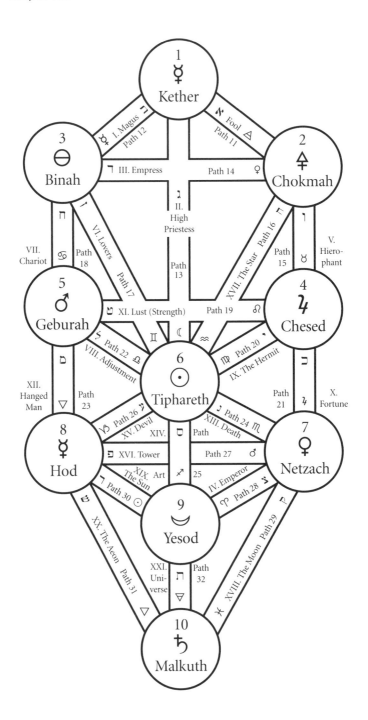

Tree of Life Ritual

The Tree of Life Ritual is the culmination of everything you've learned in this book. If you have come this far and practiced most of the exercises, then understanding and customizing this ritual will be a breeze.

The Tree of Life Ritual is literally for any purpose you can imagine. To start, pick an area on the Tree of Life you feel is related to your problem or your desire. Then customize the ritual according to the following instructions.

The essential concept is to make a clear intent, invoke the appropriate energies from the Tree of Life, and then channel the energy into either yourself or a talisman.

By now you should have a "feel" for a good ritual performance. That feeling is more important than memorizing a thousand pre-made rituals as you will be able to create your own rituals anytime and anywhere, using whatever is available to you.

The following ritual is a blueprint, but *you* are the architect and may change things as you see fit.

1. Define your intent and turn it into symbols
There is little to add from what you have learned from Chapters 4 and 7.

2. Decide which Sephirah or path
best fits the type of magick you wish to perform
Your goal here is to figure out what sort of energy will best solve your problem or achieve your desire. Here are some examples:

If you are shy, your intent might be something like: "*I have the courage to talk to men and women anytime, anywhere.*" You then have multiple choices, such as Geburah or the path of Aries (*The Emperor*). I would pick Path 19, *XI. Lust*, as it is ruled by Leo, who epitomizes courageous use of energy. This path is also well-balanced, as it connects Geburah with Chesed, the two kings.

Let's say you have been depressed, and you want to come out into the light at the end of the tunnel. You decide your intent to be, *"I am able to find happiness every day and meaning in all my suffering."* Depression is a result of an imbalance. Tiphareth is always a good choice when balance or harmony is needed. More than that, however, Tiphareth will shine warmth and hope upon you, reigniting your innate joy at being alive. Path 30, *The Sun,* would also be appropriate for this.

If you are starting college and you want to make sure you keep your GPA up, then *"I'm an intelligent and resourceful student,"* is a reasonable intent. Path 12, *The Magus,* is perfect for anything involving schools, exams, and good grades.

There are occasional overlaps in the powers of the Sephiroth/paths, in which case you can use a mixture of those Sephiroth/paths together, or simply narrow your choice down to one as I have done here.

What if I don't want a specific intent?

You can just invoke the energy into yourself to "see what happens" and it will still pull that type of energy to you in a less specific way. So go for it.

How many paths or Sephiroth can I use together?

You can make the ritual as elaborate as you like. Say you wanted to put some "fire in your gut." You might very well invoke both the path 27 (*Tower*) *and* 25 (*Art*) because of their powerful conjunction located above your navel (see Chapter 3 regarding this).

If you were going to invoke a "lust for life," you might invoke not just path 19 (*Lust*), but Chesed and Geburah as well. If you wanted wisdom, you might invoke both Chokmah and Path 20, *The Hermit.*

Nothing, in fact, stops you from invoking the entire Tree of Life at one time, except perhaps exhaustion.

However, you should still only have a single intent. If you have more than one intent you should probably split them into separate rituals, but as you advance in magick, you might very well have a good reason to combine multiple intents into a single ceremony—so even this rule is not set in stone.

3. Write out the magickal names and symbols

Do this step on scrap paper for the time being. Write everything in Hebrew *and* English. You will find all correspondences in Chapter 3 and the Appendix. What you need depends on the path or Sephirah you chose in Step 2:

If you chose a Sephirah: Write down the name of your chosen Sephirah (from Chapter 3). Then from the "Sephirothic Attributions" chart in the Appendix, write down the God name, the Archangel, and the Choir of Angels. Also write down the Sephirah's planetary symbol (given in Chapter 3).

Example: if you chose Tiphareth, you would write down: תפארת (Tiphareth), יהוה אלוא ודעת (YHVH Eloah V'Daath), רפאל (Raphael), and מלכים (Malachim), along with the symbol for Sol: ☉.

If you chose a path that is a planet:[146] Use the corresponding Sephirah to find the correct God name on the "Sephirothic Attributions" chart. Then write down the Heaven, Spirit, Intelligence, and symbol of the planet from the "Planetary Attributions" chart in the Appendix. Also make note of the appropriate Hebrew letter for your path.

Example: If you chose Path 12, *The Magus*, you would write down: אלהים צבאות (Elohim Tzabaoth), כוכב (Kokab), תפתתרת (Taphthartarath), טיריאל (Tiriel), ☿, ב.

If you chose a path that is a zodiac sign:[147] Based on the *planetary ruler*[148] of the zodiac sign in question, write down the appropriate God name,

---

146 Path 12 (Mercury), Path 13 (The Moon), Path 14 (Venus), Path 21 (Jupiter), Path 27 (Mars), Path 30 (The Sun), and Path 32 (Saturn).

147 Paths: 15 (Aries), 16 (Taurus), 17 (Gemini), 18 (Cancer), 19 (Leo), 20 (Virgo), 22 (Libra), 24 (Scorpio), 25 (Sagittarius), 26 (Capricorn), 28 (Aquarius), and 29 (Pisces).

148 These are given in Chapter 1.

Heaven, Spirit, Intelligence, planetary sign, along with the zodiac symbol and Hebrew letter.

Example: If you chose Path 18, *The Chariot*, which is the zodiac sign Cancer, ruled by the Moon, you would write down: שׁדי אל חי (Shaddai El Chai), לבנה (Levanah), חשמודאי (Chasmodai), מלכא בתרשישים ועד ברוה שהקים (Malkah Be Tarshishim va A'ad Be Ruah Shehaqim), ☾, ♋, ח.

If you chose a path that is an Element:[149] Write down the name of the element in Hebrew, the God name, Archangel, Choir of Angels, and Ruler from the "Elemental Attributions" chart in the Appendix. Also make note of the element's symbol and the appropriate Hebrew letter.

Example: If you chose Path 31, Fire, then you write down: אש (Asch), יהוה צבא (YHVH Tzabaoth), מיכאל (Michael), אראל (Aral), שרף (Seraph), △, ש.

You now have plenty of names and symbols for your ritual, but if there is anything else you want to add, now is the time to get it ready.

For example, if you wanted to use an Olympic Spirit for our example, *"I'm an intelligent and resourceful student,"* you would check the Appendix and use the Olympic Spirit listed for Mercury, in this case Ophiel.

If you still crave more, check the book *777* for more correspondences than you'll ever need. It includes lists for appropriate animals, plants, Egyptian gods, Hindu deities, Arabic heavens, and *even more* Hebrew god and angelic names.

4. Decide if you are going to invoke the energy into yourself or charge a talisman

Both ritual types are very similar, but ultimately you need to decide if you want the energy to infuse your own body, or if you are going to charge an inanimate object.

---

149 Path 11 (Air), Path 23 (Water), Path 31 (Fire), and Path 32 (Earth). For Spirit, use Tiphareth or Kether, or Path 31, which Qabalistically does double duty as Spirit and Fire.

Benefits of invoking into yourself: The effects are felt more quickly so this is better for going into situations where you immediately need a specific type of energy. This type works best for invoking energy into yourself without a long-term intent. You can perform invocations daily or weekly to keep a certain energy flowing.

Benefits of charging a talisman: You charge the object and then forget about it, going on normally with your daily life. This can be better for developing long-term goals or desires. Talismans can either be "one-offs" that you charge once and then forget about (and later burn or destroy), like the ones we have been using in this book, or you can experiment with permanent talismans that you periodically recharge.

5. Decorate your talisman or your body

In the previous steps, you gathered up and prepared the symbolism you are going to use in the ritual. Now is the time to decorate your talisman or your body with that symbolism.

Use *all* the names and symbols you wrote out in Step 3 except for the English translations.

Decorating a talisman: Choose an appropriate material basis as you've learned in the rituals from Chapters 3 and 7. You may pick one of the appropriate metals to work with. However, a piece of wood, parchment, and even poster board are good substitutes.

Let's use our example of "*I'm an intelligent and resourceful student,*" where we have decided to use Path 12 (*The Magus*), which is ruled by Mercury. Mercury's metal of choice *is* Mercury, a.k.a. quicksilver; however, quicksilver is a liquid and not easily used in a talisman, so alloys of Mercury and some other metal (often tin or silver) can be used—but these alloys aren't always easy to come by. So instead, you could just use a piece of poster board cut into the shape of an octagon (Mercury=Hod=8). You would then paint it orange (for Hod) or yellow (for Path 12). (See Appendix for a full list of colors to use). On top of this basecoat you can then paint the appropriate God names, Angels, etc., in black (because black is always good for writing names and symbols, but you may use another appropriate color). Perfect. That's all you need.

If you were going to get fancy (and expensive), you could include some precious stones (see Appendix) in the construction of your talisman. This would be appropriate for a talisman you meant to keep forever with periodic recharging. For example, you might have a gold lion statuette inlaid with Cat's Eye that you regulary infuse with Leo energy.

Decorating your body: You can paint on your body with acrylic or markers, or you can make clothing decorated with the appropriate symbolism. If you are going to paint on your body, you'll probably want to do it right before the ritual so it doesn't flake off. (You can wash everything off after the ritual.)

Where on your body you draw the symbols and magickal names is up to you. You might want to paint or draw the planetary symbol (when using a Sephirah) or the Hebrew letter (when using one of the twenty-two paths) upon your forehead. This is because the third eye is an ideal spot to focus upon when you invoke the energy into yourself.

6. Prepare the Temple

There isn't much to say regarding ritual preparation that you won't know from studying the previous rituals in this book. Only a few concerns and suggestions:

Make a note card: Write out the names and symbols from the scrap paper you used in Step 3 onto a note card. Also make note of the hexagram or pentagram you will need from the next step. If you plan to memorize everything for the ritual so much the better, but it is not necessary. Put as much information onto your note card as you need.

Magickal weapons: While not necessary, if you've constructed your magickal weapons (see Chapter 5), you may use one to perform the ritual. You can use any weapon with any path or Sephirah. Here are the enhancements granted when using one of your magickal weapons to perform the ceremony:

Wand: Brings out the active and creative side of any given path or Sephirah.

Cup: Brings out the receptive side of a path or Sephirah. The cup is good for a deep understanding of the energy you are invoking.

Dagger: Tends to stir up conflict in any given path or Sephirah, but is good for intellectual pursuits.

Earth Vessel: Brings out the material plane concerns of any given path or Sephirah and helps ground that particular energy.

How each magickal weapon reacts to a particular path or Sephirah is highly idiosyncratic, so experimentation is definitely in order. If you aren't sure which weapon to use, just leave all four on your altar, and your ritual will remain balanced between all four planes.

7. Relax and perform the Equilibrating Ritual of the Pentagram
Before you start, take time out for a ritual bath or shower, or otherwise take an extended period to relax.

Then perform the Equilibrating Ritual of the Pentagram as given in Chapter 2.

8. Invoking Hexagram or Pentagram
Stand in the center of your temple.

Face East, or another direction you deem appropriate to the ritual.

What you do next depends on which path or Sephirah you chose in Step 2. You will draw a hexagram or a pentagram depending on your chosen path or Sephirah. The Appendix lists all the hexagrams for each of the planets, and all the pentagrams for each of the elements.

Draw the hexagram or pentagram in the air with your finger (or weapon) as you know how from the Equilibrating Ritual of the Pentagram. You do not have to "see" them, but draw them large, and carefully, and *know* that they are there.

Examples will best illustrate what to do next:

If You Use a Sephirah:

For any Sephirah, draw the appropriate hexagram from the Appendix, and then chant the names you wrote down from Step 2.

Example: If you use Tiphareth, you would draw the hexagram for the Sun.[150] Follow the numbers from 1 to 8 and then finish once again in the center.

Draw the symbol of Sol in the center of the hexagram:

Then point at the center of the hexagram and chant each name in turn:

Tiphareth

YHVH Eloah V'Daath

Raphael

Malachim

Sol

If You Use a Path that is a Planet:

What you do for the paths is similar to what you do for the Sephiroth, but with a few small changes.

Example: If you chose Path 12, *The Magus*, you would draw the appropriate hexagram first, then the planetary symbol above, and then the Hebrew letter within.

Then point at the center of the hexagram and chant:

---

150 As you'll see in the Appendix, only the Sun uses a unicursal hexagram. The rest of the planets use the traditional Star of David-style hexagram. The Golden Dawn teaches an extremely unwieldy way to invoke the Sun using the traditional hexagram, but using a unicursal hexagram is far superior.

Elohim Tzabaoth
Kokab
Taphthartarath
Tiriel
Beth

If You Use a Path that is a Zodiac Sign:

Example: If you use Path 18, *The Chariot,* you would:
Draw the hexagram first, the planetary symbol above, the zodiac symbol below, and finally the Hebrew letter in the center.

Point at the center of the hexagram and chant:

Shaddai El Chai
Levanah
Chasmodai
Malkah Be Tarshishim
va A'ad Be Ruah Shehaqim
Cheth

If you use a path that is an element:

Instead of a hexagram, for Fire, Water, Air, and Earth, you will draw a pentagram.

Example: If you chose Path 31, Fire, then draw the invoking pentagram of Fire, the Fire symbol above, and end with Shin in the center of the pentagram.

Point at the center of the pentagram and chant:

Asch
YHVH Tzabaoth
Michael
Aral
Seraph
Shin

With all these examples, you may chant the names in any order, and for as long as you like. Get a little "high" on the chanting. Imagine your pentagram or hexagram growing brighter and brighter as you chant each name.

When your chanting has peaked, use your hand (or magickal weapon) to gently touch your forehead (if you are invoking into yourself), or the talisman (if you are charging a talisman).

9. Recite your odes or other spontaneous extras

If you have prepared any odes, extra invocations, or anything else you wanted to add to the ritual, now is the time to let loose with them.

If you are feeling spontaneous, now is also the time to say or do anything you feel is magickal and appropriate.

10. Climax by drawing down the light

This step is the Middle Pillar Ritual in full, but with a few key changes:

1. Replace all the usual names with the God name associated with your path or Sephirah. For example, if you chose Path 12, *The Magus*, you would chant "Elohim Tzabaoth" for all seven chakras.

2. For the entire Middle Pillar Ritual, use a single color appropriate to your path or Sephirah. For example, in the case of Path 12, the color is yellow. Therefore, all your glowing balls would be yellow, and so would your "fountain of light" be resplendent with yellow.

3. In Part IV of the Middle Pillar Ritual, as you feel your fountain of light reach its peak, channel the divine light into either yourself or your talisman:

If You are Charging a Talisman:

Take a full, deep breath, taking note of your Anahata (heart) chakra as you do so.

Slowly use the entire exhalation to chant your God name. While exhaling, hold or touch your talisman. Imagine your specific-colored energy traveling out of your chest, down your arms, and through your hands (or magickal weapon) into the talisman.

Attempt to fill the talisman with every last drop of your energy … until you reach the end of your exhalation.

Example: If you were using Path 12, you would chant "El-ohh-heeeem. Vaaa-daaa-aaaaht," while sending yellow energy into your talisman.

Put the talisman down, and before you breathe in again, make the Sign of Silence.

If You are Invoking Into Your Body:

Take a full, deep breath, paying attention to your Anahata (heart) chakra as you do so.

Slowly use the entire exhalation to chant your God name. While exhaling, touch your forehead with your fingers (or magickal weapon if you are using one). Imagine the appropriately colored light flowing into your Ajna chakra, where you have drawn a magick symbol, and down into the rest of your chakras, swirling around, filling you up with magickal energy.

Example: If you use Path 12, you would chant, ""El-ohh-heeeem. Vaaa-daaa-aaaaht," while touching the Beth symbol you would have drawn on your forehead in Step 5.

When you are completely full of energy, and have exhausted every bit of your exhalation, then seal the energy by making the Sign of Silence.

If you want to explore the path or Sephirah through "scrying" or meditating, now is the time to sit and quietly focus upon your sensations.

11. The Closing

Perform the Equilibrating Ritual of the Pentagram, or at least the Qabalistic Cross, to seal in all that magickal goodness.

Write down the details of the ritual in your magickal journal, including time, place, intent, and results. I can't stress enough how thankful you will someday be if you keep an accurate account of all your rituals.

12. Go have some fun!

If you invoked into yourself, then you are done. If you charged a talisman, put it away somewhere safe.

Now forget about the ritual and enjoy your life. Trust that your spell is already manifesting subconsciously, moving you naturally towards your goals, always attracting the right types of energy and people.

If you made a permanent talisman, one you plan to recharge periodically, then you may also wish to keep it wrapped in appropriately colored silk. If it's a talisman you keep in plain view, such as a "guardian" for your doorstep, make sure you keep it dusted and well-kept at all times. These talismans are now holy objects.

Many magicians follow big rituals with a feast or celebration of some sort. This works well to ground the magickal energies and allows you to "land" back on Earth peaceably.

Can I continue to use the talisman rituals from Chapters 4 and 7?

Using the Tree of Life Ritual and customizing it is for when you are ready. If you are content with the shorter types of rituals given earlier in the book, by all means keep using them.

How long before I see results?

Sometimes you may see results right away. Other manifestations may take weeks or months. It depends on the magician and the type of spell or magickal working. I'll try my best to give a rough estimate:

Invocations infuse you with energy right away. (If performed regularly they can transform you into an entirely new person.)

Talismans usually show results within weeks or months.

Deeper workings, which can span days or weeks, such as pathworkings, daemonic workings, and other complex rituals, can have results that manifest for years afterward.

Worrying about the spell seems to make a difference too. I've cast spells that I thought would have quick results, yet didn't manifest for more than a year, only when I had forgotten about the spell completely.

So much depends on other issues such as your self-esteem, natural and learned abilities, any mental blocks you might have, etc. You can't tell what will work for you until you've tried. For example, some people might have faster results with wealth spells over love spells (or vice versa).

My advice is to practice a wide range of spells at the beginning of your magickal career. Keep a journal and soon you will know what works best for you and what doesn't.

If you are really having a problem with results, you will have to reexamine your goals and make sure they are realistic and something you believe can truly happen.

What if a bug gets in my wine glass?
If you have an unforeseen accident during a ritual (including spilling something, fumbling words, or whatever else), either fix the problem, or move on and ignore it. Small accidents won't harm a spell. If there is something really problematic that has occurred, you can simply start over.

Customizing the Tree of Life Ritual
My hope with this book is to teach you a framework of magick that leads to success. The Tree of Life Ritual is not meant as an end, but a beginning to developing *your own ritual style.*

Here are a few specific ways you can customize the Tree of Life Ritual for a variety of needs.

Nature Rituals
All rituals in this book can be adapted to natural settings. Performing near waterfalls, streams, and fountains grants not just a beautiful locale, but would be especially appropriate for any Water-based rituals you might

perform. Outside around a bonfire, on the top of a hill, or in a field of wildflowers are also potential sites for magick.

One can hardly mention nature and magick at the same time without thinking of Dionysus. So even though what I've taught you here is high magick, I hope it's clear that I'm all for primitive carnality in rituals when it is called for, to such an extent that even the down and dirtiest pagan would be proud.

Dancing, masks, or costumes, huge gatherings, and even intoxicated reverie can be useful in magick.

Nuit Dedication Ritual for Increased Pleasure in Everything

Use the Tree of Life Ritual to invoke Path 15, *The Star*. Include some choice quotes from *Liber AL*, such as:

> "I love you! I yearn to you! Pale or purple, veiled or voluptuous,
> I who am all pleasure and purple, and drunkenness of the
> innermost sense, desire you."[151]

Then read and sign this vow:

> "I, (your magickal name), invoke an overflowing cup of sensual
> goodness. I swear to receive all pleasure as openly and as deeply as
> possible in each moment as it is presented to me. I swear this by the
> vault of Nuit's body and the red gleam in my eye. So mote it be.
> Signed _____"

You may take special care in constructing the vow and handwriting it on parchment beforehand. Sign the vow *during* the ritual.

---

151 *Liber AL*, I.61.

Consecration Ritual

Converting the Tree of Life Ritual into a consecration ritual is easy. Prepare the ritual for the proper element of the weapon you are consecrating (i.e., prepare a Fire invocation if you are going to consecrate your wand) and then treat the weapon as a talisman, which you infuse with energy just as usual.

You can also add some specific verbiage during Step 9, such as: "By the light of the Divine, in the presence of He who works in silence and whom naught but silence can express, I do hereby consecrate this wand to the element of Fire that it will assist me in serving the Holy and Most High Lord of the Universe. So Mote it be!"

HGA Ritual

Rituals to invoke your True Self are the most personal of all rituals, so feel free to follow your own intuition when developing one.

A good place to start is by using the Tree of Life Ritual to invoke Kether, Path 13 (*The High Priestess*), or both.

After you invoke your HGA, be silent and passive.

Learn to be receptive to any impressions you might receive.

Spend at least 10–15 minutes being open to anything that arises in your mind's eye.

Write down any results or issues.

Self-Dedication Ritual

Use the Tree of Life Ritual to invoke Tiphareth, then read and sign the Oath of Self-Dedication as given in Chapter 6 (or write your own dedication vow). Simple as that.

Servitor Creation Ritual

Servitor creation is about designing your own daemon.

1. Design the personality of your daemon, including name, description, and its intended purpose(s). It can be beautiful, ugly, male, female, androgynous, alien, or anything else you can imagine. It's up to you.

2. Make a sigil or symbol for the daemon as you know how. You can use any of the sigilization methods in this book to accomplish that.

3. Infuse it with life. Perform the Tree of Life Ritual using the path or Sephirah you feel best represents it. Channel the energy into its sigil, imagining its thought-form growing more detailed, realistic, and powerful.

4. Once you get some results from the servitor, you can feed it more energy with not just rituals, but by spending more time incorporating the servitor into your life. Izabael grew more powerful as I incorporated her into my artwork, my temple, and my relationships.

Lightning Bolt Ritual

The path of the flaming sword is the mythological path God used when creating the universe. The goal of this ritual is to charge your talisman (or yourself) with the same energies in the same order that created the universe.

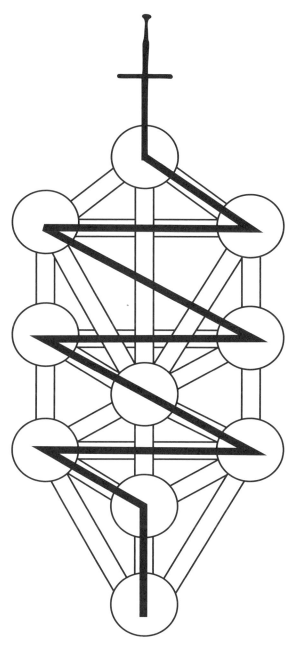

The path of the flaming sword or "lightning bolt"

1. Create an intent for your invocation or talisman.

2. Perform the Tree of Life Ritual invoking Kether, and charge your talisman (or yourself) with the resulting energies.

3. Continue down the Tree of Life. In your next ritual, you would invoke Chokmah, then Binah, then Chesed, etc.

4. After you finish the final ritual for Malkuth, your talisman is fully charged and you may put it in a safe place.

This ritual should be spread out over ten days, one Sephirah per day, though you could go "ironman" and invoke all the Sephiroth in a single ritual if you really wanted to.

The point of this ritual is to create something in the same fashion God created the universe. So you drag your intent through all the Sephiroth, where it goes from a simple idea (Kether) down to the material reality of Malkuth.

You could also perform a similar ritual with all 32 paths/Sephiroth.

Three Daily Spells for Love, Health, or Wealth

Sometimes rituals are best streamlined to the essentials. I consider these more to be "spells" than rituals, since they are so much shorter than the usual rituals we have been doing, and you do not need to perform the Equilibrating Ritual of the Pentagram when using them. These simple rituals can be used sporadically but work far better if you perform them daily.

Spell for Health

This should be performed as close to high-noon as possible. Standing bare-chested in the sun is ideal, but not necessary.

Look up to the sun as best you can without blinding yourself. If you cannot see it, then imagine it brighter than you've ever seen it before.

At this point, don't worry too much about the pronunciations. Just do your best with any unfamiliar names. Say loudly if possible; if not, you may whisper it with silent conviction:

"Hail Shabbathai, I honor thy timeless presence. I hear the call of thine impending thunder.

"Hail Zazel, I hear thy trumpet calling from afar reminding me to enjoy the now.

"Oh Shemmesh, I invoke thy sunny demeanor into my perfect now. Heal me and those I love. Teach our hearts joy. Sorath and Nakhiel, hear the golden roar of Yod Heh Va Heh El-Oh-Ah Va-Da-Ath. Bathe me in the blissful pleasure of the eternally fleeting moment. So mote it be!"

Make the Sign of Silence.

Spell for Wealth

You may do this once a day anytime, anywhere, inside or outside, but perform it somewhere you can drip candle wax onto the ground. Light the candle before you start the relaxation ritual so that there is sufficient hot wax.

Say powerfully: *"Great God AL,*[152] *lord of my fruition, send forth thy stable hand to spread your seeds of bounty."*

With the thumb of your active hand inscribe an imaginary circle in the palm of your passive hand.

Say: *"Under the skies of Tzedek, I plow my fields with dedication and marvel as thy seeds sprout with abundance and wealth."*

Drip some wax onto the ground and pause for a moment in silence.

Say: *"Hail Hismael, I feel thy blessing and mark your message upon my hand."*

With your thumb draw an imaginary "X" in the circle you previously drew upon your palm.

Say: *"So mote it be!"*

Stamp your foot on the ground and finish with the Sign of Silence.

---

152 You should verbalize this drawn out to "Ahhhhhhhhllll."

Spell for Love

Once a day (preferably in the morning or before bed), draw the Venus symbol ("♀") upon a mirror[153] with the tip of your forefinger, and then say:

"Hear me, oh Venus, goddess of love and sensual bounty. Stir up your gods, and stir up your angels to assist me in this, my most humble and passionate request:

"By the power of Yod Heh Vav Heh Tza-Bah-oth and the splendorous victory of Haniel and the Elohim, I exort you Qedemel and Hagiel, to enflame the heart of _____ with love and passion, or with the blessing of Hagith, to push him/her aside and bring me someone better.

"Call upon your consort Apollo to play upon the heartstrings of my most perfect companion. Blind him/her to my flaws, and excite his/her most intense desire. So shall my love be returned 1000-fold as I submit to pleasure not for me, but unto thee, oh Aphrodite.

"So mote it be!"

Finish by making the Sign of Silence.

(The blank space in the previous invocation is reserved for the name of someone you love or have a crush on. This can be someone you know in person, a fantasy, or even a celebrity. Choose someone who incites your strongest passions, but be open to the universe bringing you someone better suited for you.)

EXERCISE 10: CUSTOMIZE A RITUAL AND PERFORM IT

You must have something you want to work on; why else are you reading this book? Now is the time to go for it. Get out your scrap paper and start the preparations.

---

153   The symbol of Venus is a stylized representation of her hand mirror.

WHERE D⊕ I G⊕ FR⊕ⅢHERE?

"Every child is an artist. The difficulty is to remain one when you grow up."—Picasso

The End is the Beginning—The Beginning is the End

Yogis, adepts, mystics, and even scientists know there is no ultimate end or beginning to anything. Everything in the world shares the same atoms and particles, always recycled and reused. Nothing is lost and nothing is gained; rather, it's the endless interplay of molecules, atoms, and subatomic particles that gives birth to manifested existence.

This concept is expressed by the magickal image of Ouroboros, the serpent/dragon that devours his own tail.

Ouroboros symbolizes the cyclical nature of the universe, as well as the original (and underlying) unity of the universe.

In Qabalistic terms, he is the Three Veils of Negative Existence, the womb from which the Tree of Life is born.

Our connection to this primal oneness is through *The Fool*, whose tarot card is numbered zero, the shape of Ouroboros.

In Qabalah, "10" is a number of completion. Things are "done." But "11" is the number of magick, because it symbolizes the urge to change from one thing into something else entirely. *The Fool* is Path 11; coming directly after the 10th Sephirah, it marks the end of the Sephiroth and the beginning of the paths. Even if our universe has a theoretical end, it just marks the end of one phase and the beginning of the next, whereof we know not what to expect.

The Ouroboros

Ouroborus is actively consuming himself. By devouring his own quarks, fermions, leptons, and bosons[154] he gives birth to all that exists: stars, planets, the periodic table, humans—everything.

This idea of the universe having no end or beginning should relax you. There is no race to the finish line. If there is a goal at all, it is to have as much pleasure in each moment as possible.

What is the ultimate goal of magick?

Every magician will have to formulate the answer to that for themselves.

For me, the goal of magick is to increase the joy and pleasure of my life, while helping the world and those around me as much as possible.

Magick is about getting what you want, which includes not just acquiring the ability to attract the things you desire, but actually *knowing* what it is you want and understanding your relationship to the rest of the universe.

---

154   These are all elementary particles, i.e., the basic building blocks of the universe from which all other particles are formed.

Wealth, love, joy, and self-esteem are by-products of a healthy magician doing his or her True Will—and selfishly loving every minute of it.

Now what do I do?

Enjoy the riches of Malkuth with gusto.

Malkuth is the Kingdom—*your* kingdom.

The lesson of this final chapter, which is the lesson of *The Fool* as well as of this book as a whole, is this:

Enjoy what you have—while you have it.

Evolve

"Wisdom says: be strong! Then canst thou bear more joy. Be not animal; refine thy rapture! If thou drink, drink by the eight and ninety rules of art: if thou love, exceed by delicacy; and if thou do aught joyous, let there be subtlety therein!" —*Liber AL*, II.70

Variety will always help to keep your life and your magick interesting. A good magician is one step ahead of his conscious mind's short attention span.

Everyone reading this has a purpose and a perfection unique to his or herself. You have some special niche made just for you. We all do. It's just a matter of finding and appreciating it, which can indeed be a challenge, since it's already here before you. You may have to play many different roles and acquire many earthly baubles before you can appreciate the perfect simplicity of everything you *already are*—of everything you *always have* around you all the time.

Expect something amazing to happen. Your evolution will slowly live up to your expectations.

The Stonecutter

In the end, I leave you with a Japanese folktale[155] as the most *practical* thing I could find to send you on your way:

Once a upon a time, a stonecutter was working next to a mighty rock. He paused from his labor and noticed a local merchant and his entourage pass beneath the shade of the trees nearby.

"Oh, if only I were a rich merchant! How happy I would be!"

A disembodied voice answered him from the mountain, "Your wish has been granted."

When the stonecutter returned home, instead of his little hut, he found a grand and magnificent palace. The man was joyous, and in his new life, his old one was soon forgotten.

One day, while walking through a hot and humid market, he saw a fabulously dressed prince leaning cockily against his carriage, basking in the shade. "I wish I were a prince! He's got power. He's got style." And so then he was a prince.

But as a prince, he found the sun still burned his face, gave him wrinkles, and made him old. "I wish I were the sun itself." So his wish was granted.

As the sun, he at first felt mightier and more powerful than anything on Earth. But as he burned high above his old township, a large cloud moved in front of him, obscuring his view. "What is this? A cloud is mightier than me? Oh, I wish I was a cloud!"

As a cloud, he floated between sun and earth. He blocked the sun's rays, and poured rain until he flooded the town, overflowed the rivers, and drowned the crops in water. Everything was washed away and the people fled.

But after all his watery destruction, a great rock remained on the mountainside unmoved. "Ah, this rock moves for nothing! How I wish I was a rock!"

---

155   This story is traditional with no attributable original author. The following is my retelling of this classic folktale.

And a rock he became. Proud, and unmovable, unaffected by the heat of the sun, nor the barrage of rain. "This is the best of all," he thought to himself.

However, one day he heard a strange noise below him. When he looked down he saw a humble stonecutter driving tools into his surface. A trembling feeling ran through his body, and a great block broke off and fell to the ground at the stonecutter's feet.

"Is man mightier than a rock? Oh, I wish I was a man once again!"

The mountain spirit answered, "Your wish has been granted."

The man was content to remain a stonecutter for the rest of his life. Never again did he feel jealousy, covetousness, or painful longing, instead he knew only joy, relishing in his own humble perfection.[156]

EXERCISE 11: ENJOY THE MOMENT

In magick, we are not Buddhists. We don't deny our desires until they disappear, nor are we hedonists, who blindly spoil ourselves with every lust or whim. Magicians follow a path of balance, of joy, of art and creativity, thereby attaining the Great Work.

Take the day off. Put your magick away and have some fun.

---

156 The moral here is not a new one, or an unexplored one. It's basically the same message as Hermann Hesse's classic *Siddhartha*, and similar sentiments can be found in many philosophies and religions. Even the folk song "Stuck Inside of Mobile with the Memphis Blues Again" by Bob Dylan illustrates the human longing to be somewhere, or someone, we are not, unable to enjoy what is already in front of us.

APPENDIX

Invoking Pentagrams

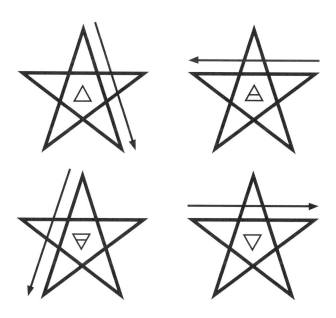

Invoking pentagrams for Fire, Air, Earth, and Water.

Elemental Attributions (Hebrew)

Element	Hebrew Name	God Name	Archangel	Choir of Angels	Ruler
Fire △	אש	יהוה צבאות	מיכאל	אראל	שרף
Water ▽	מים	אלהים צבאות	גבריאל	טליהד	תרשיש
Air △	רוח	שדי אל חי	רפאל	חסן	אריאל
Earth ▽	ארץ	אדני הארץ	אוריאל	פורלאך	כרוב

Elemental Attributions (English)

Element	Hebrew Name	God Name	Archangel	Choir of Angels	Ruler
Fire △	Asch	YHVH Tzabaoth	Michael	Aral	Seraph
Water ▽	Maim	ELOHIM Tzabaoth	Gabriel	Talihad	Tharsis
Air △	Ruach	Shaddai El Chai	Raphael	Chassan	Arial
Earth ▽	Aretz	Adonai Ha-Aretz	Auriel	Phorlak	Kerub

Planetary Attributions (Hebrew)

	Heaven	Spirit	Intelligence
☽	לבנה	חשמודאי	מלכא בתרשישים ועד ברוה שהקים
☿	כוכב	תפתרתרת	טיריאל
♀	נוגה	קדמאל	הגיאל
☉	שמש	סורת	נכיאל
♂	מאדים	ברצבאל	גראפיאל
♃	צדק	הסמאל	יופיל
♄	שבתאי	זואל	אגיאל

Planetary Attributions (English)

	Heaven	Spirit	Intelligence
☽	Levanah	Chasmodai	Malkah Be Tarshishim va A'ad Be Ruah Shehaqim
☿	Kokab	Taphthartarath	Tiriel
♀	Nogah	Qedemel	Hagiel
☉	Shemmesh	Sorath	Nakhiel
♂	Madim	Bartzabel	Graphiel
♃	Tzedek	Hismael	Uphiel
♄	Shabbathai	Zazel	Agiel

Sephirothic Attributions (Hebrew)

*	God Name**	Archangel**	Choir of Angels**
1	אהיה	מטטרון	חיות ה קדש
2	יה	רציאל	אופנים
3	יהוה אלהים	צפקיאל	אראלים
4	אל	צדקיאל	חשמלים
5	אלהים גיבר	כמאל	שרפים
6	יהוה אלוא ודעת	רפאל	מלכים
7	יהוה צבאות	האניאל	אלהים
8	אלהים צבאות	מיכאל	בני אלהים
9	שדי אל חי	גבריאל	כרבים
10	אדני מלך	סנדלפון	אשים

* Corresponds with the number attributed to the Sephirah in Chapter 3.

** of "Assiah." There are techincally four sets of god names, archangels, and angels, corresponding to the spiritual, emotional, mental, and physical planes (Atziluth, Briah, Yetzirah, and Assiah). The Assiah attributions are the ones most traditionally used in practical magick.

Sephirothic Attributions (English)

	God Name	Archangel	Choir of Angels
1	Eheieh	Metatron	Chaioth Ha Kadesh
2	Yah	Ratziel	Auphaneem
3	YHVH Elohim	Tzaphkiel	Araleem
4	El	Tzadkiel	Chasmaleem
5	Elohim Gibor	Kamael	Seraphim
6	YHVH Eloah V'Daath	Raphael	Malachim
7	YHVH Tzabaoth	Haniel	Elohim
8	Elohim Tzabaoth	Michael	Beni Elohim
9	Shaddai El Chai	Gabriel	Kerubim
10	Adonai Melek	Sandalphon	Ashim

Invoking Hexagrams

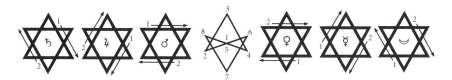

(The center, unicursal, hexagram is for the Sun.)

Olympic Spirits

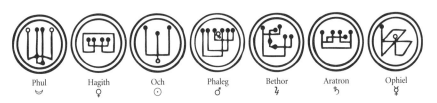

Phul	Hagith	Och	Phaleg	Bethor	Aratron	Ophiel
☽	♀	☉	♂	♃	♄	☿

The Olympics have all the charm and majesty that one should expect from planetary sigils. You may use them with or without the concentric circles surrounding them.

Magickal Alphabets*

English	A	B	C	D	E	F	G	H	I	J	K	L	M
Hebrew	א	ב	ח	ד	ה	ו	ג	ה	'	'	כ	ל	מ
Enochian**	𐤟	𐤡	𐤣	𐤥	𐤧	𐤩	𐤫	𐤭	𐤯	𐤱	𐤳	𐤵	𐤷
Theban***	ꞇ	ꝗ	ꝳ	ꝳ	ꞇ	ꝓ	ꝺ	ꝯ	ꝟ	ꝟ	ꝳ	ꝲ	ꞁ
Celestial	✕	ᶾ	⊓	⊓	⊓	ſ	⊣	⊓	△	△	⊃	↯	↗
Malachim	⧻	⅏	⊡	⫪	N	⋀	⋀	N	⌐	⌐	⊃	⊍	H
Passing of the River	∝	⊐	⊣	⫧	Ɛ	⌣	J	Ɛ	ᵐ	ᵐ	⊣	⅔	⬠
Runic†	↑	ᛒ	<	⋈	ᛘ	ᛒ	×	✳	⏐	ᚺ	<	Ⲅ	ⴲ
Dagger††	⋔	⊣	†	⧣	⫽	ⵜ	⯊	⯊	‡	⸙	Ɣ	⧟	⚼

Magickal Alphabets (continued)

English	N	O	P	Q	R	S‡‡	T‡‡	U	V	W	X	Y	Z
Hebrew §	נ	ע	פ	ק	ר	שׁ	טן	ו	ו	ו	צ	׳	ז
Enochian	✦	↗	⌂	⊔	ˢ	↖	✓	∂	∂	∂	Γ	⅂	ꝑ
Theban	ᒲ	ᴖ	ᴕ	ᒯ	ᵐ	ᴣ	ᴒ	ᴦ	ᴦ	ᴕᴦ	ᴕᴦ	ᴖᴣ	ᴖᴗ
Celestial	⅃	Ⴘ	⅂	Ͳ	ᓀ	ᗡᗝ	ᗝ꒒	⎮	⎮	⎮	Ⴟ	△	Ͳ
Malachim	˥	☐	✕	Ⴜ	V	✳𝒩	𝒩✕⫲	⋀	⋀	⋀	⏀	⊃	Ⴌ
Passing of the River	7	∣	⤬	△	∫	⊐Ⴒ	⊣Ꜫ	⌣	⌣	⌣	Γ	⌐	<
Runic	✦	⨯	ᛃ		ᚱ	ᛌ	↑	ᛈ	ᛈ	ᛈ		ᛃ	ᚤ
Dagger	⊞	⨯	✚	⤸	ᛕ	↓	⫲⫲	⬥⬥	⫲⫲	⫲⫲⫲	⨷	⤯	ᚡ

*Theban, Celestial, Malachim, and Passing of the River all appeared in Book III, Part 3 of The Three Books of Occult Philosophy by Cornelius Agrippa, published in Latin in 1533.

**Enochian comes from John Dee and Edward Kelley who "received" and worked out the basis of the Enochian language and magick system from 1582-1589.

***Theban, also sometimes called the "witches alphabet," has an additional character for a full stop: ⌘.

†These runes are a variant of Elder Futhark called "Ice-egg" Futhark (based upon a hexagonal shape). Elder Futhark, the oldest form of the runic alphabet, dates back to around 300 CE. It was used by Germanic tribes in northern Europe, Britain, Scandinavia, and Iceland. There are three other runes not on the chart: ◇ ("ng" sound), ⌁ ("i" or "æ" sound), and ▷ ("th" sound).

††The Dagger Alphabet comes to us from Crowley's Liber 418: The Vision and the Voice, a series of visions he received while working the Enochian Aethyrs.

‡‡Malachim, Celestial, and Passing of the River, like Hebrew, have two letters each for "S" and "T."

§The letter Tzaddi is placed under "X" for convenience, but the actual sound is usually the "Tz" sound, such as when "X" is used at the beginning of a word. However, when "X" comes at the end of a word like "fox," you might instead want to transliterate it as "foqs" or "foks," utilizing a Qoph or a Kaph as you see fit.

*	Colors**	Precious Stones	Scents
0	....	....	....
1	White brilliance	Diamond	Ambergris
2	Grey	Star ruby, turquoise	Musk
3	Black	Star sapphire, pearl	Myrrh, Civet
4	Blue	Amethyst, sapphire	Cedar
5	Red	Ruby	(pure) Tobacco
6	Yellow or Gold	Topaz, yellow diamond	Olibanum
7	Emerald	Emerald	Rose, Red Sandalwood, Benzoin resin
8	Orange	Opal, fire opal	Storax
9	Violet	Quartz	Jasmine, Ginsing
10	Black, green, earth tones	Rock crystal	Dittany of Crete
11	Bright pale yellow	Topaz, chalcedony	Galbanum
12	Yellow	Opal, agate	Mastic, White Sandalwood, Mace, Storax
13	Blue	Moonstone, pearl, crystal	Camphor, Aloes
14	Emerald green	Emerald, turquoise	Sandalwood, Myrtle
15	Scarlet	Ruby	Dragon's Blood
16	Reddish-orange	Topaz	Storax
17	Orange	Alexandrite, tourmaline	Wormwood
18	Amber color	Amber	Onycha
19	Greenish yellow	Cat's Eye	Olibanum

*	Colors**	Precious Stones	Scents
20	Yellowish Green	Peridot	Narcissus
21	Violet	Amethyst, lapiz lazuli	Saffron
22	Emerald green	Emerald	Galbanum
23	Deep blue	Beryl, aquamarine	Onycha, Myrrh
24	Greenish blue	Green turquoise	Benzoin resin, Opoponax
25	Blue	Jacinth	Lign-aloes
26	Indigo	Black diamond	Musk, civet
27	Scarlet	Ruby	Pepper, Dragon's Blood
28	Violet	Artificial glass	Galbanum
29	Crimson	Pearl	Ambergris
30	Orange	Yellow sapphire	Olibanum, Cinnamon
31	Glowing orange scarlet	Fire Opal	Olibanum, fiery odors
32	Indigo, Black, or earthy greens	Onyx, Salt	Asafoetida, Sulphur, Scammony, Storax

Corresponds with the number attributed to the Sephirah or Path listed in Chapter 3.

**Colors of the "Minutum Mundum."*

BIBLI⊕GRAPHY

Abraham, Ben Simeon, and S. L. Macgregor Mathers. *The Book of the Sacred Magic of Abramelin the Mage, as Delivered by Abraham the Jew Unto His Son Lamech, A.D. 1458.* New York: Dover Publications, 1975.

Alhazred, Abdul, H. P. Lovecraft, and Simon. *The Necronomicon.* New York: Avon, 1980.

Ashcroft-Nowicki, Dolores, and Billie Walker-John. *The Shining Paths: An Experiential Journey Through the Tree of Life.* Loughborough: Thoth Publications, 2006.

Austin, Osman Spare. *Writings of Austin Osman Spare: "Anathema of Zos," "the Book of Pleasure" and "the Focus of Life".* [S.l.]: Filiquarian Publishing, 2007.

Budge, E. A. Wallis. *Egyptian Religion Egyptian Ideas of the Future Life (Arkana).* New York: Penguin, 1988.

Carroll, Peter J. *Liber Null & Psychonaut.* York Beach, ME: Samuel Weiser, 1987.

Castaneda, Carlos. *Tales of Power.* New York: Simon and Schuster, 1974.

———. *The Teachings of Don Juan: A Yaqui Way of Knowledge.* Berkeley: University of California Press, 1968.

Crowley, Aleister. *777 and Other Qabalistic Writings of Aleister Crowley.* New York: Weiser Books, 1986.

———. *Konx Om Pax.* Washington D.C.: Yoga Publication Society, 1982.

———. *The Book of the Law.* York Beach, ME: Samuel Weiser, 2004.

Crowley, Aleister, and Frieda Harris. *The Book of Thoth: a Short Essay on the Tarot of the Egyptians, Being the Equinox, Volume III, No. 5.* York Beach, ME: Samuel Weiser, 1974.

Crowley, Aleister, and Israel Regardie. *Magick Without Tears.* St. Paul, MN: Llewellyn Publications, 1973.

———. *The Vision and the Voice.* Dallas: Sangreal Foundation, 1972.

Crowley, Aleister, Lon Milo DuQuette, and Christopher S. Hyatt. *Enochian World of Aleister Crowley: Enochian Sex Magick.* Scottsdale, AZ: New Falcon Publications, 1991.

Crowley, Aleister, Mary Desti, Leila Waddell, and Hymenaeus Beta. *Magick: Liber ABA, Book Four, Parts I-IV.* Boston, MA: WeiserBooks, 1997.

Cunningham, Scott. *Wicca: a Guide for the Solitary Practitioner.* St. Paul, MN: Llewellyn Publications, 1989.

Fortune, Dion. *The Mystical Qabalah.* York Beach, ME: Samuel Weiser, 2000.

Haas, Frans. *Aristotle: On Generation and Corruption, Book I Symposium Aristotelicum.* Oxford: Clarendon Press, 2004.

Hine, Phil. *Condensed Chaos: An Introduction to Chaos Magic.* Tempe, AZ: New Falcon Publications, 1995.

Hirsch, Samson Raphael. *Tefilat Yiśra'el=The Hirsch Siddur: the Order of Prayers for the Whole Year.* Jerusalem: Feldheim, 1997.

Holy Bible: 1611 Edition: King James Version. Peabody, MA: Hendrickson, 2008.

Israel, Regardie. *Golden Dawn: The Original Account of the Teachings, Rites & Ceremonies of the Hermetic Order.* St. Paul: Llewellyn Publications, 2002.

Kaplan, Aryeh. *Sefer Yetzirah.* York Beach, ME: Samuel Weiser, 1991.

Kraig, Don. *Modern Magick: Eleven Lessons in the High Magickal Arts.* St. Paul: Llewellyn Publications, 2002.

Lachman, Gary. *Turn off Your Mind: The Mystic Sixties and the Dark Side of the Age of Aquarius.* New York: Disinformation, 2001.

Lévi, Eliphas. *Transcendental Magic.* New York: WeiserBooks, 1968.

Mathers, S. L. MacGregor, Aleister Crowley, and Hymenaeus Beta. *The Goetia: the Lesser Key of Solomon the King : Lemegeton—Clavicula Salomonis Regis, Book One.* York Beach, ME: Samuel Weiser, 1995.

Plato, John M. Cooper, and D. S. Hutchinson. *Plato Complete Works.* Indianapolis, IN: Hackett Pub., 1997.

Seuss, Dr., and Theodor Seuss Geisel. *On Beyond Zebra! (Classic Seuss).* New York: Random House Books for Young Readers, 1955.

INDEX

C

D

I

T

U

V

wisdom, 2, 9, 13, 70, 73–74, 81–82, 86, 91, 131, 158, 166, 206, 228, 278, 299

wish, 12, 28, 87, 92, 110, 149, 167, 175, 188, 195, 229, 233, 277, 288, 300–301

wit, 3, 26–27, 65, 83–84, 200

witchcraft, 6, 11, 100

woman, 8, 83, 86, 89–90, 144, 148, 187–188, 219, 231, 251, 273

womb, 56, 72–73, 75, 298

women, 119, 129, 231–232, 277

wood, 111, 130, 133–134, 221, 281

word, 20, 23, 33, 40, 53, 62, 75, 83, 89, 105, 116, 124, 135, 159, 161, 166, 168, 172, 200, 207–208, 225, 228, 309

words, 4, 26, 33, 41, 60, 74–75, 81, 83, 98, 116–117, 136, 194, 202–203, 240, 250, 255, 289

world, 1, 4, 9, 15, 19, 23–24, 33, 41–42, 56, 58–63, 70–71, 74, 82–83, 91, 94, 97, 99–100, 102–104, 108, 118, 125, 131–132, 137, 148, 159, 161, 182, 186, 196, 200–201, 206, 211, 220, 226–227, 234, 239, 242, 250, 268–269, 271–272, 274, 297–298

write, 7–8, 37, 111, 114, 168, 189, 218, 226–227, 230, 241–242, 244, 246, 261, 279–280, 282, 287, 291

writing, 7–8, 19, 36, 64–65, 84–85, 105, 114, 116, 163, 192, 241–242, 249–250, 281

Y

years, 2, 6–9, 16, 19–20, 28, 32, 42, 54, 59, 72, 103, 108, 127–128, 149, 163, 169, 171, 183, 187, 204–205, 213–214, 218–219, 221, 241, 288

yellow, 22, 49, 64–66, 173, 188, 281, 286–287, 310–311

Yesod, 49, 63–64, 76–77, 141, 173, 181, 238–239, 242, 250, 256, 268

YHVH, 173–175, 189, 194, 196, 279–280, 284–285, 304, 307

Yod, 23, 50, 90–91, 223, 226, 228, 295–296

yoga, 63, 130, 147, 159, 173, 179, 252

Z

Zain, 87, 221

Zen, 154, 203